Designing Effective Feedback F in Higher Education

Feedback is one of the most powerful influences on student achievement, yet it is difficult to implement productively within the constraints of a mass higher education system. *Designing Effective Feedback Processes in Higher Education: A Learning-Focused Approach* addresses the challenges of developing effective feedback processes in higher education, combining theory and practice to equip and empower educators. It places less emphasis on what teachers do in terms of providing commentary, and more emphasis on how students generate, make sense of, and use feedback for ongoing improvement.

Including discussions on promoting student engagement with feedback, technology-enabled feedback, and effective peer feedback, this book:

- Contributes to the theory and practice of feedback in higher education by showcasing new paradigm feedback thinking focused on dialogue and student uptake
- Synthesises the evidence for effective feedback practice
- Provides contextualised examples of successful innovative feedback designs analysed in relation to relevant literature
- Highlights the importance of staff and student feedback literacy in developing productive feedback partnerships
- Supports higher education teachers in further developing their feedback practice.

Designing Effective Feedback Processes in Higher Education: A Learning-Focused Approach contributes to the theory and practice of higher education pedagogy by re-evaluating how feedback processes are designed and managed. It is a must-read for educators, researchers, and academic developers in higher education who will benefit from a guide to feedback research and practice that addresses well recognised challenges in relation to assessment and feedback.

Naomi Winstone is a Senior Lecturer in the Department of Higher Education at the University of Surrey, UK. Naomi is a cognitive psychologist specialising in learning behaviour and engagement with education. Naomi's research focuses on the processing and implementation of feedback.

David Carless works in the Faculty of Education, University of Hong Kong. His signature publication is the book *Excellence in University Assessment: Learning from Award-winning Practice* (2015), published by Routledge.

The Society for Research into Higher Education (SRHE) is an independent and financially self-supporting international learned Society. It is concerned to advance understanding of higher education, especially through the insights, perspectives and knowledge offered by systematic research and scholarship.

The Society's primary role is to improve the quality of higher education through facilitating knowledge exchange, discourse and publication of research. SRHE members are worldwide and drawn from across all disciplines.

The Society has a wide set of aims and objectives. Amongst its many activities the Society:

• is a specialist publisher of higher education research, journals and books, amongst them Studies in Higher Education, Higher Education Quarterly, Research into Higher Education Abstracts and a long running monograph book series.

The Society also publishes a number of in-house guides and produces a specialist series "Issues in Postgraduate Education".

• funds and supports a large number of special interest networks for researchers and practitioners working in higher education from every discipline. These networks are open to all and offer a range of topical seminars, workshops and other events throughout the year ensuring the Society is in touch with all current research knowledge.

• runs the largest annual UK-based higher education research conference and parallel conference for postgraduate and newer researchers. This is attended by researchers from over 35 countries and showcases current research across every aspect of higher education.

SRHE *Society for Research into Higher Education*
Advancing knowledge Informing policy Enhancing practice

73 Collier Street   T   +44 (0)20 7427 2350
London N1 9BE   F   srhe@srhe.ac.uk
United Kingdom   🐦 @srhe73

www.srhe.ac.uk

Director: Helen Perkins
Registered Charity No. 313850
Company No. 00868820
Limited by Guarantee
Registered office as above

Society for Research into Higher Education Series

This exciting new series aims to publish cutting edge research and discourse that reflects the rapidly changing world of higher education, examined in a global context. Encompassing topics of wide international relevance, the series includes every aspect of the international higher education research agenda, from strategic policy formulation and impact to pragmatic advice on best practice in the field.

Series Editors:
Jennifer M. Case, Virginia Tech, USA
Jeroen Huisman, Ghent University, Belgium

Titles in the series:

Student Plagiarism in Higher Education
Reflections on teaching practice
Diane Pecorari and Philip Shaw

Changing European Academics
A Comparative Study of Social Stratification, Work Patterns and Research Productivity
Marek Kwiek

The Education Ecology of Universities
Integrating Learning, Strategy and the Academy
Robert A. Ellis and Peter Goodyear

Designing Effective Feedback Processes in Higher Education
A Learning-Focused Approach
Naomi Winstone and David Carless

For more information about this series, please visit: https://www.routledge.com/Research-into-Higher-Education/book-series/SRHE

Designing Effective Feedback Processes in Higher Education

A Learning-Focused Approach

Naomi Winstone and David Carless

Routledge
Taylor & Francis Group

LONDON AND NEW YORK

First published 2020
by Routledge
2 Park Square, Milton Park, Abingdon, Oxon OX14 4RN

and by Routledge
52 Vanderbilt Avenue, New York, NY 10017

Routledge is an imprint of the Taylor & Francis Group, an informa business

British Library Cataloguing in Publication Data
A catalogue record for this book is available from the British Library

Library of Congress Cataloging-in-Publication Data
A catalog record has been requested for this book

ISBN: 978-0-8153-6161-9 (hbk)
ISBN: 978-0-8153-6163-3 (pbk)
ISBN: 978-1-351-11594-0 (ebk)

Typeset in Galliard
by Taylor & Francis Books

Contents

Figures

Tables

Boxes

Foreword

Feedback is a much disputed practice in higher education today. Students don't think they get enough of it and it is not of the type they want. Staff feel that they are putting a lot of effort into doing something which students don't sufficiently appreciate. In the many surveys of student satisfaction over the past twenty years, of all the things commented upon, feedback has been found the most wanting. This problem has led to much debate, many workshops and a flourishing of publications on the topic. So surely we must have sorted out the problem by now?

Unfortunately, this is not the case. While there are some signs that the quality of feedback has improved over the years, universally it continues to remain the most problematic part of the curriculum. This suggests that a new approach might be needed. Slowly, it has dawned that perhaps the solution lies not in doing better with what we presently think feedback to be, but to think about feedback differently. We could start by disentangling ourselves from our conventional assumptions to ask, what is it that feedback is supposed to do, and how might it do it? This profoundly shifts the debate: What is feedback for? Why would we devote so much time to feedback unless it was to help students in their learning? And if it is the case that it is about influencing learning, then we need to think about feedback not from the point of view of what teachers do, but what learners do. That is, what is the learner's role in the process of feedback? And how does the teacher contribute best to that?

Asking these questions has led to a profound shift in our collective thinking about the contribution of feedback. This shift has moved us from seeing feedback as a sometimes ritualistic chore undertaken after student work has been marked, towards feedback as a key feature of how courses promote student learning. By changing our perspective, we can begin to look at feedback differently and see new ways of making it relevant and potent.

We can no longer take it for granted that feedback is a simple idea referring to comments provided to students about their assessed work, with such comments offered by teachers and others in the hope that they might be taken up by students in some form. We need to ask, what is it intended to do? How does it do it? And how can its effects be best facilitated?

The commonplace notion of feedback as information-giving, as an input to students, has been accepted for such a long time that it is hard to shift. However, it is now being systematically questioned as inadequate, not least by the authors of this book, despite the fact that this misleading idea of feedback is enshrined in the very surveys of student satisfaction used to judge the performance of universities.

The view of feedback in the contemporary literature in higher education is one focused firmly on student learning. Feedback is certainly not complete when comments are sent to students. It can now be seen as a process which may be initiated by a learner or by someone else, such as a teacher, but which is essentially about the utilization of information from others to help learners improve the quality of their own work. This involves the learner as the most active feedback agent, not the person that has provided hopefully useful comments. We can no longer define feedback as just giving comments to students, we must use the word more accurately.

This stimulating book enters the feedback debate with a fresh contribution to make. Naomi Winstone and David Carless are leading feedback researchers and reformers in higher education. They have made important contributions to our understanding of assessment and feedback and the ways in which these can operate beneficially in a wide range of university courses. *Designing Effective Feedback Processes in Higher Education* brings together their complementary perspectives to provide a much-needed impetus to understand feedback better and improve feedback for students, not just to improve their satisfaction but to enhance the quality of their learning.

Based on an empirical study of feedback undertaken with UK academics and supplemented with data from elsewhere, the book takes as its starting point the major change in thinking about feedback that has occurred—which they identify as a paradigm shift—and examines the consequences of this for practice. It clearly articulates what is the new thinking on feedback and what it implies for the ways feedback is carried out in university courses. It explores this through examples across a wide range of disciplines, and it focuses particularly on the challenges for large classes.

They point out that it is not simply a matter of planning and organising new feedback activities. The move from old to new feedback practices faces barriers and constraints from students and colleagues who are trapped in old ways of thinking. The book addresses these concerns and provides practical suggestions about where to start and where the greatest impacts on student learning can be achieved.

It is a delight to read a book on feedback that is focused on the future rather than on the old nostrums that have held us back for so long. Reading this book offers the prospect of engaging with feedback with the expectation that it will make a difference and that it no longer needs to be so much of a chore.

David Boud
Director, Centre for Research in Assessment
and Digital Learning (CRADLE),
Deakin University, Australia

Acknowledgements

Naomi would like to acknowledge the support of the Society for Research in Higher Education who funded the 'Feedback Cultures in Higher Education Project' through the award of a research grant (RA1648) and for recommending David as a critical friend.

Our immense gratitude goes to the teachers who provided the material for the feedback design cases collated as part of the Feedback Cultures project and which are presented in this book: Robert Nash, Claire Tarrant, Jacqui Broadbent, Rick Glofcheski, Patrick Rosenkranz and Amy Fielden, Kennedy Chan, Hui-Tzu Min and Emma Mayhew. We are also appreciative of David Boud for contributing the Foreword.

We would like to thank a number of colleagues who commented on draft chapters as the work evolved: Liz Molloy (Chapter 2); Paul Orsmond (Chapter 3); Joanna Tai (Chapter 4); Phillip Dawson (Chapter 5); Rola Ajjawi and Rachelle Esterhazy (Chapter 6); Gavin Brown and Ernesto Panadero (Chapter 7); Teresa McConlogue and Zhu Qiyun (Chapter 8); and Edd Pitt (Chapter 9). Remaining shortcomings are, of course, the responsibility of the authors.

We would also like to thank our respective colleagues and support teams. Naomi acknowledges the contributions of the research assistants on the Feedback Cultures Project: Jessica Bourne, Emily Papps, Molly Foster, and Danielle Robinson. She also thanks her colleagues in the Department of Higher Education at the University of Surrey for their ongoing support and inspiration. Particular thanks are due to Kieran Balloo, Samuel Elkington, Robert Nash, Emma Medland, Edd Pitt, and Neil Winstone for the many discussions around feedback over the years which have shaped Naomi's thinking.

At the University of Hong Kong, David would like to thank Jessica To for her contributions and insights, and acknowledge the research and administrative support of Betty Lee and Karri Lam. And last but not least, he voices his admiration and appreciation of his two 'best friends' Amy and Alison.

Finally, many thanks to the Routledge team for their support of the project and their efficient work on the production of the book.

Naomi Winstone
Department of Higher Education,
University of Surrey, UK
David Carless
Faculty of Education,
University of Hong Kong

Series editors' introduction

This series, co-published by the Society for Research into Higher Education and Routledge Books, aims to provide, in an accessible manner, cutting-edge scholarly thinking and inquiry that reflects the rapidly changing world of higher education, examined in a global context.

Encompassing topics of wide international relevance, the series includes every aspect of the international higher education research agenda, from strategic policy formulation and impact to pragmatic advice on best practice in the field. Each book in the series aims to meet at least one of the principle aims of the Society: to advance knowledge; to enhance practice; to inform policy.

In this volume, Naomi Winstone and David Carless tackle head-on what they term 'the feedback challenge', namely the apparent difficulty in getting students to make effective use of the feedback they receive on their work. To develop the necessary student 'feedback literacy', Winstone and Carless give guidance on how teachers in higher education can redesign and manage effective feedback strategies. The work is grounded in the latest research on the topic, and the accessibility of the text is enhanced by reference to selected detailed case studies. This well-organized text is set to be an important resource for teachers and researchers who are looking to enhance the quality of student learning in higher education.

Jennifer M. Case
Jeroen Huisman

Introduction

Faced with the undertaking of designing assessment tasks, grading students' work, and providing information on students' strengths and areas for development, how do teachers decide on the design of assessment and feedback within their unit or course? To what extent do their beliefs about the fundamental purpose of feedback drive their decision-making, and how do the features of the environment in which they work, and other pressures they may experience, influence their feedback practices?

This book contributes to the theory and practice of higher education pedagogy by re-evaluating how feedback processes are designed and managed. Feedback practice should place less emphasis on what teachers do in terms of providing commentary, and more emphasis on how students generate, make sense of, and use feedback for ongoing improvement. Through eight feedback design case studies, we illustrate how active student roles in feedback can be facilitated.

The main aims of the book are as follows:

1   To contribute to the theory and practice of feedback in higher education by showcasing new paradigm feedback thinking focused on dialogue and student uptake;
2   To synthesise the evidence for effective feedback practice;
3   To provide contextualised examples of successful innovative feedback designs analysed in relation to relevant literature;
4   To highlight the importance of staff and student feedback literacy in developing productive feedback partnerships;
5   To support teachers in further developing their feedback practice.

Feedback Cultures in Higher Education project

Drawing on a project funded by the UK Society for Research into Higher Education, we set out to contribute to the enhancement of feedback processes. The project was entitled 'Feedback Cultures in Higher Education', as its primary aim was to explore the proximal and distal influences on the common ways in which feedback processes are enacted in contemporary higher education. In this context, we are referring to feedback to students, for example on their work, not from students, for example evaluations of teaching. Whilst many aspects of the feedback process might be specified in institutional regulations (e.g. the use of a specific feedback proforma, or the timeframe in which feedback should be returned), teachers are often free to consider the nature and timing of the assessment tasks they set for students, and the modality through which feedback comments are presented (e.g. written, audio, or video formats). Teachers also make decisions about the extent to which students will be part of the assessment and feedback process, for example through incorporating peer feedback or self-assessment within the assessment design. Whilst many aspects of the feedback process may rely on students' engagement (e.g. the ability to interpret feedback, understanding the purpose of feedback, and willingness to expend effort to implement feedback), teachers can still decide how and where to embed the development of these skills into the curriculum.

Teachers' pedagogic decisions are influenced by their own learning experiences and professional development, as well as external influences such as regulations and the curriculum. Thus, on a proximal level, decisions about feedback practice might stem from teachers' beliefs and values about the importance of feedback within the context of a learning process, or from the guidance and direction they might receive from colleagues within their departments. The extent to which these beliefs and values feed directly into practice is likely to be influenced by features of the local disciplinary culture, including factors such as workload, class sizes, explicit or implicit messages about the relative importance of teaching and research, or perceived agency to experiment versus conform to normative assessment practices. Decisions might also be guided by the (perceived) requirements of departmental or institutional guidelines or regulations, or the requirements of Professional or Accrediting Bodies.

Central to the book is a theoretical distinction between old paradigm transmission-focused and new paradigm learning-focused models of the feedback process, which we explore in depth in Chapter 1. As well as investigating teachers' alignment with each of these models, we aimed to bridge theory and practice by exploring how learning-focused models of feedback are enacted, as represented in the literature as well as in the work of teachers in their everyday practice.

The 'Feedback Cultures' project, conducted between January 2017 and January 2018, involved three strands of research:

Strand 1: Understanding practice

Through a mixed-mode survey distributed to academics in the UK and Australia, we explored knowledge, perceptions and practices aligned with transmission-focused and learning-focused models of the feedback process.

Strand 2: Understanding the drivers of practice

Through semi-structured interviews with 28 UK academics, Naomi explored the factors that influence decision-making around feedback practices, and features of typical feedback 'cultures' in UK Universities. Through complementary data collection in Hong Kong and Taiwan, David further investigated feedback practices in settings beyond the UK.

Strand 3: Driving practice forwards

Through an evidence synthesis and collation of feedback design cases, we set out to capture evidence of the effectiveness of learning-focused feedback practices, and characteristics of the 'feedback cultures' where such practices are adopted effectively. The cases were selected examples of good practice that illustrate different dimensions of feedback designs. According to contextual differences, a variety of data collection methods were used, including teachers' reflective accounts of practice; standard student evaluation data; interviews with teachers; interviews with students; and classroom observations.

This book focuses predominantly on the findings from the third strand of the project, but we draw upon snapshots of the findings from the survey and interviews to inform our theoretical framing and our synthesis of the learning from the project.

The structure of the book

We begin the book by framing feedback in terms of the theoretical distinction between transmission-focused and learning-focused models of the feedback process. We then move to explore practice, by presenting a series of approaches to feedback that in some way align with a learning-focused approach. Whilst the chapters provide valuable information for teachers looking to design feedback processes that are likely to facilitate student learning, the primary emphasis remains on student involvement with and driving of learning through feedback.

We begin each chapter by situating the feedback approach within a learning-focused feedback model, exploring relevant dimensions of research and practice. We then focus in greater depth on two key examples from the research literature to allow key points to emerge in greater depth. The cases in the second half of each chapter provide a window into how some of the theoretical concepts are implemented in practice. We draw connections between the approach in practice and relevant research literature.

Each chapter also contains a series of resources to bridge the divide between theory and practice, and a summary of key research findings. We learnt a lot from interviewing teachers about their practice, and we share the implications for practice pertinent to each approach. We also present a series of questions to stimulate reflection and debate; in line with a dialogic approach to feedback, we would encourage readers to engage in reflection and discussion with others. The final chapter of the book synthesises what we have learnt about feedback in the course of the project. We also share some tools, developed through our work, for use by individuals or course teams to reflect upon their current approach to feedback, and to consider how they might develop their feedback culture to be more learning-focused.

Feedback is a complex, contentious topic, and there is no single 'right' way of engaging in feedback process with students. Key to shifting from a transmission-focused to a learning-focused feedback paradigm is recognising that, whilst we can provide students with evaluative and directive information in the form of comments on their work, feedback processes cannot take place without the student's active involvement. However, by sharing real examples from teachers who face many of the challenges experienced by those working in contemporary higher education, such as growing class sizes, increasing workload, and the pressure of student satisfaction metrics, we hope to provide some indication of how a learning-focused approach to feedback can be operationalised in practice. We focus on undergraduate higher education contexts because this was the focus of our work, but we hope that many themes and practices discussed within the book will resonate with other levels of education too.

Chapter 1

The feedback challenge

Many articles on assessment feedback in higher education open by posing a commonly experienced dilemma: we know that high-quality feedback has the potential to have one of the strongest influences on students' achievement (e.g. Hattie, & Timperley, 2007), yet feedback is often framed as the dimension of students' experience with which they are least satisfied. In addition, despite recognising the value of feedback, and commonly voicing dissatisfaction with the quality and quantity of feedback received, students often appear to make limited use of feedback. This conundrum has occupied the minds of teachers who often express frustration as the effort they expend in the provision of feedback is perceived to be wasted when students do not appear to engage with the advice. However, whilst there is a wealth of research evidence regarding perceptions of feedback and how it might be delivered, there are comparatively few studies of how students use feedback. This is problematic as the simple act of delivering feedback is limited in its effectiveness, as argued by Royce Sadler: "Learners do not always learn much purely from being told, even when they are told repeatedly in the kindest possible way" (Sadler, 2015, p. 16).

In recent years, the literature on student engagement with feedback has experienced significant development; researchers are exhibiting a growing interest in how and why students engage with assessment feedback, how best to design assessment and feedback to facilitate engagement, and how to measure the impact of feedback (Henderson, Ajjawi, Boud, & Molloy, 2019). Feedback is being reframed from something that teachers do, to a process where students are involved in seeking, processing, and using feedback information. As neatly argued by Sadler (2010), feedback as 'telling' is not effective in facilitating learning because the connection between feedback comments, students' work, and future learning relies on clear and unambiguous interpretation of those comments, and in many cases key messages remain invisible to students. In this book, we look beyond feedback as the transmission of comments towards an approach where teachers design feedback sequences in ways that enable students to construct and implement their own understandings on the basis of feedback exchanges. In order for assessment and performance feedback to facilitate long-term learning and skill development, the feedback receiver needs to be open to hearing the advice of the feedback-giver, to remember how they have been advised to develop their skills, and to take advantage of opportunities to use the comments they have received. Feedback can, however, sometimes be difficult to comprehend, difficult to remember, and putting feedback into practice requires time and effort.

Discussions around feedback are often fraught with tensions and dilemmas, where "Feedback is a complex notion, often embedded in a common-sense and simplistic dominant discourse" (Askew, & Lodge, 2000, p. 1). Furthermore, whilst many guidelines for effective feedback have been published (e.g. Evans, 2013; Nicol, & Macfarlane-Dick, 2006), the translation of such guidance into practice is by no means straightforward (Barton, Schofield, McAleer, & Ajjawi, 2016). In this chapter, we first discuss different approaches to conceptualising feedback and set out the key features of old and new paradigms of feedback. We relate these to the social-constructivist approach which frames our thinking around feedback. We then move from dominant sources in the literature to the voices of higher education practitioners, to explore some of the common challenges experienced in the assessment and feedback process, and perceived barriers to reforming feedback processes, drawing upon data from the Feedback Cultures project. We conclude the chapter by considering how to move beyond a transmission-focused approach to feedback.

Defining and conceptualising feedback

One of the key challenges inherent in managing feedback in higher education is that there is much debate over what the term actually means. The term itself is broad, and has been used in widely differing ways, by different stakeholders, in different contexts. A conventional view is to see feedback as information provided by an agent, for example, a teacher, peer or self, about aspects of performance or understanding (Hattie, & Timperley, 2007). This is how feedback is commonly interpreted by teachers and students. Whilst students do need information about their performance in order to improve, this is insufficient for the implementation of effective feedback processes because students also need motivation and opportunities to make sense of comments and to use them to for improvement purposes.

Accordingly, in the recent literature on feedback in higher education (e.g. Boud, & Molloy, 2013; Carless, & Boud, 2018; Sadler, 2010; Winstone, Nash, Parker, & Rowntree, 2017a), greater focus has been placed on students' actions in response to performance information from teachers, peers and their own self-evaluation. For information to lead to action, students need opportunities to apply feedback to future tasks in order to inform the development of their learning. Building on this line of thinking, feedback is conceptualised as a process whereby students are proactive in seeking, making sense of, and using comments on their performance or their approaches to learning. This emphasis on sense-making and future actions resonates with the new paradigm feedback practices that are the focus of this book. A fundamental dimension of this conceptualisation is that a feedback process is not solely characterised by the input of comments but also by the impact in terms of changes to students' behaviour, motivation or learning strategies.

Consider the well-known philosophical thought experiment, which poses the question that if a tree falls in the forest, and nobody is there to hear it, does it make a sound? In parallel, if feedback is simply 'delivered', without leading to student uptake and impact on learning, is it merely information that leaves no trace? Sadler (1989, p. 121) aptly described information that is not used as "dangling data", which reflects the roots of the concept of feedback in cybernetic systems theory. In line with a cybernetic orientation, Wiener (1968) articulated the importance of feedback information leading to some change in output:

> Feedback is a method of controlling a system by reinserting into it the results of its past performance. If these results are merely used as numerical data for the criticism of the system and its regulation, we have the simple feedback of the control engineers. If, however, the information which proceeds backwards from the performance is able to change the general method and patterns of performance, we have a process which may well be called learning.
>
> (Wiener, 1968, p. 56)

The 'system' of feedback processes in higher education, characterised by the cognitions, emotions, and behaviours of human agents, add further layers of complexity to this process. However, the fundamental principle of a changed output in response to feedback remains of central importance. It is this response on the part of the student that characterises new paradigm approaches to feedback in higher education.

Old and new feedback paradigms

Thus far, we have outlined two different ways of thinking about feedback in higher education. The first is more focused on inputs: the provision of information or comments to students. The second is more focused on interaction, student sense-making and outputs in terms of future student action. The first more conventional view of feedback is seen as representing an old paradigm, whereas the second is termed new paradigm (Carless, 2015a). We are using the term 'paradigm' somewhat informally to represent ways of thinking about feedback. In our workshops with teachers, they seem to find it helpful to distinguish between transmission-focused old paradigm approaches mainly focused on teachers providing information and new paradigm practices adopting a more learning-focused orientation. Of course, it is more complex than that distinction implies because there is generally an interplay between inputs and outputs. The output from a system is dependent on the nature and quality of the input, so the comments that students receive on their work or learning are an important prerequisite for the impact of feedback processes. We are not arguing that we need to dispense with the old paradigm altogether, as to a certain extent this is the basis upon which new paradigm approaches can build. The problem occurs when feedback is seen *only* as comments, with no consideration given to what happens next.

New paradigm practices imply a number of features. Rather than the teacher providing information and the student being positioned somewhat passively, new paradigm feedback approaches aim for more of a partnership between teachers and students. This partnership envisages a key teacher role as designing feedback processes to facilitate students' participation in elements such as peer feedback and self-evaluation. Implicit in these practices are interactions of different forms but not those that are dominated by teachers; students can initiate feedback processes by actively seeking feedback or identifying where feedback information might help them to improve specific skills. Active student roles in feedback processes require teachers to support students to understand how to engage in productive feedback interactions. This of course raises the issue of how far the responsibility of teachers should extend: students have agency to engage with feedback processes as they wish. However, students are likely to possess greater agency to enact feedback where they have the opportunity to implement feedback on subsequent tasks, and where they feel equipped to take productive action upon feedback. Whilst it is true that you can lead a horse to water but cannot make it drink, you can make it thirsty. It is via the design of learning opportunities through feedback that students' 'thirst' for feedback can be optimised.

The seminal paper by Boud and Molloy (2013) makes the case that feedback needs to be carefully designed and integrated with curriculum and teaching sequences. Building upon this important insight, we show how meaningful and considered assessment and feedback designs can facilitate new paradigm feedback practices. The input of performance information is transformed through principled design features so that students are enabled to engage with and use feedback to facilitate their own learning. This is illustrated in Figure 1.1, whereby we conceptualise the intersection between old and new paradigm approaches as driven by design.

For example, if we want to transform feedback from the provision of information to a sense-making process where students work to develop their own representation of what it means, we need to design opportunities for students to grasp what feedback means for their own learning. Similarly, if we want to position students as active participants in feedback processes whereby they can generate comments for themselves rather than being dependent on the provision of comments from others, then we need to design opportunities for them to engage with standards and criteria to inform judgements about the quality of their own work. The notion of design is fundamental to our conceptual approach to feedback: it is design that provides a pathway for feedback information to lead to student uptake. All of the feedback cases in this book involve carefully designed opportunities for students to implement feedback. We now turn to a consideration of approaches to feedback design presented in the literature.

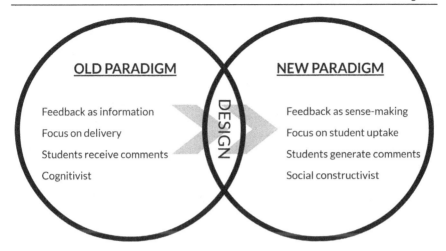

Figure 1.1 Old and new paradigms of feedback

Facilitating impact through design

Effective feedback is not merely something that happens after assessment has taken place; rather, it is designed into learning processes from the outset. Part of the impetus for a shift towards new paradigm models of feedback is a growing recognition that lack of student engagement with feedback often emanates from assessment designs which inadvertently limit student agency and action in relation to feedback. A key tenet of new paradigm feedback approaches is to promote student action, with the implication that such approaches should aim to reduce unproductive teacher commentary at times when students cannot use it.

Boud and Molloy (2013) advocate a curriculum approach to feedback, where students have the opportunity to develop their judgements of quality, and to engage in giving and receiving feedback through exchanges with peers. Fundamental to a curriculum approach to feedback is the design of multiple, sequential, and nested tasks, where comments on students' work can be applied to future tasks and learning opportunities. Their description of a curriculum approach clearly demonstrates how the design of feedback opportunities is central to a new paradigm ethos:

> Such a view enables feedback to be repositioned away from its taken-for-granted role as a feature of the ways teachers act towards students, towards being seen as an attribute of the curriculum that locates it as a central feature of student engagement. Feedback becomes therefore a key curriculum space for communicating, for knowing, for judging, for acting.
>
> (Boud, & Molloy, 2013, pp. 706–707)

This approach to feedback as a 'curriculum space' also resonates with the notion of sustainable feedback, which refers to setting up feedback processes such that feedback enables student action and learning beyond the current task, and develops students' capacities to use feedback beyond their time at University (Hounsell, 2007). In their analysis of sustainable feedback, Carless, Salter, Yang, and Lam (2011) identify four features of design that facilitate sustainable feedback: opportunities for dialogue to elucidate quality; opportunities for students to develop the capacity to monitor and evaluate their own learning; opportunities for students to develop goal-setting capacities; and opportunities to apply feedback to multiple iterations of tasks. Whilst some learning environments might incorporate all of these design features, others may not embody any at all. The survey administered as part of the Feedback Cultures project identified that the design of learning tasks to facilitate student implementation of feedback is more common in some contexts than others (Winstone, & Boud, 2019), suggesting that some feedback cultures have a stronger design stance than others.

Feedback cultures

The design of feedback processes takes place within a complex interaction of intrapersonal, interpersonal and contextual influences. Such interaction creates feedback 'cultures', which we conceptualise as representing the beliefs, values and practices that typically characterise and influence feedback processes within a given educational setting. Ajjawi, Molloy, Bearman, and Rees (2017) drew upon Bronfenbrenner's (1979) ecological systems theory to explore contextual influences on students' experiences of feedback. We follow Ajjawi et al. (2017) in applying this approach to consider the possible construction of feedback cultures that might have an impact on an individual's or a team's pedagogic decision-making in the area of assessment and feedback. Design does not take place in a vacuum: it is influenced by a range of contextual, disciplinary, and ecological factors.

An ecological systems approach would view the development of an individual's practice as being situated within a system of interdependent levels of contextual influence (see Figure 1.2). The microsystem represents the local setting in which the teacher works, and their interactions with students. Here, the teacher's approach to feedback might be impacted by dominant approaches or the practice of colleagues. Of course, an individual teacher also interacts with other microsystems, such as other academic departments or an academic development unit. The influence of the interaction between microsystems is represented by the mesosystem, and might represent the teacher being exposed to new or different ways of thinking about and practicing feedback.

Elements of the context that influence an individual's practice, but with which they do not interact directly, such as university policies and codes of practice, constitute the exosystem. The influence of the macrosystem represents broader cultural or subcultural influences, such as dominant practices in the teacher's discipline. Evidence suggests that different disciplines are characterised by variable feedback cultures, according to the dominant methods and values in this area of

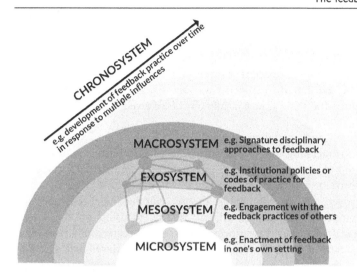

Figure 1.2 Interdependent ecological systems

practice (Watling, Driessen, van der Vleuten, & Lingard, 2014). Finally, the chronosystem represents the change in the interaction of all these influences over time, for example where a teacher develops their feedback designs on the basis of exposure to new ideas. Thus, it is possible that the extent to which an educator aligns with and adopts learning-focused or transmission-focused approaches to feedback is similarly influenced by "a complex and dynamic interaction of the implicit and explicit messages about feedback to which they are exposed, their own beliefs, values and professional development, and institutional policies and procedures" (Winstone, & Boud, 2019, p. 413).

New paradigm feedback approaches are facilitated when there are feedback cultures that encourage honesty, transparency, and an atmosphere of continuous improvement. Boud and Molloy (2013, p. 708) speak of 'learning milieu' as cultural and contextual influences on feedback processes; student involvement in these processes is facilitated where learning milieu are characterised by dialogue and trust. A further facilitating factor for the development of new paradigm feedback approaches is teacher and student feedback literacy: a core theme of the book which we elaborate as the narrative unfolds.

Learning theories underpinning new paradigm approaches to feedback

A focus on monologic feedback as the transmission of comments is cognitivist in its representation (Ajjawi, & Boud, 2017). In this old paradigm model, the role of the student in the feedback process is not fully activated. Emphasis is placed on the provision of high quality information but there is a danger that such one-way communication does not sufficiently prompt the student to engage with and act upon comments. Askew and Lodge (2000) call this dominant discourse the 'gift' model because it represents feedback that is transmitted to students. In this sense, comments could be transferred to students without any active involvement from the student, in much the same way as a gift can be received without ever being unwrapped.

A learning-focused new paradigm model of feedback, where students are actively involved in 'meaning-making' on the basis of interactions with educators and peers, and their own evaluative judgement, is aligned with a social-constructivist approach to feedback (Askew, & Lodge, 2000). Social constructivism is viewed as the dominant theory guiding feedback research (Thurlings, Vermeulen, Bastiaens, & Stijnen, 2013), focusing on the interdependence of social and individual processes in co-construction of knowledge (Palincsar, 1998). Shared and individual interpretations are developed through interaction, where feedback is a social practice guided by dialogue and influenced by relationships between participants (Price, Handley, & Millar, 2011), and where staff and students collaborate in learning communities (Evans, 2013). A social constructivist approach to feedback depends on learner agency so that students actively engage with comments they receive (O'Donovan, Rust, & Price, 2016; Rust, O'Donovan, & Price, 2005). Comments can only be implemented when they can be related by the student to what they already know and what they are motivated to do (Boud, & Molloy, 2013). This social-constructivist approach to feedback recognises that "an active and substantial feedback role for students is seen as indispensable if higher-quality learning outcomes are to be achieved" (Hounsell, 2007, p. 106). Features of new paradigm feedback approaches, such as peer interaction, dialogue, sense-making, and co-construction resonate with social constructivist learning theories, and require students to develop feedback literacy.

Student feedback literacy is defined as the understandings, capacities, and dispositions needed to make sense of comments on performance and use them for enhancement purposes (Carless, & Boud, 2018). Students need to recognise the value of feedback and appreciate their active role in its processes, and they need to learn how to make sound academic judgements about their own work and that of others. Students need to manage emotional responses to feedback in productive ways. These three elements converge on a need for action in response to feedback so that it contributes to the improvement of future work. This development of student feedback literacy is at the heart of new paradigm feedback approaches.

The teacher plays a key role in facilitating the development of student feedback literacy and teachers may need to develop their own feedback literacy in order to achieve this aim. Teachers need to design curricula and assessment in ways that enable students to gain experience in making judgements and using feedback. Teachers also need to guide and coach students towards good practices in composing and receiving peer feedback (see Chapter 8).

The role of students in feedback processes

New paradigm feedback practices place a premium on active and meaningful student roles in feedback processes. In seeking to synthesise the literature on students' use of feedback, Winstone et al. (2017a) emphasised the importance of students' 'proactive recipience' of feedback, representing "a state or activity of engaging actively with feedback processes, thus emphasizing the fundamental contribution and responsibility of the learner" (Winstone, et al., 2017a, p. 17). Conceptualising the nature of such a 'fundamental contribution' is not straightforward, and a simple analogy will serve to illustrate the difference between what might appear to be engagement with feedback on a surface level, and the kind of student-driven contribution to feedback processes inherent to the idea of proactive recipience.

Imagine that in a training session an athlete has been advised by their coach that they need to develop a particular element of their performance. Having received this information, the athlete may keep this in mind in subsequent training sessions, aiming to improve in this area. This is, on one level, representative of engagement with feedback, but not on a proactive level. Instead, imagine that the athlete chose to video-record themselves during training, and then watch back their performance to see the issue through their coach's eyes. They might then engage in specific exercises or activities targeted at the to-be-developed skill, and then return to their coach and ask for further feedback on their progress. Notice how it is now the case that the 'learner', in this case the athlete, is driving the feedback process by engaging in self-evaluation, engaging in skill development activities, and seeking targeted feedback. It is features such as these that elevate surface engagement with feedback to the level of proactive recipience. We use the term 'uptake' of feedback to represent these dimensions of feedback recipience.

The Latin root of the word 'assessment', *ad sedere*, translates as 'to sit beside'. Effective feedback processes cannot be one-sided; they require partnership, interaction, and dialogue. The comments that are given to students on the basis of their performance, whether from educators or peers, are merely advice. Students can choose to take it or leave it; a feedback process requires uptake of the advice, leading to some change in behaviour, cognition, motivation, or attitudes. In short, under a new paradigm approach, feedback is not a product but a process, driven by students and not teachers.

Challenges and tensions in feedback processes

Within the complex environment that is contemporary higher education, it is important to acknowledge that, regardless of how hard we might work towards adopting learning-focused, new paradigm approaches to feedback, there will always be forces pushing in the opposite direction. One such challenge is that many of the common metrics that evaluate the supposed quality of assessment and feedback in higher education adopt an old paradigm, transmission-focused approach, asking students to evaluate the quality of the delivery of feedback (see

Nicol, 2010; Winstone, & Pitt, 2017; Winstone, & Boud, forthcoming 2019). As a result, many action plans in response to apparent student dissatisfaction focus on improving the transmission of feedback, further exacerbating the divide between the drive to involve students within feedback processes, and the ways in which such endeavours are evaluated.

In part because of the dominance of discourses around apparent student dissatisfaction with their experience of feedback, the concept of feedback is heavily problematised and contested (Rand, 2017). Staff involved in the assessment and feedback process also express dissatisfaction (Evans, 2013), for example because of the massification of higher education, the piecemeal approach to feedback that results from modularisation, and growing student expectations in light of marketisation (Rand, 2017). Student dissatisfaction with the timing and utility of feedback, alongside staff frustration when it appears that students are not bothering to read or use feedback can lead to 'collective disillusionment' with the process (Rand, 2017, p. 33). An important step towards appreciating the drivers of such frustration involves understanding the ways in which teachers conceptualise feedback processes.

Teachers' definitions of feedback

In the Feedback Cultures project, we sought to explore the conceptions of feedback held by educators. As part of the survey administered in Strand 1 of the project, we asked respondents to define the feedback process in their own words. We received 206 responses, and we coded them thematically according to the most prominent perspective of feedback expressed by each respondent. Of these 206 responses, 96 represented a transmission-focused view of feedback as information about performance, whilst 48 represented a perspective on feedback that aligned with a learning-focused new paradigm model. We also coded 62 responses as expressing critical views denoting frustration with feedback processes.

Unsurprisingly, conceptions of feedback as the transmission of information are dominant, and the critical views suggest widespread misgivings about feedback processes as currently practised. It is encouraging to note that new paradigm feedback practices are beginning to be appreciated but there is still considerable work to be done to support their more comprehensive implementation. Of the responses that were mainly illustrative of an old paradigm perspective on feedback, many described feedback in transmission-focused language, defining feedback as the provision of "*comments on work that will help students learn and (in particular) help them with future assignments*", "*expert commentary on student work*", and "*specific comments on strengths and weaknesses, and to provide generic comments on how the students can improve study skills and marks in the future*".

In these examples, feedback is seen as being synonymous with a written product, although the focus on improving study skills and future work is promising in implying a future-oriented perspective on student development. It is important to note that detailed comments can be a valuable source of learning for students, but only if they are taken up in future work. A focus on the comments themselves overlooks this important caveat, as we cannot make the assumption that student uptake will follow the provision of feedback information. Other responses indicated that feedback was seen as a process of grade justification, which is firmly aligned with an old paradigm perspective. For some respondents, feedback was defined as "*an opportunity to justify the mark awarded*" or "*a justification of the grade and some advice for improvement*", and as a process of "*providing a summative judgement along with a statement of the evidence supporting that judgement*". These kinds of comments reinforce the major challenge that feedback carries multiple and often competing functions (Carless, 2015a; Price, et al., 2011), including support for student improvement; justification of the mark; avoidance of student complaint or dissatisfaction; and quality assurance elements, such as envisaging an external examiner as part of the audience for feedback comments. Perceptions of feedback that are aligned with a focus on grade justification are unlikely to facilitate student engagement, as emphasis is placed on individual pieces of work that have been completed, rather than the holistic process of students' learning through involvement with feedback processes.

In contrast, responses that were aligned with a learning-focused new paradigm approach described feedback as a process and not a product, involving "*a structured two-way dialogue that enables a student to understand how to develop their intellectual skills*" and "*a cyclical process that enables students to develop as independent learners*". In both of these quotations, emphasis is placed upon the impact of feedback processes on students' ongoing development, resonating with recent research focused on the longer-term outcomes of feedback processes (Carless, 2019). The impact of feedback was also represented by conceptions of feedback where teachers have as much to learn as students, with feedback processes representing "*a chance for the teacher to see whether the task was appropriate and whether the teaching prepared the students adequately for it*". This implies a perception of partnership between teachers and students in feedback processes. Other responses characteristic of new paradigm thinking emphasised the importance of students as proactive initiators rather than passive recipients of feedback processes that are "*cyclical and dialogic, with feedback owned by students rather than being imposed on them*", and the importance of feedback processes enabling students "*to appreciate and use specific criteria in self-assessment and peer assessment, aligned with the learning outcomes for that particular task, and in relation to progress towards the course developmental outcomes*". Here, the lens of impact extends beyond piecemeal course units or modules to programme objectives and graduate attributes.

The respondents who defined feedback in overtly critical terms illustrated through their descriptions many of the core challenges inherent to feedback processes in contemporary higher education. Some defined feedback as a bureaucratic "*tickbox exercise*", and others expressed frustration with the workload burden of feedback that is "*Paramount. Tedious*". Critical conceptions of feedback also alluded to a sense that in many cases feedback processes are "*broken*", thus not functioning optimally to facilitate learning, instead being described as "*very hit and *miss*" as a learning process. There was also clear evidence within respondents' definitions of frustration with a perceived lack of return on their investment of time in feedback processes, seeing feedback as "*irrelevant because the mark is all that matters to the majority of students*" and "*a waste of time, because students do not then implement it*". These indications of disillusionment with how feedback processes are currently managed signal some appetite for change, and through this book we bring new thinking as to how to make feedback processes more productive for both teachers and students.

To summarise, whilst some of the respondents to our survey did define feedback in ways that represented learning-focused new paradigm principles, they were in the minority. Many more respondents conceptualised feedback in transmission-focused ways, or expressed dissatisfaction and frustration with the way in which such processes are enacted. This is not surprising, and represents part of the impetus for a paradigm shift in feedback processes.

Perceived barriers to reforming feedback processes

As well as understanding the ways in which teachers define feedback itself, we also wanted to understand more about why they may feel it is challenging to develop their practice. To achieve this aim, we draw upon the interviews undertaken as part of the Feedback Cultures project, as they provide a window into the perceived challenges to developing practice towards a new paradigm approach. Through surfacing these barriers, we can gain insight into the difficulties perceived to limit the application of theory to practice. We return to these barriers in Chapter 10, considering how they can be tackled at individual, departmental, and institutional levels.

A key aspect of the Feedback Cultures interviews was to give participants the opportunity to consider the use of different approaches to feedback, such as audio-visual methods (see Chapter 4), dialogic feedback (see Chapter 6), student self-assessment (see Chapter 7) or peer feedback (see Chapter 8). Of the 28 people that we interviewed, very few were already using these approaches, so their discussion turned naturally to consideration of how they might implement them, which provided insight into the perceived barriers they might encounter in this process.

Thematic analysis identified four barriers: lack of expertise; time and workload pressures; growing student numbers; and the nature of the discipline (see Figure 1.3).

For many staff, a fundamental barrier to their use of such approaches to feedback was a perceived lack of experience or expertise. This is signalling a core theme of teacher feedback literacy. Some participants expressed a general lack of expertise in knowing how to enhance feedback processes, due in part to the fact that "*we don't know what good [feedback] looks like really*" (Participant 12). Limited expertise was also discussed in the context of using technology to facilitate feedback processes, where "*the thought of having to get to grips with another technology*" (Participant 10) was seen as a source of stress, requiring "*a bit of a learning curve*" (Participant 24). A lack of confidence with the use of different technological tools was cited as a reason for not moving beyond 'tried and tested'

Figure 1.3 Perceived barriers to reforming feedback processes

feedback processes: "*[audio feedback] is not something I'm overly confident in doing so I haven't used it*" (Participant 7). Nevertheless, some educators recognised that whilst they are not confident with the use of technology to facilitate feedback processes, they see the importance of overcoming this barrier:

> *[Audio feedback] is one thing which I have thought about, but I don't [do it]. Partly because I find it quite difficult to handle the technology, so there's a technical issue there. But it's on my agenda, really, I've got to come to grips with this.*
> (Participant 6)

Furthermore, some educators expressed a preference for maintaining the status quo in their approach to feedback, because they "*have a very set way of doing things, and don't particularly like change*" (Participant 2). This is a fundamental barrier to change in higher education in that teachers are generally most comfortable with what they have done before. Where such change is explored, perceived challenges can lead to a preference to revert to well-established approaches to feedback:

> *I need to explore audio feedback. I need to find out how to do it technically. And so, I guess it's partly I think oh that's just too much thinking! Go back to what we've always done.*
> (Participant 28)

It is promising to see some evidence of a desire to find out more about audio feedback in this participant's discussion, despite an overall preference for the well-trodden path.

The most commonly discussed barriers to the use of learning-focused feedback processes were time and workload pressures. For example, when discussing audio or video feedback, many participants expressed a belief that this would add significantly to their workload, so resisted exploring the tool because of "*the extra amount of work*" (Participant 11), where "*the barrier would be time*" (Participant 18). Other participants spoke about workload pressures as a more general barrier to innovation in their feedback practice, where, on a very basic level, feedback processes suffer because of time pressure: "*It is simply not possible to give proper feedback when you're acting under time pressures*" (Participant 6). This perception is likely to be accurate if a teacher's conception of feedback focuses on giving detailed comments to students. As we exemplify in this book, there are other ways of engaging students in feedback processes that do not require the production of detailed comments for each student, including with large classes.

Barriers to developing feedback practices were also discussed in the context of managing the tension between the time required for research and teaching activities. These challenges were seen as particularly pertinent to those at an early stage of their career, where building a strong research profile was seen as taking priority over educational innovation:

> *I do think that the primary thing is time. You know, staff are under pressure to succeed at research ... a lot of my colleagues will say, 'teaching is not the thing that's going to get me my next promotion, so I need to deliver on research'.*
>
> (Participant 14)

> *An ambitious young academic in his or her first years of the job who needs to get his PhD published, who might be thinking about moving to a better academically rated institution, doesn't have time for feedback.*
>
> (Participant 6)

Whilst the majority of participants who discussed time pressures saw it as an impediment to the development of feedback practices, one participant saw the issue differently:

> *I think one of the greatest challenges is that many academics think that improving the feedback process means giving more, or more time, or putting in more resources, erroneously, rather than seeing it as from the outset building into their programme, ways of shaping up students to be part of that process. The assumption that many academics might make is 'we're doing lots already, does that mean we have to give more?' but it's not about that.*
>
> (Participant 5)

This thoughtful comment is congruent with new paradigm feedback practices aimed at making feedback processes more effective and efficient. By circumventing transmission-focused approaches where teachers end up doing more and more unproductive marking, our orientation is towards developing and designing practical and impactful feedback strategies.

Aligned with concerns about workload were discussions about the impact of growing student cohort sizes on feedback processes. For some participants, the constraints of class sizes related to the mere provision of teacher-generated feedback; for others, student numbers were seen as a barrier to opportunities to innovate in feedback processes. With regard to the former, the challenge was expressed in terms of the ability to provide 'constructive' and 'lengthy' feedback to large groups of students:

> *I know some of my colleagues who have classes of 180 would say 'how can I possibly give constructive feedback when I've got to mark all of these things?'*
>
> (Participant 9)

> *The only real limitation on the way we do it is just number of students. I mean I've got two hundred test papers to mark and I can't sit down and write a lengthy report on each paper with recommendations of how the student can improve.*
>
> (Participant 23)

Perceived barriers to innovation in feedback processes as a result of growing student numbers were primarily discussed in the context of dialogic feedback, which in almost all cases was interpreted to require face-to-face oral feedback to students on an individual basis:

> *It's a crazy ideal. We've got 200 and odd students just in one year, there's no way we have the time to do oral feedback, so given the current time constraints I think there's not much more we can do.*
>
> (Participant 7)

> *Yeah, the numbers, the amount of students who you have to give feedback to and the time you get to do it in ... what stops us doing more is that we'd use up all our available time on just assessment and feedback.*
>
> (Participant 4)

As we explore in Chapter 6, bringing dialogue into the feedback process does not necessarily require individual discussions in a face-to-face setting; new paradigm feedback approaches emphasise student-generated dialogues, peer-to-peer feedback, student self-evaluation, and the development of student feedback literacy. What the data above vividly illustrate is that old paradigm feedback approaches do not work with large classes because it is often impossible to provide detailed teacher comments to numerous students within stipulated turnaround times. Large classes require a different way of thinking, including features such as pre-assessment guidance rather than post-task comments; the skilful use of exemplars embedded within the curriculum; and supporting students in developing an active role in self-monitoring their own work in progress. A key feature of the book is to showcase new paradigm feedback practices with large classes (as seen in the cases in Chapters 2, 4, 5 and 6). These illustrate that large class sizes can actually act as an incentive to find innovative ways to develop learning-focused feedback approaches.

Finally, participants expressed a belief that some feedback processes were more appropriate for particular disciplines, and that innovations in feedback processes would be difficult to carry out in their discipline. For example, one participant discussed how all assessments in their department consisted of examinations, where *"students don't get feedback, they get a grade. That is it. There is no feedback with that type of exam"* (Participant 13). This underpins the perspective that *"the opportunity to give good feedback is discipline-specific"* (Participant 12). In Chapter 5, we share some ideas on how to provide exam guidance and practical forms of exam feedback in various disciplines. It is also worth acknowledging that there are inevitably going to be occasions when disciplinary conventions are such that defensible practices which involve some compromise between new and old paradigm thinking may be the least unfavourable option.

The responses of participants when discussing different feedback processes gives us some preliminary insight into feedback cultures in higher education. Experimentation with new approaches to feedback (e.g. through audio or video media) may be inhibited where individuals have not been given support to try new tools, such as would be provided through Continuing Professional Development (CPD) training. It is also possible that within a culture where maintenance of the status quo in an area of practice such as assessment and feedback is the norm, then innovation and experimentation will be limited. Finally, it is likely that the voices of champions akin to our participant who explained that improving feedback processes does not mean providing more feedback, are likely to facilitate new paradigm thinking within a local and institutional feedback culture. The role of local champions is important and we return to this issue in Chapter 10, where we also discuss in further detail barriers and enablers to new paradigm thinking, drawing together lessons learned about the development of feedback cultures.

Exploring new paradigm approaches to feedback

In this book, we showcase eight different approaches to enacting feedback processes that all incorporate features of learning-focused new paradigm thinking. We begin by considering the development of students' feedback literacy (Chapter 2). If students are to be able to play a more significant role in feedback processes, and use feedback to facilitate their development, they need to reach an understanding of the purpose of feedback, to develop the skills to judge the quality of their own work and that of others, and to manage emotional responses to feedback. The development of student feedback literacy is thus central to new paradigm approaches to feedback as it represents the skills and attributes that enable students to become more active partners in feedback processes. Staying with student skills and attributes, in Chapter 3 we focus specifically on how we can nurture students' proactive engagement with feedback processes. Students' engagement with feedback is essential for the enactment of new paradigm feedback processes because it is only through student engagement and action that feedback processes move beyond transmission and 'telling', as demonstrated by the quotation from Royce Sadler at the beginning of this chapter.

In Chapter 4, we consider the use of technology in feedback processes. It is important to emphasise at this point that the use of technology in feedback is not by itself a new paradigm approach to feedback. In fact, as we discuss in Chapter 4, technological tools could be used in such a way that the feedback process merely replicates the transmission of comments through different media. Thus, we focus specifically on the ways through which technology can afford new paradigm approaches to feedback. We then turn to the relationship between assessment design and feedback processes in Chapter 5, by exploring how patterns of assessment can be designed in ways that facilitate student generation and application of feedback. By providing conditions through which assessment designs encourage uptake of feedback, students' role in the feedback process is facilitated, in line with a new paradigm focus.

Dialogic approaches to feedback align with a new paradigm focus because within this approach, feedback is not something 'done to' students, but a process where their involvement as an active interlocutor is central to its impact. We explore ways of bringing dialogue into feedback processes in Chapter 6, through peer-facilitated, technology-enabled, teacher-orchestrated, and student-generated forms of feedback. A particular strategy we discuss is the use of interactive coversheets to enable students to request feedback from markers or to summarise what previous feedback comments they are acting upon. A key point is that interaction with students should be neither teacher-dominated nor excessively labour-intensive.

We then turn to a consideration of the different 'actors' in feedback processes. In Chapter 7, we explore the relationship between internal and external feedback; students' ability to evaluate the quality of their own work is central to their involvement in feedback processes within a new paradigm approach. Internal feedback from the learner can be calibrated against external feedback from peers or teachers. Similarly, peer feedback processes, whereby benefits accrue for both partners in the feedback exchange, facilitate students' development through feedback (Chapter 8). A key issue is the need to train and support students in composing and receiving peer feedback productively. In Chapter 9, we emphasise that feedback is a relational process whereby the nature and enactment of interactions within the process can influence the likelihood of feedback having an impact on students' learning and development.

Each of these topics provides a piece of the puzzle to understanding new paradigm feedback processes, because they focus on students' action, engagement, uptake, motivation, and, fundamentally, their involvement in feedback. The approaches themselves are not mutually exclusive; in many cases, a particular feedback process will likely embody features of many of these approaches. Our final chapter draws together these individual approaches into the larger picture of new paradigm feedback cultures, by exploring relevant features of environments that recognise the importance of, and seek to foster, these skills in students.

Conclusion

Assessment and feedback are often described by teachers as one of the most challenging aspects of their role. The workload associated with these tasks is significant, and due to the fact that in contemporary higher education students commonly submit work, and teachers return feedback, via Virtual Learning Environments or Learning Management Systems (hereafter LMS), teachers rarely see evidence that their feedback has been read and implemented. Coupled with the discourse about the poor quality of many feedback practices following the release of student satisfaction surveys or course evaluations, developing practice in this area is commonly perceived to be challenging. These systemic challenges provide impetus for new ways of thinking about feedback.

In this chapter, we have also taken a snapshot of teachers' conceptions of feedback and perceived barriers to innovation in feedback practices, by drawing upon data from the Feedback Cultures project. We have chosen to start the book by adopting a critical stance on feedback, and surfacing the views of a variety of teachers, such that we can explore the literature and examples of practice in the light of these barriers. Facilitating a shift from old to new paradigm approaches to feedback is predicated upon tackling the challenges experienced by those involved in feedback processes.

Box 1.1 Questions for reflection and debate

- How would you have responded to the question in the Feedback Cultures survey asking you to define the feedback process? Would your definition be more closely aligned with an old paradigm, new paradigm, or critical perspective?
- How do you manage tensions between feedback as information for learners, and feedback for student uptake?
- What do you currently do in your own practice to support students' use of feedback? Where does the teacher responsibility for student use of feedback end and the student responsibility begin?
- What do you see as the biggest challenges in the practices of assessment and feedback?
- To what extent is it easier to innovate in feedback practices in some disciplines than others, and what can you do to enhance feedback processes in your discipline?
- What do you see as the features of the feedback 'culture' in which you work? How is feedback discussed and enacted? Do such discussions place greater emphasis on the process of transmitting feedback comments, or student involvement in feedback?
- What are the facilitating and inhibiting factors for the adoption of new paradigm feedback practices?

Chapter 2

Developing student feedback literacy

Anyone wishing to develop expertise in a particular domain needs to possess relevant literacy. Such literacy consists of pertinent competencies and knowledge, such that an individual can engage in dialogue through interpreting and utilising domain-specific terminology, and participate in associated practices and processes. Thus, students becoming part of a learning community in higher education need to develop new academic literacies. Inculcating students into tertiary-level study often involves supporting the development of skills such as essay writing, critical thinking, and alignment with academic conventions. Much less common in this context is facilitating the development of skills required to understand and act upon feedback, yet the latter is just as crucial an academic skill. Perhaps more importantly, the ability to use feedback effectively is a critical life skill that is needed for effective functioning in the workplace and in interpersonal relationships. Whilst feedback literacy may be a subcomponent of the broader concept of assessment literacy, arguably feedback is so crucial to students' development that it warrants a term of its own. As argued by Carless and Boud (2018, p. 1323),

> The development of student feedback literacy is central to the enhancement of feedback processes and broader attempts to improve student learning outcomes. Feedback literacy is not just a tool for doing better in university studies but a core capability for the workplace and lifelong learning.

In their comprehensive book on assessment literacy, Price, Rust, O'Donovan, Handley, & Bryant (2012) suggest that student assessment literacy encompasses: an appreciation of the relationship between assessment and learning; a conceptual understanding of assessment; understanding of the nature and meaning of assessment criteria and standards; skills in self- and peer-assessment; familiarity with assessment techniques; and the ability to select and apply appropriate approaches to assessment tasks. Smith, Worsfold, Davies, Fisher, & McPhail (2013) view assessment literacy as students' understandings of the rules of assessment in context, their use of assessment tasks to monitor or further their learning, and their ability to use criteria to support the production of work of an appropriate standard. One of the significant common strands within these two views relates to student capacity to use criteria to monitor performance in relation to standards. Appreciating and using feedback are implicit in these descriptions of assessment literacy; part of learning through assessment is using feedback to calibrate evaluative judgement and to inform future study behaviour. We return to the roles of assessment and feedback literacy in supporting engagement with feedback in Chapter 3.

In this chapter, we argue that it is important for students in higher education to be supported to develop the knowledge, skills and mindset to be able to participate in feedback processes and use feedback to maximum effect. Such active participation in feedback processes is central to a new paradigm approach to feedback. The assessment and feedback environment in higher education is likely to be very different to that which students experience at school or college. Beaumont, O'Doherty, and Shannon (2011) discuss how assessment and feedback processes in school and college are often characterised by frequent formative feedback, and opportunities for resubmission of work. In contrast, a common model in higher education is for students to receive a single summative judgement of a piece of work that has been completed independently, meaning that many students are "thrown in at the deep end" in their experience of assessment and feedback at university (Beaumont et al., 2011, p. 677).

It is perhaps surprising that students often have limited opportunities to develop these skills. Weaver (2006) asked Business and Design students whether they had received any guidance on how to understand and use feedback. Of the students that responded, 50% reported that they had received no guidance; of those who had, 26% were provided with this information prior to starting university, with 14% gaining this understanding in their first year of university, and 4% acquiring this knowledge for themselves by engaging with study skills texts. In a follow-up study by Burke (2009), only 39% of a sample of students (humanities, languages, and social sciences disciplines) reported that they had received guidance on how to use feedback prior to starting university; 46% of students reported that they had not, and a further 15% claimed to have received 'limited' guidance prior to starting university. It is clear that many students do not arrive on higher education programmes fully equipped with the skills needed to make use of feedback, and it is a mistake to assume that they will automatically know how to make best use of the developmental advice provided by their teachers. Thus, the development of students' feedback literacy should be a core concern of higher education practitioners. We focus here on the development of students' feedback literacy, but it is worth emphasising at this point that the development of teachers' feedback literacy is equally important, even though the research base has not yet developed rich conceptualisations of teacher feedback literacy. An initial investigation suggests that teacher feedback literacy involves: appreciation of the role of feedback in developing student self-regulation; strategies to support students in generating peer feedback; and attentiveness to socio-cultural, relational and affective elements (Xu, & Carless, 2017). We consider the role of teachers' feedback literacy in greater depth in Chapter 10 in the light of the evidence presented throughout the book.

Conceptualising feedback literacy

In an initial conceptualisation of student feedback literacy, Sutton (2012, p. 31) described it as "the ability to read, interpret and use written feedback". Sutton drew upon the academic literacies approach in higher education (e.g. Lea, & Street, 1998), arguing that an approach based on academic literacies overcomes deficiencies inherent in the study skills approach and the academic socialisation approach in higher education. The study skills approach places emphasis on students' acquisition of a skills 'toolbox'; in this sense, difficulties using feedback arise because students possess a deficit in this particular skill (Sutton, 2012). In contrast, the academic socialisation approach emphasises the importance of students' inculcation into the academic culture. Thus, difficulties using feedback can be attributed to students' failure to grasp the model of feedback held by the academic culture into which they are becoming socialised. Sutton summarises the deficiencies with both of these viewpoints; a study skills approach is reductionist in that it focuses on 'fixing' missing or deficient skills, and an academic socialisation approach fails to recognise the nuances of different disciplinary cultures, and the importance of identity change and development during the period of socialisation. In contrast, the academic literacies approach encompasses epistemological, ontological, and practical dimensions. Similarly, Sutton identifies three dimensions of feedback literacy: the epistemological dimension (understanding the influence of feedback on and for knowing), the ontological dimension (understanding the influence of feedback on one's academic identity), and the practical dimension (knowledge of how to act upon feedback).

In a more recent and comprehensive treatment (Carless, & Boud, 2018), feedback literacy was defined as "the understandings, capacities and dispositions needed to make sense of information and use it to enhance work or learning strategies" (Carless, & Boud, 2018, p. 1316). The notion of students' sense-making of feedback exchanges is central to the authors' conceptualisation of feedback itself, which leads naturally to a consideration of the attributes needed to facilitate this process. Carless and Boud identify four dimensions of feedback literacy: appreciating feedback processes; making judgements; managing affect; and taking action. The framework proposed by Carless and Boud represents an important advance on earlier discussions of feedback literacy as their paper discusses the implications of feedback literacy for teaching and course design. Students need opportunities and means to use feedback for improvement purposes because without action, feedback comments cannot facilitate learning.

All of the practices discussed in this book are in some way predicated on their potential to develop student feedback literacy through supporting students to develop a deeper understanding of the meaning and purpose of feedback, in line with a new paradigm focus. We now discuss challenges to the development of feedback literacy, before exploring key examples from the literature that represent ways forward in overcoming these challenges. We focus on the importance of learning to appreciate the purpose and process of feedback, to harness the emotional impact of feedback, and to take productive action upon feedback.

Learning to appreciate the purpose and process of feedback

One of the most fundamental barriers to student involvement in feedback processes is that teachers and students may not share a common understanding of the purpose of feedback, and students may not recognise many of the means through which they receive and generate feedback. Misalignment between students' and teachers' views of feedback is clearly evident in the literature (e.g. Adcroft, 2011; Carless, 2006; Mulliner, & Tucker, 2017; see also Chapter 6). In exploring different perceptions of feedback, Adcroft (2011, p. 406) draws upon the concept of 'mythologies', defined as "a set of underlying assumptions and beliefs that determine interpretation and behaviour". He set out to explore whether teachers and students shared a common 'mythology' of feedback, or whether dissonance was evident in their perceptions. Through the administration of a survey to teachers and students in Business and Law disciplines, he demonstrated that, in contrast with teachers, students showed a lower level of agreement with a learning-focused conception of feedback, for example the role of feedback in explaining gaps in knowledge and understanding, the role of feedback in directing students to appropriate study practices, and the role of feedback in helping self-assessment and self-correction. In contrast, students showed greater agreement than teachers with the conception of feedback as improving performance. In addition, teachers agreed to a greater extent than students that feedback occurs frequently beyond the bounds of assessed work, for example through dialogue and other non-written forms. Conversely, students agreed to a greater extent than teachers that a mark or grade constitutes the most important form of feedback, and that written feedback is the most useful form of feedback. Adcroft argues that it is important to build a shared set of beliefs with greater alignment of perspectives. This is particularly important in the context of feedback cultures, as an effective new paradigm feedback culture requires the explication of shared goals and a meaningful division of responsibility in the feedback process (Nash, & Winstone, 2017). There is a need for teachers and students to enter into partnerships in feedback processes.

Within the epistemological dimension of feedback literacy, it is important for students to come to view feedback as an important source of learning, informing them not only how their understanding is developing (feedback *on* knowing), but how to further develop their skills and knowledge (feedback *for* knowing; Sutton, 2012). This brings us to one of the key challenges in the development of feedback literacy: that students often ascribe greater importance to the grade awarded (more closely aligned with feedback *on* knowing) than on developmental advice for improvement (feedback *for* knowing). This is probably inevitable due to the importance of students' obtaining a competitive honours classification but it is a barrier to the kind of improvement that would enhance that very same honours classification.

Although students claim to value feedback that directs them towards future improvement (e.g. Winstone, Nash, Rowntree, & Menezes, 2016), they are much more likely to forget this form of feedback when compared to evaluative feedback *on* knowing (Nash, Winstone, Gregory, & Papps, 2018). Students' focus on grades is inadvertently reinforced when summative feedback is framed as a way of justifying grades or marks rather than as a learning device in its own right. Thus, both teachers and students need to develop feedback literacy to see feedback as a source of learning, rather than a grading mechanism or one that satisfies the requirements of quality assurance procedures. Calvo and Ellis (2010) draw an important distinction between a 'cohesive' conception of feedback, where feedback is linked to the development of learning, and a 'fragmented' conception of feedback characterised by an emphasis on task completion. Four different conceptions of feedback, increasing in sophistication, are identified by McLean, Bond, and Nicholson (2015), moving from feedback as 'telling', through feedback as 'guiding' and 'developing understanding' to feedback as 'opening up a different perspective'. They argue that limited feedback literacy, characterised by a focus on feedback as 'telling', might explain why students do not recognise all forms of feedback they are exposed to, such as oral and peer feedback. Thus, an important challenge for the development of feedback literacy is for teachers to share with students their own beliefs about the purpose of feedback, such that students can advance their own conceptions in line with those of their teachers (Orsmond, & Merry, 2011), and engage in dialogue and debate to develop shared definitions.

Learning to harness the emotional impact of feedback

As discussed in Chapter 9, the affective and interpersonal dimensions of feedback are important to acknowledge. Meaningful engagement with feedback processes can be "obscured by emotional static" (Chanock, 2000, p. 95), where emotions can impede cognitive processing of feedback exchanges (Boud, & Falchikov, 2007). The ontological element of feedback literacy requires students to appreciate the impact of feedback on their own identity as a learner, and to manage their emotional reactions to feedback. Within the affective dimension, Carless and Boud (2018) suggest that feedback-literate students are able to maintain emotional equilibrium and avoid defensiveness when receiving critical feedback, and develop habits of striving for continuous improvement on the basis of internal and external feedback.

There is evidence from Weaver's (2006) study that feedback elicited negative emotions in students, with 39% of Business students and 45% of Design students reporting that negative feedback left them feeling demoralised or angry. As would be expected, 91% of Business students and 90% of Design students reported that they received a confidence boost from positive comments. However, despite the elicitation of emotion, there was little evidence that students allowed these emotions to colour their engagement with feedback. Only 9% of Business students and 20% of Design students reported that they had ignored negative or critical feedback, and only 8% of Business students, and 25% of Design students, reported that they felt like giving up on the basis of negative feedback. Whilst there are clear disciplinary differences here, it appears that many of these students were able to separate emotional and rational responses to feedback. Other evidence supports this assertion; findings from group and individual interviews in a study by Small and Attree (2016) reveal that many students were able to stand back from their initial emotional reactions and rationally appraise the quality and purpose of the feedback, as illustrated in these two narratives:

> ... yeah, you've got to be able to cop that to be able to improve. There's no point in saying that it's fantastic when it's completely wrong.
>
> (Small, & Attree, 2016, p. 2088)

> I think you need the criticism ... that's the point. That's why you hand it in, to find out what you're doing wrong.
>
> (Small, & Attree, 2016, p. 2088)

The ability to manage emotion in feedback situations does not mean that students do not experience negative emotion; rather, that they recognise the importance of moving beyond these feelings to implement guidance on their work, as strongly exemplified in the following narrative from a student participant in the study reported by Shields (2015, p. 620):

> I was really hurt. I was devastated. Although I knew that I haven't done well the feedback was quite negative only the first sentence said it was a nice attempt, but then a long row of negative things ... For the first few days I was just in an upset mood. And I couldn't get over it and then I said to myself the approach is not correct. And if I have this approach I'm never going to make it. The advice they are giving me is to improve myself so I started working off the words.

Developing adaptive emotional responses to feedback is a core element of feedback literacy, and one we return to later in the chapter as well as in Chapter 9.

Learning to take action on feedback

Feedback literacy requires students to act upon comments that they have received (Sutton, 2012); indeed, as argued in Chapter 1, if no action is taken, those comments are merely information. Students need to engage actively in making sense of information and using it to inform their later work, thereby closing some form of feedback loop (Boud, & Molloy, 2013). This imperative for students to take action is a critical aspect of feedback processes underpinning our new paradigm perspective on feedback; feedback-literate students develop and hone a repertoire of strategies for acting on feedback.

Students need motivation, opportunities, and means to act on feedback (Shute, 2008). Unless students see themselves as agents of their own change and develop identities as proactive learners, they may be unable to make productive use of comments about their work (Boud, & Molloy, 2013). One of the most useful things teachers can do to encourage student use of feedback is to design curricula and assessments in ways that facilitate students' processing and implementation of feedback (Carless, & Boud, 2018). These ideas are illustrated in the discussions of practice throughout the book, and specifically in Chapter 5.

There is a danger of making the implicit assumption that students know how to make use of feedback (Orsmond, & Merry, 2011). Students need feedback literacy to recognise where and how comments from one piece of work can be transferred to another (Douglas, Salter, Iglesias, Dowlman, & Eri, 2016; Duncan, 2007), which can often be difficult for students (Hepplestone, & Chikwa, 2014). Research has revealed that comments which may seem very transparent and actionable to a teacher may not appear so to a student, as these student narratives demonstrate:

> Occasionally you get 'be more evaluative' and I think – I don't know what you mean with that comment because I think I have been very evaluative.
>
> (Brown, 2007, p. 40)

> I got told that a piece of work was more like an essay than a literature review. This is not helpful as it does not tell me what should be contained in a literature review or how it should be presented.
>
> (Weaver, 2006, p. 388)

These examples serve to illustrate the difficulties that some students can experience when decoding and taking action upon feedback. In Weaver's (2006) study, Business students were presented with a series of comments, and were asked how confident they were in interpreting what was meant by them. Whilst 67% of the sample were very confident that they could interpret the meaning of the comment 'key concepts identified', only 17% were very confident that they could interpret the comment 'underpinning theory', with this figure being just 5% for the comment 'superficial analysis'. Weaver identifies that students may thus need support to develop the requisite feedback literacy to be able to 'decode' feedback language, arguing that:

> more guidance in interpreting and using feedback is needed; many students may lack the understanding necessary to accurately interpret academic discourse.
>
> (Weaver, 2006, p. 384)

This leads us to consider how we can support students to develop a repertoire of strategies for implementing feedback as an important dimension of their feedback literacy, which we explore further in Chapter 3.

In summary, we have seen how feedback literacy is epistemological (Sutton, 2012), requiring an appreciation of the purpose and process of feedback, and the ability to make evaluative judgements (Carless, & Boud, 2018); it is ontological in that it requires an awareness of the impact of feedback on identity (Sutton, 2012), and the ability to manage emotions arising from feedback (Carless, & Boud, 2018); and it is practical in requiring knowledge and skills in using feedback information (Sutton, 2012; Carless, & Boud, 2018). We have seen how the development of feedback literacy can be hampered by difficulties 'learning the language' of feedback, and by misaligned conceptions of feedback between teachers and students. We have seen how it is important for students to be able to stand back from their initial emotional reactions to feedback, and develop rational plans for action. Finally, we have seen how it is important to avoid the assumption that students know *how* to translate comments into actions; developing such skills is an important dimension of feedback literacy. With these issues in mind, we now move to a consideration of two examples from the literature where the development of students' feedback literacy formed a central purpose.

Key examples from the literature

Having considered the key challenges inherent to the development of feedback literacy, we now consider two examples from the literature where the aim has been to overcome such challenges and implement practices to support the development of students' feedback literacy. The first example (Quinton, & Smallbone, 2010) recognises the importance of reflection on feedback, supporting students to better understand and implement comments, and to overcome knee-jerk defensive reactions that can be stimulated by emotion. The second example (Winstone, Mathlin, & Nash, 2019) describes an approach specifically designed to develop students' feedback literacy, using a set of resources to equip students with the skills needed to take action upon feedback.

The approach reported by Quinton and Smallbone (2010) was built upon their recognition that, in many transmission-focused models of feedback, it is not known whether students understand and make use of comments, and, teachers are not aware how well their comments are understood and used. Thus, Quinton and Smallbone recognised that it may be beneficial to dedicate some class time to provide a space for students to reflect upon feedback, and for students to share these reflections with teachers. They argue that:

> If learning from feedback is to be effective, programmes should be designed to include classroom time allocated for reflection on written feedback, thus providing an opportunity for feeding forward and for self-development.
>
> (Quinton, & Smallbone, 2010, p. 125)

In the context of a Business School, second and third year undergraduate students received marked assignments in a tutorial, and then took part in an individual reflective activity through the use of a carbon-paper reflection sheet. The reflection sheet consisted of three key questions for students selected from a wider set of prompts in a well-known framework for reflective learning (Gibbs, 1988). Gibbs' framework incorporates processes of description ('what happened?'), feelings ('what did I feel about it?'), evaluation ('was it a positive or negative experience?'), analysis ('what sense can I make of the experience?'; 'where does it fit within my personal development?'), conclusion ('what else could I have done?'), and action planning ('in a similar situation, what would I do now?').

The first question on the reflection sheet (see Box 2.1) was designed to encourage students to recognise and record their immediate emotional reactions to feedback, such that these could be separated from more deliberate, rational reactions. Common responses to this question revealed that many students were able to identify honestly and accurately their initial emotional responses to the grade and the associated feedback; many students reported emotions such as 'happy', 'relieved', 'gutted', 'upset', and 'worried' (Quinton & Smallbone, 2010, p. 130).

Box 2.1 Reflection questions used by Quinton and Smallbone (2010)

1 What do I feel about this feedback?
2 What do I think about this feedback?
3 Based on this feedback, what actions could I take to improve my work for another assignment?

The second question was based upon the 'evaluation' and 'analysis' dimensions of Gibbs' framework, and was designed to encourage students to engage with and break down the feedback comments they had received. It is pertinent that whilst many students reported experiencing negative emotions in response to their feedback, they were then able to process the feedback rationally, noticing for example that it was 'fair', 'useful', 'constructive' and 'justified' (Quinton, & Smallbone, 2010, p. 130).

Finally, Gibbs' stages of 'conclusion' and 'action planning' underpinned the third question, which represents the fundamental importance of student uptake of feedback in a new paradigm model. Quinton and Smallbone (2010, p. 130) report that most students were able to identify actions on the basis of feedback, albeit simplistic in some cases, such as 'make more of a plan for my essay', 'provide more evidence', 'leave time to review piece once written', and 'make sure I focus on the question asked'. However, not all students were so adept at identifying actions, suggesting that further support may be needed in order for this approach to facilitate the development of feedback literacy. One student noted as an action, "These comments reflect other pieces of coursework" (p. 131), thus noticing that they were being given consistent feedback, but not identifying a way forward to address these comments. Quinton and Smallbone argue that students should be encouraged to keep a portfolio of their reflection sheets, so that they can identify recurring themes in feedback, and track their emotional reactions over time. A further benefit of this approach is that students can give a copy of their reflection sheet to the marker, giving teachers greater insight into the impact of their feedback which is central to a new paradigm feedback focus. Quinton and Smallbone also argue that this approach, whilst valuable in providing students with the space to engage in structured reflection, should be a catalyst, not substitute, for further reflection on the basis of feedback. Furthermore, this example does not provide evidence of whether students actually followed through on the actions they identified, which would require the collection of follow-up data at a later point in time. The potential impact of the process requires student action, and this is central to a new paradigm focus.

At the beginning of this chapter, we identified that feedback literacy is more than just an academic skill, also being an important dimension of professional competence in the workplace. In line with this focus, Quinton and Smallbone (2010, p. 132) identify that the reflective sheet has the potential to "enable students across disciplines to develop reflective habits which they need in order to support their future role in the workplace". Thus, this approach facilitates the development of feedback literacy by helping students to overcome initial emotional reactions, and to consider how to implement feedback in future work. It is thus a sustainable approach to the development of feedback literacy, but would perhaps be best facilitated through the use of technology in order to meet the demands of electronic management of assessment now commonplace in higher education. For example, students could respond to the reflective questions as part of an e-portfolio housed within the LMS.

Our second example specifically relates to the concept of feedback literacy, involving a toolkit of resources to support the development of the requisite skills underpinning effective use of feedback. In collaboration with students, Winstone and Nash (2016) developed a toolkit of resources that can be used to support students in the development of their feedback literacy. Whilst students did not receive any specific training in feedback literacy prior to collaborating in the design of the resources, they worked closely with academic staff and a research assistant, who facilitated dialogue around the use of feedback as part of the process. The toolkit comprises a student-authored feedback guide (providing advice and strategies for understanding and implementing feedback, including a glossary of common terms used within feedback), a set of feedback workshop resources, and the building blocks for a feedback portfolio. The toolkit is freely available (see Box 2.4), and is designed to be flexible, such that teachers can edit the resources to fit their educational context. The feedback portfolio is further discussed in Chapter 4, so for our present purposes we focus on the feedback workshop component of the toolkit.

Winstone and Nash (2016) specifically structured the workshop activities around the three dimensions of feedback literacy as identified by Sutton (2012): the importance of feedback for *knowing*, developing a sense of *being*, and the importance of *acting* upon feedback. The aim of the activities is that they can be used within lectures, seminars, tutorials or workshops, providing space for the development of feedback literacy. Winstone and Nash (2016) designed three activities and associated resources addressing each of the three domains of feedback literacy. Developing students' awareness of the learning potential of feedback is achieved through activities involving teachers and students developing a shared definition and agreed purpose of feedback, students engaging with standards and criteria, and students identifying the potential for learning from different types of feedback comments. The ontological dimension of feedback literacy is targeted through activities exploring how feedback influences our sense of identity, developing strategies to overcome defences and barriers to engagement with feedback, and exploring how to harness the emotion elicited by feedback in a positive way. Finally, the workshop helps students to develop the capacity to act upon feedback through activities wherein students share ideas for the implementation of feedback, identify actions that could be taken on the basis of common feedback comments, and develop action-planning skills. Over two successive academic years, Winstone et al. (2019) delivered a feedback workshop to first-year Psychology undergraduates as part of an academic skills development programme. Winstone et al. (2019) assessed students' self-reported feedback literacy in the domains of *knowing, being* and *acting* before and after participation in a feedback workshop through the use of a questionnaire measure, reporting statistically significant gains in feedback literacy. This example demonstrates how the provision of opportunities for students to develop the skills needed to make productive use of feedback can lead to gains in their self-reported feedback literacy.

Box 2.2 Key research findings

- Many students begin their university courses without any experience of being supported to learn how to use feedback effectively (Burke, 2009; Weaver, 2006).
- Being 'feedback literate' requires the capacity to appreciate feedback processes, make judgements about the quality of work, manage emotion in response to feedback, and take meaningful action on feedback (Carless, & Boud, 2018).
- Students and their teachers can hold very different perceptions of the purpose of feedback, and its utility (Adcroft, 2011; Carless, 2006; Mulliner, & Tucker, 2017).
- Whilst teachers might believe that feedback comments are transparent in terms of required action, students may not understand how to enact feedback information (Brown, 2007; Weaver, 2006).
- Supporting students to reflect upon feedback is useful in supporting the development of action plans (Quinton, & Smallbone, 2010).
- Directly training students to manage and use feedback productively can lead to gains in students' self-reported feedback literacy (Winstone, et al., 2019).

The case: Embedding feedback literacy within the curriculum

Context

The context for this case study is a large first-year compulsory Social Psychology module with around 240 students at Aston University in the UK. The course is taught by Dr Robert Nash, a Senior Lecturer in Psychology, and a Senior Fellow of the Higher Education Academy. At the time that Robert took over the teaching of this module, he had for quite a while been conducting research on the topic of students' engagement with feedback. He realised that taking on this module represented a great opportunity to 'put your money where your mouth is', so to speak, through trying to build the development of feedback literacy into the fundamental curriculum design.

As a result of his research in the area of feedback, Robert came to appreciate its role in improving students' performance and skills over time. His approach recognises that, without feedback, students are restricted to blind trial-and-error guesswork, with no concrete idea whether past or current actions are appropriate or effective. Robert wanted to find a way of supporting new undergraduates to develop a wider appreciation of the purpose of feedback, and to develop relevant skills to put it into practice. Robert aimed to interweave the development of feedback literacy within the curriculum, rather than as an 'add-on' academic skill, such that students were simultaneously learning about feedback and their disciplinary content.

The feedback design

Robert embedded an overt 'Receiving Feedback' theme into the existing social psychology module design, from the course material, to the assessment methods, to the teaching style. In terms of course material, Robert continued to teach the usual basic content that is required at this introductory level; however, at the end of each lecture he illustrated a psychological study that linked the week's topic to an insight on how people receive feedback. For instance, when teaching 'Self and Identity', Robert outlined a study that demonstrates how people tend to exaggerate their own groups' positive traits whenever they receive feedback that rival groups have outperformed them (Cadinu, & Cerchioni, 2001).

Throughout the initial weeks of the module, students complete a portfolio of short writing tasks, all oriented around one of these feedback studies, each designed to promote a variety of fundamental academic skills (e.g., referencing, professional writing style, and self-evaluation). About halfway through the module, they submit these initial tasks together and Robert reads a sample of portfolios and provides group-level formative feedback in the form of an online audio-narrated slideshow. In the same week that this feedback is released, Robert runs a series of workshops for the students to engage in smaller groups with the concept and purpose of feedback, the difficulties in receiving feedback openly, and the strategies they might use for making feedback more effective. These workshops are based on the Developing Engagement with Feedback Toolkit (Winstone, & Nash, 2016; see Box 2.4).

Following the feedback and workshop, students then complete a fifth portfolio task in which they must reflect on which aspects of the group-level feedback they personally could benefit from taking on board. This element of the design is a clever way of supporting students to make the most of all feedback opportunities, even generic class-level feedback. Finally, having completed all of these portfolio tasks, students complete their main assignment: a reflective essay. In this essay, they must consider some of their past experiences of receiving feedback from others, and apply social psychological theories and evidence to interpret how they had reacted to that feedback. The intent of this assignment is, therefore, that students should implement the feedback they have received and the skills that they have learned, whilst demonstrating their substantive knowledge and understanding of the core subject material.

After one year of running this approach, Robert made two changes to the approach. First, he decided to make the completion of the initial portfolio exercises contribute a small amount towards students' final grades. Whilst it was important that the purpose of these exercises was explicitly formative, it was nevertheless clear that a minority of students were not engaging with them at all. Adding a small grade-weighting ensured that most of this minority had a motivation to engage, albeit instrumental, and that the stronger students were not demotivated by seeing others receiving formative feedback despite doing nothing.

Second, the fifth portfolio task, in which students are required to write their reflections on the group-level formative feedback that Robert had provided, was an addition to the portfolio following the first trial year. He did this because in the first year he saw that a fair number of students did not even watch the feedback presentation, and many who did watch it perceived that because the feedback was group-level rather than individualised, it therefore did not apply to them. Robert wanted the students to pause to reflect on how they can take personal advice even from general, non-personalised feedback. Again, then, he decided to make their reflection on the feedback an explicit requirement, and added this as a fifth portfolio task. Where students fail to appreciate the value of potential feedback exchanges, including those that are generic in nature, this could be seen as an indicator of limited feedback literacy.

Student response

In their evaluations of the module, overall student satisfaction has thus far been exceptionally high, and individuals often comment on the feedback-related content and the workshops as being the most valuable part of their entire academic year. The students' written reflections on the formative feedback have been a further source of insight into the impact of the approach. For Robert, these have often been rewarding, and show great insight into the skills the students have developed, highlighting for instance their awareness of how they can seek out and use specific resources, rather than passively awaiting evaluative feedback at the end of the module once it is too late. The students' actual essays at the end of the module also frequently demonstrate this same kind of insight – showing that they have developed stronger feedback literacy by being able to reflect critically on how they react and respond to challenging feedback. However, despite this module involving an assignment on the use of feedback, it is perhaps frustrating that not all students open the file containing feedback on their essay. This presents us with an interesting conundrum: in order for students to benefit from practices that may enhance their feedback literacy, they may need some pre-existing level of feedback literacy in order to appreciate the value of engaging with the process. Put another way, could this perhaps be another example of the so-called 'Matthew Effect' in education, whereby initial advantage begets further advantage (Rigney, 2010)? Those who are more competent in a given domain may stand to benefit more from associated interventions, as they are better able to access and progress through engagement with opportunities for development. In contrast, those who perhaps have most to gain from the intervention do not benefit to the same degree as they are unable to access, or do not value, these development opportunities. If this applies to the development of feedback literacy, then it is important to uncover ways of supporting those with more limited levels of feedback literacy to benefit from practices, such as Robert's, that stand to confer gains in skills and attitudes towards feedback.

Enabling factors

A key enabler in this case was the fact that Robert had recently moved to his current institution in the middle of an academic year, and so his administrative and teaching-related workload were relatively low for the remainder of that year. Having this mental space enabled him to pause to really think about and plan for good practice, in a way that is so difficult to achieve in the midst of a normal, chaotic academic cycle. Robert is also an active researcher in the psychology of feedback, so his engagement with the literature on new paradigm approaches to feedback is likely to also act as an enabler in this context. Thus, the feedback culture in which Robert is situated, where he engages with other scholars working in this area, is likely to facilitate his thinking and innovation.

Challenges

The main challenge experienced was that those students who in principle stand to gain most from the innovation – those with the lowest grades – were typically those who engage least with it. Indeed, after completing a module with so much emphasis on how and why to use feedback effectively, and after writing an essay on this topic, it is somewhat ironic that some of these students still don't fully engage with feedback! One potential reason for this is that the 'reflective essay' form of assessment is a highly unfamiliar one for most students, and some of Robert's students expressed anxiety about undertaking an assessment task that they had not experienced before. Whilst Robert explains that this new reflective style may not be appropriate in all of their written work, he takes several steps to help the students understand how the process of reflection is valuable even if they will not normally be asked to write in a reflective style. One of the potential complications, though, is that students might perhaps judge that receiving feedback on their reflective writing is less useful to them if they are not usually going to have to write in this way.

Another issue is that this module runs at the end of the first year, and so after completing all of these exercises the students go away for the summer, and it is not clear whether many of the messages are lost by the time they return for second year. Robert came to believe that reaping the real potential value from these kinds of teaching practices will probably require a systemic, programmatic approach, rather than the students merely receiving these messages and opportunities from individual academic staff in individual modules. We take up this issue of programme-wide approaches to assessment and feedback in Chapter 5.

Relationship to the literature

Central to this design is developing students' readiness to engage proactively with feedback, and their sense of having both the agency and the responsibility to do so. To this end, the 'SAGE' feedback recipience processes outlined by Winstone, Nash, Parker, and Rowntree (2017a; see Chapter 3) – self-appraisal, assessment literacy, goal-setting and self-regulation, and engagement and motivation – are all targeted in one or more ways through the different components of the portfolio assessment and the module content. Students also have the opportunity to reflect upon their own use of feedback, which resonates with Quinton and Smallbone's work (2010). Learning about research from their discipline relevant to their own engagement with feedback has the potential to enable students to appreciate the purpose and influence of feedback, as well as to manage their own affective responses to feedback, both core dimensions of feedback literacy according to Carless and Boud (2018).

Significance of this practice

This case is an excellent example of developing students' feedback literacy in a way that is fully embedded within the curriculum. The seamless integration between the development of academic skills and conceptual knowledge is distinctive, particularly as this integration extends beyond methods of teaching to assessment methods too. It is often believed that students are unlikely to engage with material unless it relates to assessment; by relating the exploration of feedback directly to assessment, this practice enables students to harness their motivation to complete an assessment to learn about and reflect upon the psychology of engaging with feedback information.

This approach works especially well in the context of teaching social psychology because the barriers that prevent people from taking feedback on board can be so easily demonstrated through the lens of social psychological evidence and theory. However, there are likely to be analogous ways of delivering this kind of approach effectively and creatively in other disciplines (for example in the context of feedback use in business environments; see Box 2.5). It is also important to ensure that students fully appreciate the rationale behind the integration of feedback literacy into curriculum design and that this rationale is communicated on multiple occasions during the module.

Box 2.3 Implications for practice

- There are powerful benefits of integrating feedback literacy within the curriculum, as learning about feedback is not an 'add-on' but a central part of students' courses.
- A portfolio assessment design is a useful facilitator for student engagement and action on feedback (see also Chapter 5).
- Students need to be motivated and encouraged, often repeatedly, to engage in feedback activities.
- A pragmatic, yet instrumental option, is to incentivise student participation in meaningful feedback activities through awarding marks/grades for students' use of feedback.
- Working with students to explore and agree the purpose of feedback, and how it can be implemented, is an important part of a student's orientation to a course or unit, and can avoid misaligned perceptions between teachers and students.
- Students benefit from direct support and training to help develop their feedback literacy.

Conclusion

Teachers invest a significant amount of time and effort in providing detailed comments to students. In a new paradigm approach to feedback, this is merely the start of the process; how students understand, assimilate and implement these comments is paramount in ensuring the impact of feedback. In order to navigate this process, students need to be literate in the domain of feedback, from understanding standards and criteria prior to submitting an assignment, to engaging in meaningful dialogue with peers and teachers about their work, to managing the emotional response to feedback, and understanding what feedback is and why it is important. All of these factors are likely to support students in taking meaningful action on the basis of feedback. This is a complex set of processes, yet often less time is invested in helping students to develop these attributes in comparison to other academic skills.

In this chapter, we have explored students' perspectives on the support they have been given to develop feedback literacy, before discussing the dimensions of feedback literacy as articulated by Carless and Boud (2018). We then considered research evidence that illustrates the often misaligned perceptions of feedback held by teachers and students, arguing that the development of shared feedback literacy is likely to be crucial. We briefly considered the importance of managing emotional responses to feedback (this topic is explored in more depth in Chapter 9), and saw examples of students having difficulty determining what actions they should take on the basis of feedback. Our two key examples from the literature demonstrate the value of supporting students to reflect upon feedback (Quinton, & Smallbone, 2010), and giving students the opportunity to develop feedback literacy skills in dedicated workshops (Winstone, et al., 2019).

As we have argued here, the importance of supporting the development of students' feedback literacy cannot be underestimated. Regardless of a student's programme of study, not only are these skills central to students' success at university, they are essential workplace competencies. As part of our commitment to developing our students' graduate attributes, and supporting them to develop as lifelong learners, we need to pay attention to the development of feedback literacy.

Box 2.4 Key resources

- The Developing Engagement with Feedback Toolkit, containing a feedback guide, feedback workshop resources, and feedback portfolio tools (Winstone, & Nash, 2016): www.heacademy.ac.uk/knowledge-hub/developing-engagement-feedback-toolkit-deft
- Why should we focus on assessment and feedback literacy? A blog from the University of Edinburgh, UK: www.teaching-matters-blog.ed.ac.uk/why-we-should-focus-on-assessment-and-feedback-literacy/
- David Carless talking about student feedback literacy: https://tinyurl.com/DCarless-FL
- Guidance on promoting students' assessment literacy: www.cetl.hku.hk/teaching-learning-cop/wp-content/uploads/2015/08/wise-assessment-briefing7.pdf
- Evaluative judgement and the development of student feedback literacy: a blog post from the Centre for Research in Assessment and Digital Learning (CRADLE; Deakin University): https://blogs.deakin.edu.au/cradle/2018/05/10/evaluative-judgement-and-the-development-of-student-feedback-literacy/
- A case study from University College London on student reflection on feedback: www.ucl.ac.uk/teaching-learning/case-studies/2016/jul/reflecting-feedback-using-forms-formalise-process

Box 2.5 Questions for Reflection and Debate

- To what extent does the nature of feedback literacy vary according to academic discipline, or are there core elements of feedback literacy relevant to all disciplines?
- How does the feedback literacy of teachers influence the feedback literacy of their students and what are the implications of this influence?
- To what extent are a) schools/colleges and b) universities responsible for developing students' feedback literacy?
- Do you think that your conception of the purpose of feedback aligns with that of your students? If not, how could you work towards a shared understanding?
- How does feedback literacy relate to relevant graduate attributes in your discipline?
- How do you currently support the development of your students' feedback literacy, and what else could you embed into your practice?
- How do we convince students of all ability levels of the benefits of developing feedback literacy, and that it is worth the effort?
- How could you integrate the development of feedback literacy with your disciplinary content? For example, has resistance to feedback played a role in momentous historical decisions, political policies, or social movements for example? Will students on this career path be involved in communicating difficult feedback to patients, job applicants, or managers?

Chapter 3

Facilitating student engagement with feedback processes

Even the very highest quality feedback will have limited impact on student learning unless the information is used to develop skills, understanding and motivation. Central to new paradigm conceptions of feedback is the notion of student uptake of feedback, which necessarily requires students to engage with and enact the information provided through feedback exchanges. It is student engagement with and action upon feedback that moves feedback from comments as "dangling data" (Sadler, 1989, p. 121) towards processes that change students' thinking, behaviour, and motivation. As argued neatly by Price, Handley, and Millar (2011, p. 894), "Feedback without engagement is completely unproductive".

What might student engagement with feedback look like?

How we conceptualise engagement with feedback will likely differ according to our conception of feedback itself. For example, if the purpose of feedback is viewed as informing students about their performance and identifying errors, then we might be satisfied to know that they had received and read it. However, if we view feedback as facilitating learning, then we need to know how well that feedback has led to changes in behaviour, performance and understanding (Price, Handley, Millar, & O'Donovan, 2010). The latter perception, where teachers seek evidence of the impact of feedback, represents what Boud (1995a) calls 'consequential validity'; however, research suggests that the practice of seeking such evidence is far from common (Winstone, & Boud, 2019).

Handley, Price, and Millar (2011) bring further clarity to the notion of student engagement by discussing the concept of 'doing time': paying lip service to engagement by collecting feedback but only skim-reading the comments. Such surface engagement contrasts with 'mindful' engagement which involves reflection and interpretation, and application of the feedback to develop understanding and adjust learning behaviour. This conceptualisation of mindful engagement gives us an indication of what behaviours we might expect to see in a student who is engaging with and making use of their feedback. Such engagement might exist on a continuum from reading and considering how comments could be implemented, through using feedback whilst working on the next assignment, to seeking skill development opportunities and setting goals for improvement on the basis of feedback. These higher levels of engagement require investment of time and effort; commitment and willingness to invest such time and effort is described by Handley et al. (2011, p. 547) as a student's "readiness to engage".

There is also evidence that students' engagement with feedback differs according to their level of ability; through a series of focus groups and interviews with undergraduate students, Orsmond and Merry (2013) demonstrated that high-achieving students showed stronger personal responsibility for acting in response to feedback than their lower-achieving counterparts. The higher-achieving students also self-assessed their own work against work they had completed in the past, and discussed feedback with their peers. In contrast, lower-achieving students favoured external regulation, with limited evidence of self-regulation. Similarly, Sinclair and Cleland (2007) reported that more academically able students were more likely than their less able counterparts to collect written feedback.

We conceptualise student engagement with feedback processes as consisting of two interrelated activities: mindful processing and sense-making of comments, and reasoned decision-making for uptake. Whilst uptake requires sense-making, students can process feedback thoroughly and choose not to take action. A conscious decision not to take immediate action or to file the comment for future use still represents uptake; the student may recognise that the comment is valid and potentially useful, but consciously decide that acting upon the comment at the present time would not be appropriate. Instead, they may plan to revisit the comment at a later date. Where we discuss engagement with feedback, we are referring to feedback *processes*, thus emphasising that students can engage prior to receiving comments, for example by requesting and negotiating feedback exchanges (Blair, & McGinty, 2013).

In an attempt to understand the skills and behaviours that underpin engagement with feedback processes, Winstone, Nash, Parker, and Rowntree (2017a) conducted a systematic review of literature on student engagement with feedback. Within papers that reported interventions to develop students' engagement with feedback processes, Winstone et al. (2017a) sought information about the authors' rationale: what skills were they trying to develop in students? Winstone et al. (2017a) classified these skills into a taxonomy of processes underpinning engagement with feedback, the 'SAGE' taxonomy (see Figure 3.1).

Self-appraisal represents the ability to look critically at one's own attributes, and recognise strengths and areas for development. If an individual is not open to this process of self-evaluation, defensive reactions to feedback can result, which can hamper strong engagement (e.g. Smith, & King, 2004). *Assessment literacy* (see also Chapter 2) requires knowledge of standards and criteria used within the process of assessment. When students develop the capacity for evaluative judgement (e.g. Tai, Ajjawi, Boud, Dawson, & Panadero, 2018), they become less reliant on external sources of feedback, being better able to generate feedback for themselves.

Feedback typically contains valuable information about how to improve future assignments; however, knowing *what* to improve, and *how* to improve, require

Figure 3.1 The SAGE Taxonomy of recipience processes
Source: Winstone et al., 2017a.

different levels of engagement. *Goal-setting and self-regulation* are thus important dimensions of engagement with feedback, enabling the student to adopt the goal-directed behaviours needed to realise the impact of feedback information (Winstone, et al., 2017a). Finally, Winstone et al. (2017a) identified *engagement and motivation* as an important dimension of feedback recipience; students have to be willing to scrutinise feedback and to engage in what can be hard work to develop their skills.

The skills identified within the SAGE Taxonomy are complex; it is likely that students need opportunities to practice and hone their ability to effectively engage with and implement feedback (see Chapter 2). Before we can consider ways of facilitating student engagement, we need to understand the barriers students might face to meaningful engagement with feedback.

Why might students show limited engagement with feedback?

Anecdotal reports from practitioners in Higher Education often paint a poor picture of student engagement with feedback. To a certain extent, the literature provides support for these anecdotal reports. Students do not always collect feedback or open feedback files on the LMS, and not all students read feedback in depth (Mulliner, & Tucker, 2017). When they see students failing to make the most of feedback opportunities, some teachers might assume that students lack motivation and commitment. Rather than just assuming that students are not interested in receiving feedback, it is important to try and understand what lies beneath this apparently disengaged behaviour. Jönsson (2013) addressed this question by reviewing the literature on students' use of feedback, uncovering five challenges that might prevent productive use of feedback. First, Jönsson draws attention to the fact that the feedback has to be useful in order to be used; if the feedback comes too late to be implemented on subsequent assessment tasks, or if assessments are not designed to enable students to transfer feedback, then an important prerequisite for engagement is not in place (see Chapter 5). Second, Jönsson argues that students demonstrate a preference for specific, detailed and individualised feedback, so engagement may be limited if these criteria are not met. Jönsson recognises that what students say they want is not necessarily what will best support their learning; indeed, such a focus on the level of detail within feedback comments aligns closely with an old paradigm perspective on feedback. Third, Jönsson discusses the role of emotion in feedback, arguing that authoritative feedback is unlikely to have strong impact. Jönsson also stresses that the tone of feedback is important, whereby feedback-givers should not frame their opinions on student work as definitive facts (see Chapter 9). Fourth, according to Jönsson, students may not know which useful strategies they should use to implement feedback, and fifth, they may find it difficult to engage with feedback because they lack an understanding of the academic terminology used within feedback. The barriers identified by Jönsson give us insight into the range of affective, cognitive, and behavioural dimensions encompassing engagement with feedback.

More recently, Winstone, Nash, Rowntree, and Parker (2017b) identified four distinct barriers to students' engagement with feedback information, through a thematic analysis of focus groups with undergraduate students. In these focus groups, students were not asked directly about barriers to engagement, but discussion of what prevents them from using feedback emerged spontaneously as students discussed a series of feedback comments, exploring the actions they would take on the basis of these comments.

The first barrier identified by Winstone et al. (2017b) was termed awareness, representing students' difficulty decoding the language used within feedback, understanding the purpose of feedback, and recognising where feedback comes from. This aligns closely with Jönsson's discussion of students' difficulty understanding academic terminology commonly used within feedback. The next barrier identified by Winstone et al. (2017b) also resonates with Jönsson's discussion: the term cognisance was used by Winstone et al. (2017b) to represent students' difficulty in knowing which strategies they should use to implement feedback. The barrier of agency represents students' difficulty in feeling empowered to act upon feedback; a common issue arising here is the difficulty transferring feedback across assignments in a heavily modularised curriculum (see also Hughes, Smith, & Creese, 2015). Finally, the barrier of volition represents an unwillingness to put in the 'hard graft' (Carless, 2015a) required to realise the impact of feedback.

It is useful to hear directly from students the difficulties they face when implementing feedback. Whilst some of these barriers are motivational, it would be dangerous to assume that students are simply not interested in feedback. Indeed, evidence suggests that students are eager to receive performance information beyond the numerical grade. Based on questionnaire data from 94 Undergraduate students, Higgins, Hartley, and Skelton (2002) reported that 82% of students agreed that they paid close attention to their feedback. They followed up the questionnaire through interviews with Business and Humanities students, and their analysis revealed evidence of intrinsic motivation to use feedback to support broad skill development. In a recent survey study, Mulliner and Tucker (2017, p. 277) presented data illustrating a wide gulf in the perspectives held by teachers and students with regard to students' engagement with feedback. For example, whilst 68% of the students surveyed agreed that they "refer back to feedback from a previous assignment when starting a new related assignment", only 15% of staff respondents held the same view about students. In a similar vein, 93% of students agreed that they always read qualitative feedback; only 35% of staff agreed. Most strikingly, 82% of students agreed that they always act on feedback, whereas only 4% of staff agreed that students always act on feedback.

Why might the views of teachers and students regarding students' engagement with feedback be so discrepant? First, in an old paradigm transmission-focused approach to feedback, students' recipience of feedback is hidden from teachers, as evidence is rarely sought that might demonstrate how students have utilised the information. As a result, teachers may be able to speculate about students' engagement with feedback, but these assumptions are based on little hard evidence, due to the "invisibility of engagement" (Price, et al., 2011, p. 882). The same issue applies to the research literature; behavioural research on engagement with feedback is scant (Jönsson, 2013; Winstone, et al., 2017a). Recent developments in the use of learning analytics for pedagogic purposes offer some scope to resolve this issue. For example, Zimbardi et al. (2017) tracked how long students engaged with feedback that had been posted on the LMS, and then sought to explore how this engagement related to students' improvement on subsequent assignments. In terms of practice, this approach is valuable as it serves to surface the hidden recipience of feedback; in terms of research, these large datasets can provide valuable insight into students' behavioural responses to feedback information.

A second potential reason for wide differences in teacher and student perceptions of engagement with feedback is that teachers and students might conceptualise engagement in different ways. For example, in Mulliner and Tucker's (2017) study, when responding to the statement "Students/I always act on feedback", students might believe that they are taking action, but this action might be on more of a surface level than teachers might expect from students (Burke, 2009). There may also be different interpretations of what 'taking action' means; some might argue that merely reading the comments is an action.

Regardless of the underlying reasons for discrepant beliefs about students' engagement with feedback, teachers' and students' views coalesce around the purpose of feedback as a tool to facilitate learning and improvement (e.g. Dawson, et al., 2019; Mulliner, & Tucker, 2017). Thus, if we are to explore how to support students' engagement with feedback, it is important to build upon agreement regarding the purpose of feedback, and develop a shared perception of what we mean by 'engagement' in the context of feedback processes. On this basis, we can then start to consider the roles that teacher and student need to play in promoting engagement, and how we might work to nurture the skills that support meaningful and impactful engagement with feedback information. It is to these crucial issues that we now turn.

How can we facilitate student engagement with feedback?

One of the primary aims of higher education is to develop autonomy within students. In this vein, it could perhaps be argued that once the teacher has provided feedback on students' work, the responsibility is then passed to students to engage with the advice and take action. However, it is crucial to recognise that important environmental facilitators need to be in place that support student engagement with feedback (Price, et al., 2011). For example, ensuring that students feel empowered and supported through feedback is important, as negative emotional experiences in prior feedback exchanges can limit future engagement with feedback (Price, et al., 2011; see also Chapter 9). Furthermore, an assessment culture that places heavy emphasis on summative assessment can also limit students' engagement with feedback, by shifting students' motivations towards passing the unit of assessment, and away from engaging with developmental feedback (Harrison, Könings, Schuwirth, Wass, & van der Vleuten, 2015).

Nicol (2010) speaks of teachers and students 'sharing the burden' within the feedback process, and Price et al. (2010, p. 280) clearly state that "Student engagement with assessment feedback is not entirely the responsibility of students". Thus, it is also important to consider the roles and responsibilities of teachers and students in overcoming some of the common barriers to engagement with feedback. Nash and Winstone (2017) argued that whilst both teachers and students share roughly equal responsibility for overcoming such barriers, in some cases teachers possess the greatest responsibility, and in others, so do students. This sharing of responsibility is indicative of the interplay between teacher and student feedback literacy. For example, teachers have a responsibility to make sure that feedback is clear, and that students know the purpose of feedback and all of the different sources of feedback available. They also have a responsibility to ensure that students are equipped with strategies to make productive use of feedback, and to create an environment in which students have the opportunity to implement feedback (see Chapter 5). If these conditions are put in place, students should be able to shoulder the weight of responsibility for being willing to put in time and effort to engage with feedback and to improve their skills. Students also need to be willing to engage in meaningful dialogue, seeking further guidance where necessary (Nash, & Winstone, 2017). These dialogic elements are scrutinised further in Chapter 6. Crucially, then, the key responsibility of teachers is to create the conditions under which students possess the agency and volition to implement feedback, by supporting the development of their awareness of the meaning and purpose of feedback, and their cognisance of appropriate strategies for implementing feedback. How can such ends be achieved?

Perhaps the first step to facilitating students' engagement with feedback is to ensure that students have the opportunity to implement feedback, by paying attention to assessment design (see Boud, & Molloy, 2013). For example, producing a draft and then reworking it affords students opportunities to engage with feedback and rework the assignment before final submission (O'Donovan, Rust, &

Price, 2016; see also Chapter 5). Other elements of a design approach to facilitating engagement with feedback are to ensure that feedback is timely, occurring at a time where it can be put into practice on the next assignment, and involves dialogue to build strong relationships between teachers and students (O'Donovan, et al., 2016). Furthermore, engagement with feedback can be facilitated by providing strong cohesion between assessments in different modules, so that transfer of feedback is supported (O'Donovan, et al., 2016; see Chapter 5).

In their systematic review, Winstone, et al. (2017a) identified within the literature many different examples of interventions that have been developed with the aim of supporting students to engage with and implement feedback. They uncovered a diverse range of practices and initiatives, and clustered the interventions into four broad categories (see Figure 3.2). It is important to note that not all of these interventions are reported to have equivalent efficacy, yet evidence attests to the potential

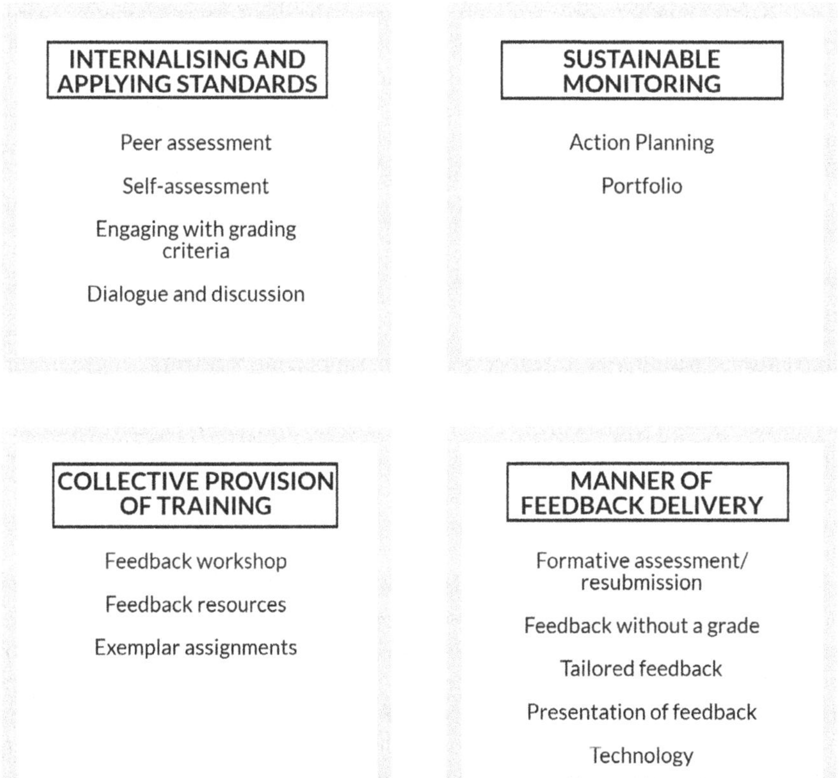

INTERNALISING AND APPLYING STANDARDS	SUSTAINABLE MONITORING
Peer assessment	Action Planning
Self-assessment	Portfolio
Engaging with grading criteria	
Dialogue and discussion	

COLLECTIVE PROVISION OF TRAINING	MANNER OF FEEDBACK DELIVERY
Feedback workshop	Formative assessment/ resubmission
Feedback resources	Feedback without a grade
Exemplar assignments	Tailored feedback
	Presentation of feedback
	Technology

Figure 3.2 Interventions to support student engagement with feedback
Source: Winstone et al., 2017a.

of these approaches in developing students' skills and motivation to engage proactively with feedback information. We now turn to a brief exploration of these interventions, also drawing upon an additional focus group study exploring students' perceptions of each of these interventions (Parker, & Winstone, 2016).

Internalising and applying standards

This group of interventions focuses on supporting students to understand how the assessment process works, and to gain understanding of the criteria and standards against which their work will be assessed. Such practices support engagement with feedback because as students internalise these standards, they should over time become less reliant on others for feedback, being better able to generate such feedback for themselves. Internalisation and application of standards might be facilitated through students discussing work with teachers and peers. However, some evidence suggests that students can be reticent to take advantage of opportunities for dialogue with markers (Parker, & Winstone, 2016). Furthermore, students recognise the benefits of engaging with grading criteria (Parker, & Winstone, 2016; cf. Bloxham, & West, 2007), but can also find it difficult to understand the terminology used within rubrics and mark schemes (Cartney, 2010; Parker, & Winstone, 2016). Some students express concerns about possessing the necessary expertise and objectivity to comment on their own or others' work (e.g. Moore, & Teather, 2013; Parker, & Winstone, 2016), which can be overcome by emphasising the developmental function of the activity.

Sustainable monitoring

Interventions within this category focus on supporting students' engagement with feedback processes by enabling them to track their use of feedback, and the impact of this engagement on their academic and personal development. Feedback portfolios can be utilised to support students to synthesise feedback from multiple assignments, and to gain a more coherent perception of their strengths and areas for development (Parker, & Winstone, 2016; see also Chapter 4).

Targeted action planning interventions can also be used to support students' engagement with feedback. For example, Enomoto (2012) reported an innovation where University students on a Japanese Language course were supported to understand and use feedback, and to develop skills of reflection and self-regulation (see also Chapter 7) through 'Study Skills Action Plans'. Students are generally very positive about action planning interventions. For example, students in Parker and Winstone's (2016) study reported that setting goals helped them to feel more in control of acting upon feedback, seeing concrete actions "like a solution, rather than a stab in the dark" (Parker, & Winstone, 2016, p. 60).

Collective provision of training

Many interventions to support student engagement with feedback can be carried out with large cohorts of students, either as additional sessions or as part of the timetabled curriculum. In the discipline of Law, Withey (2013) developed a feedback guide for students explaining what feedback is, how to use it and explaining typical comments that students might receive on their work. The guide was introduced to students through a lecture presentation, and 80% reported that the guide had enhanced their engagement with feedback. Large cohorts of students can also be collectively introduced to exemplar assignments as a means to develop evaluative judgement, supporting them to internalise criteria and standards. These cohort-wide interventions can be seen as part of the broader process of building students' assessment literacy, which is an important contribution to the development of self-regulation (see Chapter 7). Providing structured support to students in this way does not necessarily constitute spoon-feeding (Balloo, Evans, Hughes, Zhu, & Winstone, 2018), but can provide the conditions for independence through empowerment.

Manner of feedback delivery

Some approaches to supporting students' engagement with feedback focus on the way in which feedback is structured and delivered, including provision for formative assessment or resubmission of work following feedback on a draft, or changing the presentation of feedback using different feedback proformas or through a different medium (e.g. oral feedback). In some interventions, students are able to request feedback on specific elements of their work, which can lead to stronger engagement with the advice provided (Bloxham, & Campbell, 2010; see Chapter 6). Other approaches include withholding the grade until students have engaged with feedback (e.g. Sendziuk, 2010), as discussed in Chapter 4. Whilst students recognise that this might make them pay more attention to the feedback, those in the study reported by Parker and Winstone (2016) expressed frustration with this approach, and said that when reading the feedback they would be seeking to ameliorate anxiety by 'guessing' the grade they had achieved, rather than mindfully processing the qualitative feedback. Other interventions within this category utilise technology as a way of strengthening students' engagement with the assessment and feedback process (see Chapter 4).

Key examples from the literature

We now turn to consideration of the work of key scholars who have developed our understanding of the process and importance of student engagement with feedback: Margaret Price, Berry O'Donovan and Chris Rust who carried out a programme of work at Oxford Brookes University, UK; and Paul Orsmond and Stephen Merry from Staffordshire University, UK. The work of Price and colleagues has been influential in providing the impetus for a shift in feedback scholarship and practice towards consideration of student engagement. They have argued that many responses to student dissatisfaction with feedback, such as increasing the quantity of feedback, can be well-meaning but limited in failing to consider whether the feedback is having an impact:

> There is a danger of merely trying to respond to student dissatisfaction with *more of the same*, but this is likely to exacerbate rather than address the problem. Therefore, a new perspective on the feedback process, focused on the process of *engagement* rather than the technicalities of feedback, needs to be explored.
>
> (Price, et al., 2011, p. 880, italics in original)

This quotation is indicative of new paradigm thinking; by warning against a focus on the delivery of comments, rather than on students' engagement with feedback, Price and colleagues were hinting at the importance of shifting the dominant model of feedback in higher education.

Based upon a three-year project on engagement with feedback in business students, Price, et al. (2011) proposed a model of engagement with feedback as a process, with multiple points in the process where students can potentially disengage. The first point where disengagement with feedback could potentially occur is collection of feedback. Evidence suggests that if students perceive the feedback to be useful, and if they have an opportunity to apply it, then they are more likely to collect it (Price, et al., 2011). If students collect their feedback, the next potential point of disengagement occurs if students do not pay attention to the feedback. In order for students to engage on this attentional level, it is important that they can understand the comments (Price, et al., 2011). The next point of disengagement in Price et al.'s model is at the cognitive level, at the point where students might apply the feedback to their own learning. Price et al. (2011) argue that in order for engagement to be supported at this level, students need to understand that feedback is intended to improve their long-term learning and skills development. It is thus crucial that feedback comments target this developmental process, and do not merely serve as justification of the grade that has been awarded for an individual piece of work. Price et al. (2011) further argue that students need to know how to take action, and implement the developmental advice they have been given. Finally, they actually have to take action. Disengagement could potentially occur at either of these final two points in the feedback process and even if students are engaged at each prior stage of the process, this does not guarantee that they will take the final action (Price, et al., 2011). Finally, Price et al. (2011) caution that there are varying degrees of action and not all are substantive.

The work of Orsmond and Merry has also been influential in developing our understanding of *how* students engage with feedback. In one study, Orsmond, Merry, and Reiling (2005) conducted semi-structured interviews with 16 third-year biology undergraduates. Students were engaged in discussion around their experiences of receiving formative and summative feedback, their perceptions of the purpose of feedback, and their beliefs about the contribution of feedback to learning.

The first thing that Orsmond et al. (2005) report is a summary of the behaviours of their sample in response to feedback. Of the 16 student participants, three reported that they did not read feedback, with one further student claiming that they only read feedback if the mark is unexpected. Five of the students believed that the mark is more important than the feedback; the other 11 students believed that both are equally important. In terms of the application of feedback, five students reported that they make use of every comment, whereas ten reported that they took away the gist of their feedback.

In their analysis of the student interviews, Orsmond et al. (2005) discuss four ways in which the students in their sample appeared to use feedback:

1 **To motivate.** Some students discussed how feedback comments are used to encourage them in their further learning, and to give them confidence in their skills: "Feedback enables you to develop and become more confident. You are motivated to approach lecturers to talk to them about your work" (p. 374). However, it is notable that Orsmond et al. (2005) also discovered that students' response to feedback in terms of seeking further dialogue with staff is dependent upon how comfortable they feel approaching tutors for further guidance: "Yes, if you get on with a tutor you will seek clarification; if you do not understand feedback from an unapproachable tutor, you ignore it" (p. 377).

2 **To enhance learning.** For some students, feedback had a clear use in terms of supporting their ongoing development and enhancing their learning behaviour: "Feedback helps with other modules and exams; you can avoid making the same mistakes. It helps learning. You can pick up points you might have missed" (p. 375). In some cases, students demonstrated that they use feedback to make direct changes to their learning behaviour: "Feedback changes your direction of learning, no feedback no change" (p. 375).

3 **To enhance reflection.** There was evidence that some students engaged in reflection and self-appraisal, and attempted to synthesise feedback from multiple assessments in order to inform their approaches to future work: "I think the role of feedback is to make you assess what you are doing. I reflect on weaker points more than in previous years and compare feedback from different assignments to look for common themes" (p. 375).

4 **To clarify understanding and expectations.** The final way in which students seemed to use feedback was to help them clarify the level of their understanding, and the expectations of their tutors. For some, this led to a perception that feedback serves the purpose of grade justification: "For me, feedback shows how a mark has been achieved" (p. 376).

This study is important in demonstrating a range of behaviours and cognitions in response to feedback, ranging from less sophisticated to higher level responses.

In their recommendations, Orsmond et al. (2005) echo Boud's (1995a) notion of consequential validity by arguing for the importance of teachers seeking evidence of how their feedback has been used. They also suggest that students should be provided with opportunities to explore and discuss how prior feedback can be applied to their current assignments: "Previous student feedback could be linked to 'feedforward' discussions and so could provide a focal point for assignment preparation" (p. 382). It is with this recommendation in mind that we turn to exploration of a specific case of this approach in practice.

Box 3.1 Key research findings

- The provision of comments in the absence of student engagement and action can be viewed as "dangling data" (Sadler, 1989).
- In order to use feedback effectively, students need to engage at the point of collection of feedback, then attend to the feedback, apply it, and take action (Price, et al., 2011).
- The skills needed to implement feedback include self-appraisal, assessment literacy, goal-setting and self-regulation, and engagement and motivation (Winstone, et al., 2017a).
- Students use feedback in a variety of ways: to motivate; to enhance learning; to enhance reflection; and to clarify their understanding and the expectations of markers (Orsmond et al., 2005).
- Students may struggle to engage with feedback because the feedback is not useful, not sufficiently individualised or specific, too authoritative, or because they do not understand the language used by markers and do not know how to implement it (Jönsson, 2013).
- Students may also be prevented from fully engaging with feedback because they lack awareness of what the feedback means, they lack cognisance of how to implement feedback, they lack agency to enact comments, and they lack volition to put in the effort needed to transfer feedback from one assignment to another (Winstone, et al., 2017b).
- Evidence suggests that the perspectives of teachers and students with regard to students' level of engagement with feedback are not well-aligned (e.g. Mulliner, & Tucker, 2017), perhaps because students' engagement is often not visible to teachers (Price, et al., 2011), or because 'engagement' may mean different things to different people (e.g. Burke, 2009).
- Supporting students' engagement with feedback is a shared responsibility of both teachers and students (Nash, & Winstone, 2017; Nicol, 2010; Price, et al., 2010), and there are many opportunities to help students develop the skills needed to enact feedback (Winstone, et al., 2017a).

The case: Motive, means and opportunity to use feedback

Context

This case focuses on the work of Claire Tarrant, a Teaching Fellow in the Faculty of Health and Medical Sciences at the University of Surrey. Claire teaches across a range of pre-registration programmes in Operating Department Practice, Nursing and Midwifery, and Paramedic Science, and post-registration programmes in Mentorship and Anaesthetic Practice. This particular case focuses on an initiative used with a cohort of 27 Operating Department Practitioner (ODP) students. Whilst this is a relatively small cohort, the heavy practice placement requirements of the programme mean that students spend a lot of the year working away from campus. Claire's perspective on feedback is aligned with a new paradigm approach, as within her practice she embeds opportunities for students to implement feedback as a way to support their development. Claire is the recipient of a teaching excellence award, in recognition of her innovative approaches to pedagogy.

Claire also recognises the importance of dialogue within the feedback process (see Chapter 6), as she has seen students struggling to understand the meaning of the feedback they receive on assignments and to take useful follow-up actions. An ideal response to these challenges would be to schedule individual sessions with students after they have received feedback, in order to support them to make sense of feedback, and to support them in putting it into practice but this is highly workload-intensive and unsustainable. Claire wanted to develop a strategy to facilitate this kind of dialogic interaction in a way that did not rely on individual face-to-face discussions.

The feedback design

Central to the feedback design was supporting students to apply feedback from a previous assignment when later working on a similar one. In the second year of their ODP programme, students focus on the development of skills and knowledge pertaining to emergencies and complex care needs across a broad range of patient groups. Students need to problem-solve, analyse, and critically evaluate their own actions as well as the care being delivered by the team. One assessment requires students to undertake an evidence enquiry; a 2000-word critical evaluation of two research papers thematically linked to one of three topics. Claire ran a session focused on preparing students for this Intraoperative Evidence Enquiry, and asked them all to bring along a copy of one of their first-year assignments, an 'Understanding Research' poster, with the marker's feedback attached. Claire saw clear links between the two assignments, and wanted to support students to revisit, unpack and make sense of the feedback from the poster, and develop strategies for applying it to the Intraoperative Evidence Enquiry assignment.

In the session, students were first asked to review the feedback by themselves, thinking about what was written and what they felt about their work. Next, Claire wanted to replicate the kind of dialogic exchange she might have with each individual student in a one-to-one tutorial, but in a way where students could feel comfortable sharing their questions and concerns. In order to achieve this, Claire used Poll Everywhere, an online Audience Response System (www.pollevery where.com/; see Chapter 4), to invite students to share their thoughts on a series of anonymous questions (see Box 3.2).

Box 3.2 Questions posed to students

- What are you pleased with about your poster?
- What was identified as an area of strength in your feedback by the marker?
- What was identified as an area for development in your feedback by the marker?
- What would you like to improve on?
- What do you need to achieve this?

Students were given a link to Claire's Poll Everywhere page, where they were presented with the questions followed by open-response text boxes. Poll Everywhere then anonymously presents all of the responses, on a screen visible to all students. Having shared their responses, Claire then engaged in dialogue with the students, responding to each of their posts, opening up discussion around developing their assignments and their future work, and directing students to strategies, resources, and support structures that might help them when working on their Interoperative Evidence Enquiry. The aim of this practice is that students take away not only a deeper understanding of the feedback, but also a clear strategy for applying that feedback to the assignment they were working on at that time.

Student response

In an evaluation at the end of the session, many students commented positively on the opportunity to develop their understanding through dialogue, even though some showed a preference for individual tutorials. All students participated in the discussions, and asked further questions following Claire's responses. In this sense, the dialogic interaction extended beyond just Claire and the student that submitted a particular question; all students were engaged in the dialogue. Students also reported that having the opportunity to engage with prior feedback was an incredibly valuable activity, as they had not remembered feedback from the previous year of their programme. Without this activity, they would not have realised that the comments contained highly relevant information that they could apply directly to their current assignment.

Students also responded positively to seeing that other students were posting similar concerns to themselves, so students were fully engaged in discussion and felt more confident sharing their ideas and concerns with peers as a result. Thus, whilst the posts were anonymous, students consequently felt comfortable engaging in dialogue not just with Claire but with each other.

Enabling factors

Poll Everywhere does not require any specific technology; it is a web-based system that students can access on their laptops, tablets, or smartphones. At the time when Claire developed and implemented this innovation, she was just over a year in post and was completing her PGCE for Professional Practice. She felt empowered to develop teaching strategies that met the outcomes of the sessions and the needs of her students, as well as being fun to teach. Claire also felt that the department in which she worked had a climate that fostered development and excellence in teaching, where there was a real appetite for development of innovative teaching strategies for the benefit of the student experience. Within the department, there is a culture of experimenting and sharing the outcomes of teaching innovations, which is likely to facilitate a feedback culture characterised by trust and shared purpose.

Challenges

Whilst most students were enthusiastic about the session, some students were not keen on the group discussion, and expressed a preference for just getting on with their assignments. Even though some students may have preferred a one-to-one tutorial, this was not feasible from a timetabling perspective, given the students' practice placement schedules. Furthermore, the benefit of Claire responding to queries and concerns whilst all students were present means that students were able to benefit from hearing Claire's responses to other students' questions. This is an inclusive practice that ensures all students are able to ask, and share responses to, assignment queries. However, not all students will recognise this benefit, and may feel that generic feedback is neither beneficial nor applicable to them. This may indicate that further development of feedback literacy is required in order for students to appreciate the benefits of this opportunity.

Relationship to the literature

Recent experimental research has demonstrated that students' memory for feedback information is poor, even after a very short delay (Nash, Winstone, Gregory, & Papps, 2018). Thus, supporting students to revisit prior feedback that is relevant to an assignment they are working on is likely to facilitate transfer of the feedback, and was one of the recommendations made by Orsmond et al. (2005) in their study on students' use of feedback. Claire's practice promotes three out of the four 'recipience skills' in the SAGE taxonomy (Winstone, et al., 2017a). This approach facilitates self-appraisal, by asking students to look back at their previous work and identify strengths and areas for improvement, and goal-setting/self-regulation, by asking students to identify the skills they would like to improve on the basis of the prior feedback, and to identify the strategies they need to take to achieve these goals. The practice also facilitates engagement and motivation, by supporting students to see the transfer of feedback from one assignment to the next, and motivating students by reminding them of the pride they have felt in their work.

Shute (2008) argues that students need motive, means and opportunity to enact feedback. In this case, the opportunity is provided by the direct relevance of feedback from one assignment to another, and the means is provided by supporting students to deconstruct and consider ways of using the feedback. It could be argued that part of the motivation for using feedback comes from seeing that other students may be asking similar questions, thus encouraging students to see that implementing feedback and realising improvement on this basis is fully achievable.

Significance of this practice

This is a simple strategy, but one that is highly effective in facilitating uptake of feedback and developing students' feedback literacy. Providing space for students to revisit and explore the relevance of prior feedback is essential, yet pedagogic practices that facilitate reflection on previous feedback are rare. This practice is also inclusive in first giving students time to reflect individually on their feedback before submitting responses to the questions, and by enabling students to respond anonymously. Students benefit from hearing Claire's responses to all posts, meaning that no student is advantaged or disadvantaged individually. This practice is also a good example of technology being used for a specific purpose, where the affordances of the technology (in this case, anonymity and instant presentation of all responses) are central to the feedback design (see Chapter 4).

The questions that Claire posed to students could be applied to any situation where the transfer of feedback is of relevance; in this case, the transfer was from one academic year to an assignment drawing on similar skills in the following academic year. The same approach could be used from one assignment to the next, or used to help students apply feedback between what might appear to be very different assignments. Similarly, these questions could be used in any discipline, and on any type of assignment. The strategy could be implemented within programme-wide feedback approaches. Course teams could identify parallel tasks in the programme where there would be potential to revisit previous feedback and apply it to a future assignment. A by-product of such an approach would be enhanced teacher and student feedback literacy.

Box 3.3 Implications for practice

- Supporting students' engagement with feedback begins at the point of assessment design: students should be provided with opportunities to apply feedback from one task to another (see Chapter 5).
- There is a need for designs which prompt students to revisit and apply previous feedback.
- Effective implementation of feedback draws upon a complex set of skills, and students are likely to benefit from opportunities to develop and practise these skills (see Chapter 2).
- As the views of teachers and students on what constitutes 'engagement' with feedback are often misaligned, it is valuable to discuss with students what engagement might look like, and to find out why students may find this process difficult.
- There is also an important role for teachers in seeking evidence of the impact their feedback has had on students.

Conclusion

Engagement with feedback processes does not just involve behaviour; there are cognitive, emotional, and motivational dimensions of engagement. When students demonstrate what appears to be limited engagement with feedback processes, it is easy to assume that they are simply not interested in feedback. However, apparent disengagement with feedback can be an important sign that assessment design is not facilitating student uptake (see Chapter 5), and hence diluting the learning potential of feedback.

Whilst there are many things that teachers can do to facilitate student engagement with feedback, there is equal responsibility shared between students and their teachers in ensuring that feedback has an impact on learning (Nash, & Winstone, 2017). Whilst teachers have a responsibility to design assessment to facilitate use of feedback, and to ensure that students understand what feedback means and how to use it, students need to take responsibility for seeking further feedback and for putting in the 'hard graft' needed to implement feedback (Carless, 2015a). The development of feedback literacy is needed in order for students to appreciate the importance of their own participation in feedback processes.

A common theme that links much of the research and practice discussed in this chapter is that the implementation of feedback is likely to be facilitated through meaningful discussion between teachers and students. We have seen that the perceptions of teachers and students regarding engagement with feedback are often misaligned, and that students can struggle to 'decode' the often opaque academic language used within feedback. The case that we examined in this chapter had dialogue at the core of the practice, and many of the interventions that might support student engagement with feedback rely on effective dialogue. Teachers also need to be on the receiving end of feedback information, by seeking evidence of the impact of their feedback. We cannot simply 'deliver' feedback and cross our fingers that it reaches or engages the receiver and has an impact on their future work. We need to design assessment with such impact in mind, and follow up to see that feedback information has initiated some change in the behaviour, knowledge, skills, or motivation of our students.

Box 3.4 Key resources

- Exploring the impact of feedback on students: https://theconversation.com/universities-are-failing-their-students-through-poor-feedback-practices-86756
- A teacher reflects upon effective feedback and students' opportunities to use it: www.learningscientists.org/blog/2018/8/9-1
- Naomi Winstone talking about the SAGE Taxonomy and interventions to support engagement with feedback: https://apadiv15.org/podcast-series/
- The Developing Engagement with Feedback Toolkit for higher education (www.heacademy.ac.uk/knowledge-hub/developing-engagement-feedba ck-toolkit-deft) and for 16–19 year-olds (available at www.surrey.ac.uk/depa rtment-higher-education/learning-lab/outputs).
- A discussion of interventions to support engagement with feedback: www.lea rningscientists.org/blog/2018/8/9-1
- A case study from Advance HE (formerly the Higher Education Academy) on students' use of feedback on a Business programme: www.heacademy.ac.uk/knowledge-hub/student-engagement-feedback

Box 3.5 Questions for reflection and debate

- When you return feedback to students, how do you expect students to engage with the information? What do you see as your responsibilities, and the responsibilities of your students, in this process?
- If students are viewed as 'free agents', what do you see as the challenges that might arise when considering the roles and responsibilities of teachers and students in facilitating engagement with feedback?
- Look back through some feedback comments that you have returned to students. For each one, consider what actions a student could be expected to take on the basis of the comment. If this is not apparent, then consider whether it might be more effective to give fewer comments, and focus instead on comments that are more likely to be 'actionable'.
- What makes feedback memorable? Is it where feedback is provocative or surprising? Does it fit with or challenge existing assumptions of the student?

- Map the assessment journey for a student on your course/unit/module, including the types of assessments and submission dates, and the dates when marked work will be returned to students (you might find the 'Map My Programme' tool useful for this purpose; https://sites.google.com/site/mapmyprogramme/). Are there opportunities for students to enact comments from one assessment to the next? Where does formative assessment fit into your programme or unit?
- Consider how you might know whether or not your feedback has had an impact on your students. For example, would you see evidence in future work that students produce? Would you perhaps notice that students were demonstrating more sophisticated conceptual understanding in class discussions? If it is difficult to see how you might gather this evidence, consider whether redesigning your assessment pattern might enable you to do so.
- 'Engagement with feedback' is a dominant way of thinking in existing literature but does it risk promoting old paradigm thinking of teacher delivery followed by student response? Might it better seen as a more equal partnership of feedback exchanges, feedback interactions, or feedback negotiations?

Chapter 4

Technology-enabled feedback processes

Contemporary higher education is characterised by a proliferation in the use of educational technology, perhaps as a result of the belief that education can be "transformed through technology" (Fullan, & Langworthy, 2013, p. 2). However, in recent years lively debate regarding the use of educational technology has emerged in the research literature, on social media, and within institutional dialogues. Important questions have been asked about the impact of technology on students' learning, and the perhaps unanticipated outcomes of its use in the classroom. These debates have been seen most prominently in discussions around lecture capture and student attendance (e.g. Edwards, & Clinton, 2019), and the use of laptops for notetaking in class (e.g. Luo, Kiewra, Flanigan, & Peteranetz, 2018). What these examples serve to illustrate is that the rationale for the use of educational technology, not just in pragmatic terms but also in pedagogic terms, is crucial. In the domain of assessment and feedback, technology has the potential to streamline the process or facilitate practices not possible without the use of technology. However, technology can merely be used to replicate feedback as 'telling' in a different medium, and it is important to consider how the use of technology adds further educational value to existing processes (Weston, & Bain, 2010). Sanders and George (2017) caution that "the medium is not the solution", where technology is "merely a tool like any other in a teacher's repertoire, and its effective use depends on its pedagogical use by teachers" (p. 2923). In this chapter, we consider the role of technology in feedback processes from a design stance, seeking to explore the affordances of technology in facilitating a new paradigm approach to feedback.

Technology and the new paradigm of feedback

When new technological tools come to the market, or when we hear about innovative pedagogical uses of existing tools, the novelty can be enticing. We perhaps think that students will value the use of technology in feedback processes, given the ongoing rhetoric regarding our students as 'digital natives'. In reality, many uses of technology in the area of assessment and feedback are not designed with a particular pedagogical purpose in mind but are adopted just because the technology is new and available, or because we hope the tool might be the magic bullet that concurrently saves us time in the marking process and raises student satisfaction.

In a new paradigm approach to feedback, of central importance is students' engagement with and use of feedback, such that the feedback process facilitates learning and future development. Deeley (2018, p. 439) argues that "assessment and feedback processes can be enhanced through creative uses of technology"; however, the direction of enhancement should be towards superior student generation and uptake of feedback. Hepplestone, Holden, Irwin, Parkin, and Thorpe (2011, p. 123) argue that technology "has the potential to enhance student engagement with feedback". However, others have cautioned that many uses of technology in assessment and feedback merely replicate old paradigm models of the transmission of comments, albeit through a different medium (Pitt, & Winstone, 2019).

Technology-enabled feedback in a new paradigm model places emphasis not on how educators produce and deliver comments, but on what students do with feedback, and the development of feedback literacy. That is not to say that systems designed to streamline the production and delivery of comments (e.g. statement banks and electronic annotation tools) cannot serve new paradigm functions, but feedback designs would need to focus on their use in facilitating student uptake of feedback. For our present purposes, the affordances of technology within a new paradigm approach to feedback is of central importance. With this in mind, we explore three such potential affordances: enabling timely feedback; enabling synthesis of feedback; and enabling feedback uptake.

Affordances of technology: enabling timely feedback

A key dimension of new paradigm feedback processes is that the timing of feedback is not as important as its timeliness; feedback information should come at a time within a learning cycle where it can be implemented and utilised to inform understanding, learning, and future behaviour. It has been argued that feedback is often unable to facilitate learning because it comes too late; the notion of 'just-in-time' feedback represents the importance of students receiving feedback at a time where they can directly use the information it provides. Thus, feedback designs can facilitate students' uptake of feedback by using technology to provide feedback comments at a time where they can directly influence students' understanding (Hepplestone, et al., 2011). For example, in the context of teacher education, Gibson and Musti-Rao (2016) reported a feedback design where trainee teachers wore earpieces through which mentors relayed real-time feedback on the enactment of practical skills in-situ. Without this 'bug-in-ear' technology, the feedback would likely come in a debrief session after the lesson, thus not facilitating immediate application of the advice.

A common use of technology to facilitate timely feedback involves computer-based assessments (CBAs), which typically take the form of online quizzes for which students receive immediate feedback. Whilst there are specific programmes designed for this purpose (e.g. i-assess, WebCT-Quizzes), most LMSs have inbuilt quiz functions. Such systems are described as "indispensable" (Förster, Weiser, & Maur, 2018, p. 100) for the provision of immediate feedback on a regular basis. As well as providing prompt feedback on students' understanding, targeted feedback on CBAs can direct students towards further learning materials such as articles, websites, or specific pages of the course text (Miller, 2009). This form of immediate, directive feedback would not be feasible if human intervention were required to correct answers.

Technology can also be used to facilitate timely feedback within class settings. Systems such as Poll Everywhere, Mentimeter, and Zeetings (web-based audience response systems) enable the presentation of different types of questions to which students can respond using their laptops, smartphones or tablets. Students' anonymous responses are displayed instantly, thus facilitating class discussion around common misconceptions. Hand-held student response systems (or 'clickers') can also be used for this purpose. Whilst similar ends could be achieved without the need for technology, for example by a show of hands, there are specific affordances of technology in this context, including the option for anonymity of responding, and the opportunity for all students to see a distribution of responses as a form of immediate feedback. In their meta-analysis of clicker use, Hunsu, Adesope, and Bayly (2016) report that clickers have little overall benefit in terms of cognitive outcomes in comparison to conventional teaching methods. However, clickers do show an advantage in terms of student engagement and participation, indicating that the affordance of anonymity may facilitate students' involvement in feedback processes.

As well as helping students to monitor their learning during lectures, the use of clickers can also facilitate students' use of feedback to support learning in other areas of the course. For example, receiving feedback on clicker questions in class can lead students to pay greater attention to detail in course readings (Ludvigsen, Krumsvik, & Furnes, 2015). In this study, there was also evidence that the feedback design led students to adjust their long-term approach to learning, with one student explaining that

> This is something I will carry with me the rest of my life, in my work life as well. If I shall learn something, I can just ask: Ok, did I understand this? Do I know this? Just to check for myself.

(p. 59)

Ludvigsen et al. (2015) argue that students see the clicker questions in lectures "as a real feedback space that invites them to reflect on their understanding of concepts" (p. 60).

When using clickers in classrooms, the immediacy of feedback is an advantage, as it can enable students to correct misconceptions in a way that can facilitate their future approaches to learning. However, the use of clickers in classrooms does not, in and of itself, represent a new paradigm feedback design; the design needs to consider *how* this use of technology can facilitate uptake. If the focus of the use of clickers is just on the provision of answers, without space for student sense-making through further elaboration and discussion, then the practice is arguably more closely aligned with an old paradigm feedback model. Thus, a key affordance of the use of clickers in classrooms is the provision of opportunities for discussion with peers (Hunsu, et al., 2016; Ludvigsen, et al., 2015), whereby upon the display of correct answers to clicker questions, students can share and clarify their own understanding, providing further feedback to each other.

Affordances of technology: enabling feedback synthesis

The impact of feedback is not realised through a single event, but through the synthesis of multiple feedback processes (Winstone, 2019). In a new paradigm approach to feedback, in order for students to act upon feedback they need to recognise the commonalities and trends in feedback that they might access from different sources and on different elements of their work and on different occasions. Such an approach has the potential to facilitate self-assessment, reflection, and self-regulation (Kabilan, & Khan, 2012; Lam, 2014; see also Chapter 7). Thus, a specific affordance of technology in a new paradigm model would be to support students to synthesise multiple instances of feedback to inform future learning behaviour. This is an important part of student feedback literacy as at present students generally seem to see feedback exchanges as one-off episodes. Through sense-making and reflection upon varied feedback exchanges, students can develop a more sophisticated plan for uptake.

Learning Analytics Dashboards (LADs) present feedback on students' progress, based on the synthesis of multiple sources of data regarding students' engagement with learning activities, effort, and performance (Sedrakyan, Malmberg, Verbert, Järvelä, & Kirschner, in press). Visual presentation of the synthesised data can inform regulatory processes and monitoring of progress towards learning goals (Sedrakyan, et al., in press). LADs can be combined with e-portfolios, to enable students to curate artefacts and feedback that chart their learning journey. In the context of medical education, van der Schaaf et al. (2017) used learning analytics to generate personalised feedback based upon "many multi-sorted assessment moments" (p. 361), which was presented to students as an interactive chart showing their performance over time with associated feedback.

A good example of the use of technology to facilitate synthesis of feedback comes from Ajjawi, Schofield, McAleer, and Walker (2013) within the context of an online distance learning course in medical education at the University of Dundee. They developed a system called InterACT (interaction and collaboration via technology) using a Wiki tool in the LMS, comprising a feedback journal to enable students to collect feedback together, and to encourage students to reflect on previous assignments. In this chapter, we focus on the use of the system to collate and synthesise feedback; InterACT also incorporates an interactive cover-sheet for students to complete when submitting work, requiring them to self-assess against assessment criteria, ask for feedback on specific elements of their work, and describe how they have used previous feedback to inform the current piece of work. This latter element of the system is discussed in Chapter 6.

The system enables students to look back through feedback and their reflections from previous assignments. Data from interviews with students who had used InterACT revealed that through synthesis, students were better able to see how to apply feedback:

> You are then a bit more mindful of what your feedback was from the first one [assignment] to any changes that you might make in the subsequent assessments. I suppose in a way before you would just think about your answer a bit and the feedback that you have got but not writing it and writing it down makes a difference.
>
> (Barton, Schofield, McAleer, & Ajjawi, 2016, p. 60)

The importance of synthesising multiple feedback events in order to inform future action is demonstrated by perceptions of feedback "as a complex *system* that needs to permeate the curriculum, rather than an activity that appears within it from time to time" (Molloy, & Boud, 2013, p. 25, emphasis in original). Clarke and Boud (2018) argue that e-portfolios can be an effective means to manage the complexity of the feedback 'system', as a way to consolidate feedback and to see where action has been taken. They discuss "curation for feedback" (p. 484), whereby "students transform individual feedback instances into an overview or create a commentary requesting feedback on specific points of a piece they are working on" (p. 484).

The Feedback Engagement and Tracking System (FEATS; Winstone, 2019) is a good example of an affordance of e-portfolios in the feedback process as identified by Clarke and Boud (2018):

> An ongoing collection where feedback comments from all assessment tasks, whether graded or not, can be easily accessed and built up over time, and where giving, receiving and working with feedback from teachers, peers and others is required, valued, evidenced and included at some point(s) in the assessments.
>
> (p. 481)

FEATS was developed through a co-design process involving students, academic staff, learning technologists and learning developers, and consists of three sections (see Figure 4.1). This partnership approach with salient student input is an important strand of student involvement in enhancing feedback processes. In Section A, students collate multiple instances of feedback, both formal and informal, formative and summative, and from teachers, peers, or self-assessment, by completing a 'feedback review'. The feedback review requires students to deconstruct feedback and enter the main strengths as identified by the feedback-giver, and the main suggestions for development. For each of these areas, students are

Figure 4.1 The FEATS Feedback Portfolio

able to tag each comment against a list of academic skills (e.g. critical evaluation; citation and referencing skills). They can then see a visual summary of the most common skills being identified as strengths and areas for development across multiple feedback reviews.

After students have identified their priorities for development, Section B of FEATS enables students to access a comprehensive resource bank providing them with the tools they need to enact development of those skills. Finally, in Section C, students can create a personalised action plan setting out how they plan to implement feedback, promoting dialogue with teachers. All actions taken on the basis of feedback are stored by the system, and can be linked with a grade tracker to see the impact of engaging with feedback on attainment.

Evaluation of FEATS (Winstone, 2019) has demonstrated that, by engaging with the system, students can develop both in terms of the use of feedback, and their perceptions of the value of feedback. One specific affordance of the technology is that it enables synthesis of multiple instances of feedback, giving students a clearer picture of how they should implement feedback, as expressed by this student: "[FEATS] enables me to condense all of my feedback into one place, so that I can identify any patterns in my strengths and weaknesses which is important to know how to improve." Furthermore, FEATS has facilitated students' uptake of feedback, which is central to a new paradigm approach to feedback: "[FEATS] has got me to look at feedback more often and I know how to apply it more now."

Feedback designs that afford the synthesis of multiple feedback exchanges can facilitate student uptake, by enabling students to visualise the 'bigger picture' of how feedback can support their learning beyond an individual unit or task, and by supporting reflection and goal-setting. This also encourages a more long-term perspective on making sense of and using feedback (Carless, 2019).

Affordances of technology: enabling feedback uptake

The use of audiovisual tools (e.g. audio, video, or screencast technology) for the provision of feedback has been reported to result in a greater volume of comments as compared to written feedback (e.g. Anson, Dannels, Laboy, & Carneiro, 2016; Mayhew, 2017; Thomas, West, & Borup, 2017), hence markers are able to provide more detailed advice on what has been done well and where improvement is needed. Yet the provision of feedback comments, however detailed, through alternative technological media does not in itself constitute a new paradigm approach. New paradigm feedback designs involving audiovisual technology should be focused upon facilitating superior uptake of feedback, and in creating opportunities for students to generate and respond to feedback comments.

In terms of student uptake, there is some evidence that audiovisual feedback holds promise. Students are generally very positive about their experiences of audiovisual feedback; for example, Crook et al. (2012) reported that 60% of the students in their study claimed to take greater notice of video feedback in comparison to other forms of feedback, leading to the conclusion that the videos "enhanced [students'] active engagement with feedback" (p. 395). When using the screencast software Camtasia to produce feedback on students' work, Deeley (2018) reported that some students claimed to have paid more attention to screencast feedback in comparison to written feedback. Similarly, in a study reported by West and Turner (2016), 55% of students said that they had spent more time reviewing feedback in video than in written format, and 70% said that video feedback would enable them to improve their work to a greater extent than written feedback.

Where merely paying attention to feedback information is perhaps indicative of a surface approach to uptake, evidence of students working with comments in more productive ways would make a more compelling case for the affordance of technology in new paradigm feedback designs. Students report that video feedback can prompt reflection on their current work and consideration of strategies to be adopted in future work (Henderson, & Phillips, 2015). Henderson and Phillips note that some of these benefits are not specific to video feedback, but did argue that the video format affords the opportunity to spend time focusing on not just *what* to improve in future work but *how*. Similar affordances have been reported for audio feedback, where all 12 students interviewed by Merry and Orsmond (2008) about their experiences of this form of feedback spoke about working differently with audio feedback in comparison to written feedback; for example,

> I'd listen to it and write my own comments and then I'd go back through it a second time looking at the notes I had written for each paragraph ... and I'd thought of things in my head that I could put (in).
>
> (Merry, & Orsmond, 2008, p. 4)

Merry and Orsmond also analysed the nature of feedback comments and uncovered some interesting statistically significant differences. In written feedback, markers were more likely to identify errors, but in audio feedback they were more likely to demonstrate correct practice. It is likely that the latter focus would better enable student uptake.

Whilst audiovisual feedback seems to hold promise in promoting student uptake of feedback, it is important to note that the majority of evidence relies on student preferences and self-reported behaviour (see Pitt, & Winstone, 2019), rather than students' behaviour or the impact on learning (see Boud, & Molloy, 2013).

Moving beyond students' self-reported behaviour, it is possible that audiovisual technology may also facilitate student response to feedback in a more visible way. It has been reported that audiovisual feedback may be more likely than written feedback to encourage students to engage in further dialogue with their teachers. Video feedback, where students can see the face of the marker, is believed to hold particular affordance in this regard, as identified in a recent synthesis of the evidence on video feedback: "It strikes us that video feedback holds potential due to its affordances over written or audio feedback in promoting a social interactional approach" (Mahoney, Macfarlane, & Ajjawi, 2019, p. 158). Such forms of feedback are perceived by students to be more personalised (see Pitt, & Winstone, 2019), which can build a sense of rapport with teachers (West, & Turner, 2016), and enable students to feel more comfortable approaching teachers to engage in face to face dialogue (e.g. Anson, et al., 2016; Vincelette, & Bostic, 2013). In Henderson and Phillips' (2015) study, this affordance was built into the feedback design, where they included within the videos an explicit invitation to engage in further discussion with the teacher regarding the feedback and future assignments. The enhanced interpersonal dimension of audiovisual feedback also extends to peer feedback exchanges. In a study by Hung (2016), students provided two-minute feedback videos for peers relating to short online presentations, shared via a virtual learning community on Facebook. Students reported that because the video feedback encouraged them to engage in further dialogue with their peers, they were better able to understand the content of the feedback, in comparison to written feedback.

Perhaps the most compelling evidence for the affordances of audiovisual feedback designs in facilitating student uptake would be if such technology could be used to enable students to respond to feedback comments; however, this practice is rare. In their synthesis of the evidence on video feedback, Mahoney et al. (2019) concluded that: "Feedback dialogue or an opportunity for students to respond to feedback was not deliberately incorporated into the feedback processes of any studies we reviewed." (p. 166). It is important to emphasise that uptake of audiovisual feedback is likely to be facilitated through feedback designs such as those discussed in Chapter 5, whereby opportunities to respond to feedback are embedded into task sequences. For example, screencast technology might enable students to reveal how they respond to feedback from their teachers (Fernández-Toro, & Furnborough, 2014). In the context of a distance learning Spanish programme, Fernández-Toro and Furnborough used the screencast software Jing to enable students to record their responses to feedback, directly affording dialogue between students and teachers. A group of ten students were asked to 'think aloud' for five minutes whilst going through feedback they had received. This technique provided teachers with insight into how students engaged with feedback. Whilst the primary purpose of this approach was to conduct research into student response to feedback, rather than acting as a pedagogic practice *per se*, there is much promise in this technique for completing the feedback loop and facilitating dialogue. It is also useful for students to have access to their recordings to look back through, as identified by Fernández-Toro and Furnborough: "The use of screencast technology in the present study offers a further advantage, as it gives students time and space to reflect instead of just responding to the feedback", which can "inform and enhance subsequent dialogue between students and tutors" (p. 45). Thus, using screencast technology for 'feedback on feedback' "can effectively be implemented as a means of getting learners to articulate their responses to feedback in an explicit manner" (p. 46). As we have seen in this section, audiovisual feedback can be positioned more effectively in line with new paradigm approaches if students have the opportunity to respond using technology, and if technology is used to facilitate peer feedback exchanges. There is an urgent need for technology-enabled feedback processes to do more to activate students in the process, and to be more than merely teacher-telling in a more engaging form.

Thus far we have seen how technology can be used to facilitate students' engagement with feedback, by providing timely feedback, facilitating synthesis of feedback, as well as enhancing the attention paid to feedback and facilitating dialogue with teachers (see Table 4.1). We now turn to two specific examples from the literature that illustrate some of these affordances.

Table 4.1 Summary of the affordances of technology in a new paradigm approach to feedback

Affordances		*Examples*
Facilitating uptake of feedback by ...	... providing **timely** feedback with opportunities to implement it	'Bug-in-ear' technology 'Clickers' Computer-based assessments
	... encouraging **attention** towards and **mindful processing** of feedback	Audiovisual feedback
	... encouraging engagement with feedback opportunities by providing **anonymity**	'Clickers'
	... encouraging further **dialogue** in feedback processes	Audiovisual feedback
	... enabling the **synthesis** of multiple feedback processes	E-portfolios Learning analytics

Key examples from the literature

There are many examples within the literature of specific projects that have aimed to develop the use of technology in the assessment and feedback process, and the first example that we explore represents one such project, carried out at Sheffield Hallam University in the UK. This project is a good example of an institution-wide approach to using technology to enhance feedback processes. Our second example illustrates the potential uses of learning analytics to support the feedback process, which we have included here as the field of learning analytics is an emerging area of research and practice that is gaining traction worldwide.

At Sheffield Hallam University, a project entitled 'Technology, Feedback, Action!: The impact of learning technology upon students' engagement with their feedback' focused on three technology-enabled feedback processes: the publication of grades and feedback through the LMS; adaptive release of grades; and the use of an electronic rubric to generate feedback comments. As well as a literature review on the impact of technology on student engagement with feedback (Hepplestone, et al., 2011), the group also synthesised the learning from the project in a paper published in 2012 (Parkin, Hepplestone, Holden, Irwin, & Thorpe, 2012). Through semi-structured interviews with 23 undergraduate students from computer networks, psychology, diagnostic radiography, and events management programmes, they explored student perspectives of the perceived benefits and drawbacks of the three technology-enabled feedback practices of central interest to the project.

Students' perspectives on receiving feedback within the LMS were positive in recognising that they would be more likely to revisit feedback that had been provided electronically, perhaps because they believed it would be easier to create a storage system for electronic feedback in comparison to hard copy assignments. A further perceived benefit to online return of feedback was the opportunity to collate grades and track progress electronically, although Parkin et al. (2012) caution that this could lead to an instrumental approach to progress. Students also valued the opportunity to engage with feedback in private, rather than in the somewhat public environment typical of hard copy submission and return. Students perceived the feedback process to be faster with electronic submission and return, but in some cases this was because grades were published online before feedback was uploaded, which then minimised student engagement with the often detailed comments on their work.

The adaptive release of grades was facilitated by a system whereby students were provided with detailed comments on their work in advance of receiving the grade, with the grade only being released once students had submitted a reflection on their feedback. Students recognised that through the requirement to engage with feedback prior to receiving the grade, they benefited from more mindful processing of feedback, and that by reflecting on feedback they were better able to remember it in future. However, in some cases students resisted this process as 'enforced' reflection; Parkin et al. (2012) stress the importance of sharing the rationale with students so that they are aware how this process stands to benefit them. Adaptive release can also be stressful for students, and their processing of feedback can be limited to trying to 'second-guess' the grade they have achieved (Parker, & Winstone, 2016).

The final technology-enabled practice of focus in this project was the use of an electronic rubric tool called Feedback Wizard. The tool consisted of a feedback template, containing a matrix of assessment criteria and associated feedback comments. Few students participating in the interviews had experienced the use of this tool, yet they recognised and valued the benefit of the enhanced transparency of marking. Whilst the data regarding students' perceptions of these technology-enabled approaches to feedback come from students' self-reported beliefs about the benefits and drawbacks to these approaches, Parkin et al. (2012) report that "the online publication of grades and feedback and the adaptive release of grades were found to significantly enhance students' engagement with their feedback" (p. 971). However, further data on a behavioural level would provide stronger support for this statement.

Our second example (Pardo, Jovanovic, Dawson, Gašević, & Mirriahi, 2019) represents a different deployment of technology to facilitate feedback processes: the use of learning analytics to provide feedback to a total of 414 undergraduate engineering students. Whilst the provision of feedback through the use of learning analytics might, at first glance, appear to be more closely aligned with an old paradigm model of feedback as transmission, it is one particular affordance of this method that has new paradigm features. The timing of the feedback, which is designed to directly facilitate student uptake and application, provides opportunities to implement feedback and correct any misunderstandings. Pardo et al. (2019) draw upon the notion of multiple 'cycles' of learning and feedback, where the feedback from one cycle is designed to be applicable to the next cycle of activities. Each cycle lasted for one week, and consisted of tasks for students to complete in the LMS, such as watching a video and then completing a set of multiple-choice questions. Based on data representing students' interaction with the activities within the system, students receive automated feedback; instructors write feedback messages targeted at different levels of engagement and performance with the tasks, and an algorithm selects the appropriate comment for each activity, and collates comments across all activities the student has completed to form a detailed feedback narrative. The intention is that this information directly informs students' behaviour during the next learning cycle, and students experienced four such cycles over weeks 2 to 5 of the course, before taking a mid-term examination in week 6.

This approach was evaluated using two sources of data: student satisfaction and student performance in the midterm examination. Students in the cohort experiencing this new approach were compared to students in the two previous cohorts ($N = 291$ and $N = 315$) who did not receive such an intervention. There was a significant increase in students' perception that feedback has utility in supporting learning when compared with students who did not receive this approach. More importantly, academic performance also increased significantly, as measured by students' grades on a multiple-choice mid-term exam, compared with a previous cohort who did not experience the personalised feedback cycles. Whilst it is important to recognise that the nature of the counterfactual comparison in this study (students in a cohort prior to the introduction of an intervention) does not enable us to draw firm conclusions about the impact of the initiative, these data provide promising indications that students' use of feedback can be facilitated through the use of learning analytics to deliver prompt, personalised feedback at a time where it can directly influence students' learning. If statement banks and feedback algorithms are used purely as a way to minimise educators' workload, without consideration for improving the timing and impact of feedback, then transmission continues to drive the feedback approach. If emphasis is placed on student action and the impact of feedback, then the use of learning analytics and algorithms to provide feedback can fit within the ethos of a new paradigm approach to feedback.

Box 4.1 Key research findings

- Online quizzes can be used to provide immediate, regular feedback and correct student misconceptions. The use of such tools can support learning (Miller, 2009).
- The use of 'clickers' in classrooms can also provide immediate feedback that can lead to students adjusting their learning strategies (Ludvigsen, et al., 2015).
- Technological tools can be used to good effect to enable students to synthesise multiple instances of feedback, facilitating reflection and uptake (Ajjawi, et al., 2013; Winstone, 2019).
- Audiovisual feedback can facilitate stronger engagement with feedback (Crook, et al., 2012; Deeley, 2017; West, & Turner, 2016), and encourage further dialogue through enhanced rapport building (Mahoney, et al., 2019; West, & Turner, 2016; Henderson, & Phillips, 2015).
- There is also great promise for screencast technology to be used in a way that enables students to demonstrate their response to feedback (Fernández-Toro, & Furnborough, 2014).
- Adaptive release of grades in LMSs can lead students to report more mindful processing of feedback (Parkin, et al., 2012).
- The use of algorithms based on learning analytics to provide timely feedback that students can act upon can have a positive effect on students' attainment (Pardo, et al., 2019).

The case: The affordances of technology for feedback in large cohorts

Context

This case study represents a good example of how technology can facilitate feedback processes with large cohorts of students. Dr Jaclyn Broadbent is Associate Head of School (Teaching and Learning), in the School of Psychology at Deakin

University, Australia. The unit in question is a Health Behaviour module taken by first year undergraduate students from a variety of courses. The cohort is very large; the course runs three trimesters a year with a total of more than 2100 students, with the largest group size ranging from 1300–1700 students in one trimester. The course consists of weekly two-hour lectures (ranging from 50–700 students) and 1-hour tutorials of around 30 students.

Jaclyn's approach stems from her belief that feedback enables students to understand and make sense of their performance, with feedback ideally being used by students to enhance their future performance on similar tasks. However, Jaclyn recognised that large student numbers can create a tension between time and budget constraints and the aim of providing personally meaningful or relevant feedback to students. In a unit with a large cohort size and multiple assessment points, it was challenging to give useful and high-quality written feedback. Furthermore, assessment of large cohorts typically requires teams of multiple markers, where moderation is a time- and effort-intensive process that is often exclusively grade-focused rather than feedback-focused.

The feedback design

In Jaclyn's unit, assessment and feedback design are inextricably linked. The assessment involves three reflective journal entries spaced over the course of the unit, where students are required to reflect upon their own health behaviour change. For each of the three entries, students receive three forms of feedback: their grade aligned with assessment criteria in a rubric; a short written explanation of how their entry links to the learning outcomes; and a five-minute audio feedback file. The marking team for this unit consists of up to 30 markers, with each student having their three entries marked by the same person.

This feedback design affords timeliness of feedback; students are receiving regular feedback throughout the unit, rather than at the end of the unit, and at a time where they are able to use the feedback to improve future work. Because audio feedback takes less time to produce than written feedback, students receive feedback on their journal entry 17 days after it has been submitted, and at least seven days before the next entry is due.

Jaclyn's approach affords feedback synthesis by virtue of the continuity of the sender–receiver partnership. As the marker will have seen the student's previous entry, they are able to comment directly on students' personal progress, and how they have implemented previous feedback. They are also able to provide personal recommendations for further improvement in the subsequent entry. In this sense, the three instances of feedback are synthesised into an ongoing dialogic thread, rather than representing isolated advice.

The affordance of this design for uptake is also carefully considered. Markers open the audio file by explaining the feedback design to students, so students are aware how they should be using the feedback for future work. In the audio file, markers refer to specific paragraph numbers so that students can easily locate the focus of the comments. Furthermore, markers are instructed to link their feedback to the next assignment, facilitating direct transfer of the information. Jaclyn also sees that audio feedback affords uptake because of the conversational and personalised feel in comparison to written feedback, where markers' tone of voice can enhance the meaning of the developmental advice given to students. The use of technology, where the audio files are released via the LMS, enables Jaclyn and her team to see whether the file has been opened, but not how long students engage with the audio feedback for.

Student response

Since implementing audio feedback in 2011, student evaluations for the question "the staff gave me helpful feedback" have risen significantly, from 79% to a peak of 99% agreement, surpassing both Faculty and University averages. The feedback has also made a dramatic difference to student learning. After submitting three journal entries, students sit an in-class test applying the knowledge learnt in the journals to a novel situation. Students' scores on this test have shown consistent increases. Comments from students also demonstrate the impact that the feedback has had on their wider learning. In their course evaluations, students expressed a belief that the audio feedback enables them to better understand the teachers' comments, that the audio feedback feels more personal, and that they feel like the markers care for them. There was also evidence in students' evaluations that the audio feedback enabled uptake; students discussed how they felt empowered to apply the feedback to future assignments, and motivated to use comments to develop their learning strategies.

Enabling factors

This case is a good example of how assessment design facilitates effective feedback; whilst the use of audio feedback adds further value, a key enabler of this approach is the fact that students' use of feedback is built into the assessment design. A further enabler is the technological infrastructure; the marking platform has an inbuilt audio feedback function, meaning that staff have access to a one-step recording process, with no need to learn how to use a new piece of software. Finally, the leadership of this unit is a significant enabler. Jaclyn has a strong vision for seeing the impact of feedback, and through her commitment to supporting a large team of markers, and her personal reflection, the unit continues to develop. This indicates that Jaclyn creates an effective feedback culture whereby colleagues who might never have tried audio feedback are supported to develop their practice. This is also likely to facilitate further scaling-up of the practice beyond this particular module. Jaclyn has strong knowledge of the literature on assessment and feedback, having contributed to the evidence base herself (see, for example, Broadbent, Panadero, & Boud, 2018).

Challenges

The biggest challenge to this feedback design stems from the large cohort size, and ensuring consistency of marking and feedback with such a large team of markers. The moderation process is quite time-consuming, but to Jaclyn this process is crucial, to ensure that all students experience the same quality of feedback. The moderation process involves the unit leaders blind-marking and reviewing the audio feedback file for two assignments from each marker at the beginning of the marking process. Beyond the quality assurance function, this process is designed with the ethos of building the feedback literacy of the markers. Each marker receives an audio feedback file containing advice on their marking and feedback, mirroring the one provided for students on their work. Half way through each marker's batch of marking, this moderation process is repeated. Jaclyn argues that this is beneficial as it enables the teachers to develop their own practice, and to experience the process from the perspective of their students.

Relationship to the literature

This case serves to illustrate how audio feedback communicates more than just the content of the marker's comments. For example, in their discussion of audiovisual approaches to feedback, Henderson and Phillips (2015) emphasised as a specific affordance of these technologies that markers can demonstrate *how* to improve. This echoes the findings of Merry and Orsmond (2008), where it was identified that, whilst errors were more likely to be identified in written feedback, in audio feedback, markers were more likely to demonstrate how to correct the error. Jaclyn's use of audio feedback mirrors these affordances identified in the literature.

Significance of this practice

This case illustrates the provision of timely, personalised cycles of feedback at scale, with cohorts of around 1500 students. The audio feedback is designed to coach students to improve their work. The comments help clarify what good performance encompasses, facilitate self-reflection, and aim to elicit a student's best possible performance in subsequent journals. This case is also an excellent example of how educators can develop their own feedback literacy through a values-driven moderation model, where markers are able to take the perspective of their students.

Box 4.2 Implications for practice

- The use of technology in feedback processes should focus on the specific affordances in terms of student uptake and learning, not just the practicalities.
- Teachers can make use of analytics tools within LMSs to gain insight into how many students access feedback.

- Students like the personal touch of audio/video feedback, which can facilitate greater uptake.
- Many LMSs have built-in functions that can be used to facilitate uptake of feedback, such as quiz tools and audio feedback capability.
- As well as considering how technology can be used in more traditional approaches to feedback, it is also worth exploring how technology could afford further examples of new paradigm approaches to feedback such as peer feedback and self-evaluation.

Conclusion

In our exploration of technology-enabled feedback, we have focused on three interrelated considerations: rationale, design, and affordance. The use of technology in a new paradigm approach to feedback requires careful consideration at the point of design, such that the use of a particular tool or approach is built upon a specific rationale according to its particular affordance in facilitating student learning through feedback. This approach to design is illustrated by Sanders and George (2017, p. 2923), who argued: "Don't ask what [technology] you should use, but rather identify what you need to do, and then see how [technology] might help you achieve that." There is an inherent danger that the availability of a new piece of technology can be appealing because it might appear to streamline the process, or facilitate 'copy and paste' approaches to commenting on students' work. However, in these cases, old paradigm transmission processes are merely replicated in a different medium (Pitt & Winstone, 2019). Transformative use of technology instead focuses on the end point: how does the approach involve and empower students?

We have focused here on three such affordances. First, we saw how the use of technology such as online quizzes and 'clickers' can directly facilitate students' learning, by providing feedback at a time where it can be used to correct misunderstandings and enable students to solidify their conceptual knowledge. Next, we explored the potential for technology to enable students to reflect upon feedback and synthesise feedback from multiple assignments to inform their ongoing development. Synthesis is an important outcome in a new paradigm approach to feedback because it encourages students to see how feedback can be applied beyond a specific module or unit. It is also a critical dimension of student feedback literacy, facilitating students' appreciation and implementation of feedback. Finally, we considered how the use of audiovisual technology can enable students' uptake of feedback, for example by demonstrating how to correct errors, and by encouraging students to engage in dialogue through the rapport-building properties of seeing and/or hearing their teachers engage in quasi-dialogic exchanges.

We have also identified a series of challenges that will need to be addressed if technology is to be used to facilitate new paradigm feedback designs. Primary sources of data for the influence of technology on uptake of feedback come from student self-report methods, and evaluating the use of technology on behavioural responses to feedback is a priority for future work in this area. Perhaps most importantly, we see much untapped potential for technology to be used to directly enable students to respond to feedback, for example, using screencast technology for students to submit a response (Fernández-Toro, & Furnborough, 2014). One of the exciting things about technology is that tools can often be repurposed beyond their original design function to provide solutions to common challenges inherent to feedback processes. Thus, there is much scope for creativity and discovery in the use of technology within feedback processes. However, in the context of new paradigm approaches to feedback, design, rationale, and affordance should be our guiding principles.

Box 4.3 Key resources

- "Effective Assessment in a Digital Age" – a JISC guide to using technology to enhance assessment and feedback processes. Available at www.webarchive. org.uk/wayback/archive/20140614115719/http://www.jisc.ac.uk/media/docum ents/programmes/elearning/digiassass_eada.pdf
- To see how the FEATS portfolio works, see these screencast tutorials: http:// tinyurl.com/FEATSPortfolio
- Using technology to facilitate feedback processes: http://blog.ascilite.org/levera ging-technology-to-support-effective-assessment-feedback-practices/
- "10 ideas for enhancing feedback with technology" – a resource from the Higher Education Academy (now Advance HE): www.heacademy.ac.uk/ system/files/resources/10_ideas_for_enhancing_feedback_with_technology.pdf
- A case study on the use of clickers from the Y1Feedback Project: http:// y1feedback.ie/wp-content/uploads/2017/01/AIT-1-Anne-M-OBrien-5.pdf
- A case study on the use of screencast feedback from the Y1Feedback Project: http://y1feedback.ie/wp-content/uploads/2017/01/DKIT-6-DCranny-2.pdf
- The 'Floop' tool (www.floopedu.com/) is a feedback tool that enables two-way dialogue; students can respond to specific feedback comments by asking questions or seeking further clarification, to which their teachers can then respond further.

Box 4.4 Questions for reflection and debate

- Consider the ways in which you have used technology within assessment and feedback processes. What was your rationale for using this tool? Was your approach driven by practicalities (e.g. it saves time, or because it is required by the institution), or by a specific rationale that focuses on improving students' learning?

- How could you reframe your use of this technology to facilitate students' learning through feedback? How could design facilitate a more active student role in audiovisual feedback processes?
- How do you think students view the use of technology in the feedback process?
- What evidence is there that students are using technology-enabled feedback? How might technology-enabled feedback be designed specifically to promote student uptake?
- If audio or video feedback were used more widely, would their novelty eventually wear off, limiting their impact on uptake?
- What kinds of technology-enabled feedback particularly support the development of student feedback literacy?
- Find out what tools and support are available through your University's Technology-Enhanced Learning department, and whether they hold examples of how they have been used to good effect in your institution.

Chapter 5

Enabling feedback through assessment design

For better or worse, assessment has long been recognised as being the main driver of students' learning behaviours. Students prioritise their study time and choose their approaches to learning based on how they perceive they are going to be assessed. An important starting point for this chapter is that how assessment is designed impacts on what kind of feedback practices are feasible. In fact, assessment and feedback designs are fundamentally interlinked. At the heart of new paradigm feedback approaches are assessment designs that involve students in making academic judgements and using feedback to enhance their work. This chapter discusses the role of assessment design in facilitating or inhibiting effective feedback processes. It makes the case for staged designs and iterative sequences of tasks in which students are encouraged to improve their work and performance over time. In this way, "Feedback is repositioned as a fundamental part of curriculum design, not an episodic mechanism delivered by teachers to learners" (Boud, & Molloy, 2013, p. 699).

As we acknowledged in Chapter 1, the influential work of Boud and Molloy (2013) has highlighted the importance of feedback designs. The above quotation reinforces this notion by proposing that feedback needs to be seen as a core element of curriculum and assessment design, not something that is delivered after students submit their work. Within this conception, design facilitates a number of features. It creates opportunities for students to develop the capabilities to operate as judges of their own learning; it involves students seeking and offering feedback; is driven by sequences of tasks that progressively build student capacity to deploy internal feedback; and requires student action to demonstrate that feedback loops have been closed (Boud, & Molloy, 2013). The active positioning of students in eliciting and acting on comments is a fundamental principle of new paradigm feedback practices.

Also highlighting the need for students to be active participants in feedback processes is the concept of sustainable feedback (Carless, Salter, Yang, & Lam, 2011; see also Chapter 1). These authors talk about designing assessment tasks to facilitate student engagement over time in which feedback from varied sources is generated, processed, and used to enhance performance on multiple stages of assignments. To develop sustainable feedback processes, there needs to be less emphasis on feedback as telling and increased focus on the development of student autonomy and the promotion of self-directed learning. The ideas of feedback designs and sustainable feedback are central to the new paradigm approach that we introduced in Chapter 1.

Assessment designs for feedback

The kind of assessment designs that enable students to engage with feedback are two-stage or multi-stage assessments; a series of overlapping, interlinked or integrated tasks; or iterative sequences in which feedback from an earlier task can be applied to a later one. Two-part or multi-stage assignments are a particularly useful means of promoting student engagement and uptake of feedback. In these kinds of design, a series of tasks enables students to apply internal or external feedback as well as self-monitor their own performance. Staged assessment task designs also encourage dialogue and iterative development of student capacities.

A good example of feedback uptake facilitated by a series of overlapping tasks is reported by Zimbardi et al. (2017) in the context of large classes in years 1 and 2 in the biomedical sciences. The assessment tasks focused on the conventions of scientific report writing and then producing a report targeting levels of publishable scientific research articles. An innovative web-based system facilitates marker provision of audio, typed, and handwritten comments and also enables the tracking of student engagement with feedback; 92% of first year students, and 85% of second year students were found to have accessed their feedback, with the analytics evidence indicating that 58% accessed their feedback for more than an hour (Zimbardi, et al., 2017). The amount of time students spent interacting with the feedback was significantly related to their progress in subsequent tasks. Two key implications arise. When assessment tasks are designed to build on earlier tasks, and the links in a sequence are made explicit, students are more likely to draw on feedback from preceding tasks. It is more efficient to focus feedback provision on the earlier tasks in a sequence as students are less likely to use and demonstrate learning gains from feedback on final tasks (Zimbardi, et al., 2017). This is particularly the case when the same learning outcomes are being evaluated.

A further practical and user-friendly example of a two-stage design is an individual or group oral presentation, including peer and teacher feedback followed by a written assignment on the same topic. In the context of civil engineering, oral presentations on a bridge design task included student questioning and teacher guidance, and informed the development of the written report which was submitted later (Carless, et al., 2011). In that way, the student experience of preparing, delivering, and reflecting on the presentation is integrated with feedback from peers and teachers, and is followed up to allow some uptake of comments received.

There are also multi-stage assessment designs which for reasons of variety involve a series of different tasks. Variety allows students to showcase different learning outcomes but if tasks are not aligned then it is harder for students to apply latent learning from feedback on earlier assessed work (Bevitt, 2015). Too much variety in assessment design may inhibit students' capacities for judgement because they need to accustom themselves to what the task requires and how it needs to be represented (Boud, Lawson, & Thompson, 2015; see also Chapter 7). So perhaps it may be fair to conclude that, for feedback purposes, it is more favourable to develop an assessment design with interlinked rather than different tasks unless the transfer of feedback between different types of assessments is made salient to students.

Students will spend more time on task and be more interested in seeking and engaging with feedback if they can shape assessed work to their preferences or capabilities (Bevitt, 2015). Partnership approaches to assessment and feedback, including negotiated assessment tasks, can play a role in encouraging an active student role in assessment and feedback design (Deeley, & Bovill, 2017). Students often appreciate authentic assessment tasks focused on real-life problems because they support them to develop as participants of a disciplinary culture and engage with methods of enquiry which are valued in particular academic disciplines (Sambell, McDowell, & Montgomery, 2013). When they tackle real-life assessment tasks, students are putting knowledge into practice in ways in which they are used in the discipline to which they are being inducted (Eddy, & Lawrence, 2013). There is also potential for authentic feedback, involving students in feedback exchanges similar to those in the real world of their discipline (see also Box 5.4). Our thinking is that this kind of authentic assessment and feedback is a facilitator for new paradigm feedback practices and we illustrate this further through the case discussed later in the chapter.

Guidance, rubrics, and exemplars to facilitate feedback processes

Another pertinent strand of assessment design involves considering pre-task guidance and anticipatory feedback in tandem rather than prioritising post-task feedback (Hounsell, McCune, Hounsell, & Litjens, 2008). Guidance is congruent with new paradigm feedback practices because it supports students in understanding expectations and facilitating the self-monitoring of their performance. In many circumstances, especially with large classes, guidance before the task is likely to be much more practical and impactful than feedback after the assessment task is completed. Weaknesses in guidance coupled with unfamiliar assessment tasks place undue pressure on teacher feedback to facilitate learning through assessment (McCune, & Rhind, 2014). In fact, not knowing what is expected of them is both a source of student frustration as well as being a hindrance to effective feedback processes (Balloo, Evans, Hughes, Zhu, & Winstone, 2018; Hounsell, et al., 2008).

Guidance encompasses setting out expectations; providing relevant clarifications; and scaffolding ongoing progress. This interplay between guidance and feedback has also been referred to by Hounsell as 'flipping feedback' in view of the implicit change to sequencing (see also Box 5.4). Through analogy to the concept of flipped classrooms, thought is given as to when feedback can most profitably lead to students engaging with information that is available to them. Through conceptualising guidance and feedback as a series of loops, students are involved in cycles of engagement, including ongoing efforts in understanding expectations; active involvement in feedback processes; and integrating learning into future performance (McCune, & Rhind, 2014).

Rubrics, grade descriptors, or lists of criteria can be helpful in clarifying expectations but teachers need to promote some form of student engagement with criteria. This is challenging because rubrics are often not designed particularly well. Rubrics seem to have potential to support learning when they are co-created or negotiated with students; they make the expectations for an assignment transparent; and students use rubrics to guide peer evaluation and internal feedback (Reddy, & Andrade, 2010). A point of debate is when to share rubrics with students (see also Chapter 7). No less an authority than Royce Sadler argues that providing rubrics in advance may inadvertently inhibit holistic student appraisals of quality (Sadler, 2015).

When the way rubrics are used encourages student self-regulation, they are likely to have a positive impact on achievement (Panadero, & Jönsson, 2013). Rubrics can facilitate the understanding and use of feedback in that, by making criteria explicit, they support understanding of feedback messages and appreciation of what needs to be done to improve (Jönsson, & Panadero, 2017). Rubric use does, however, need to avoid the danger of criteria compliance when quality is interpreted in a formulaic, instrumental way that can lead to a limited student learning experience (Torrance, 2007).

A useful way of clarifying rubrics involves sharing and analysing exemplars of work to support students in developing understanding of what quality work looks like, and in appreciating how quality can take different forms. Exemplars are tangible rather than abstract so they are often perceived by students as more useful than lists of criteria in illustrating what needs to be done and this kind of clarification is particularly useful in relation to innovative assessments or tasks with which students are less familiar (Carless, 2017). Exemplars of student work provide concrete embodiments of work of different levels of performance to illustrate how quality is achieved and there is plenty of evidence that students are positive about being exposed to exemplars (e.g. Hendry, Armstrong, & Bromberger, 2012).

There are legitimate teacher concerns that students may inappropriately copy material from exemplars (Handley, & Williams, 2011) but this can be tackled by designing variation between the exemplar and the live task. Probably the most important element of the use of exemplars is the role of dialogues in supporting students to develop their appreciation of the nature of quality work (Carless, & Chan, 2017). By producing accounts of strengths, weaknesses, and potential improvements to exemplars, students gain experience in making academic judgements and comparing them with those of the teacher (Sadler, 2010). Dialogues around exemplars have potential to support student engagement with feedback because they make expectations more explicit, which can facilitate students' sense-making of teacher comments (To, & Carless, 2016). Exemplars also act as guidance which is often more effective than post-hoc forms of feedback.

Assessment tasks and prospects for feedback

How do the prospects for new paradigm feedback approaches relate to frequently practised forms of assessment? The most common tasks in contemporary assessment tend to be examinations; extended pieces of writing, such as essays; oral presentations; group assessment, usually in the form of a group project; and portfolios or e-portfolios. All of these assessment tasks have their strengths and limitations, and for our current purposes, the potential or constraints for engineering productive feedback processes are paramount.

In Chapter 1, informants expressed some of the well-known challenges of providing feedback on examinations. Examinations have traditionally been something of a 'no feedback zone' and it has been common for students to receive little or no comments on examination performance. This is starting to be challenged in the literature (e.g. Blair, Goodwin, Shields, & Wyburn-Powell, 2014; Scoles, Huxham, & McArthur, 2013) and university practice is diversifying, including take-home exams, open-book exams and online exams. Many universities now offer the possibility of one-to-one exam feedback on request, or in failure cases. Generic feedback posted on the LMS is also a common option but students often doubt whether it applies to them and uptake of messages is likely to be modest. There are limited prospects for useful exam feedback if old paradigm practices are adopted. Individualised comments are time-consuming for staff to produce and there is limited potential for student action on comments which come at the end of an academic year. Thinking about feedback in relation to examinations through a new paradigm lens prompts us to consider timing and uptake in different ways.

A strategy developed in the hard sciences and popularised by Nobel prize-winning physicist Carl Wieman is two-stage exams (see also Box 5.4). Students first complete the exam individually and submit their answers in the normal way. Then they work in small groups to complete a variation on, or a selected part of, the exam with the proviso that they should negotiate answers and submit one answer script per team. The individual exam performance can count for 80–90% of the exam grade and the group stage for the other part of the weighting. Students are involved in a motivating form of collaborative learning and are providing immediate peer feedback on each other's answers. Recent research into two-stage exams evidenced both positive responses from students and improved achievement when working collaboratively (Levy, Svoronos, & Klinger, in press). The strategy seems particularly appropriate for exams that involve multiple-choice or short answer questions, so seems suitable for subjects such as science, mathematics, and engineering.

Building on the earlier discussion of guidance, we can also identify that for examination purposes students need guidance or practice prior to the exam. A mock test or integrated series of tasks culminating in an examination could allow students to gauge progress and receive actionable feedback. Pre-emptive guidance as part of exam preparation can draw on the experiences of previous cohorts of students. Through facilitating the typing up of hand-written examination scripts, Scoles et al. (2013) enabled a large group of students in the Life Sciences to have the opportunity to review exemplars of previous student exam performance prior to taking the exam. Key findings of the study were that students who accessed the exemplars performed better than those who did not, suggesting that exemplars play a role in enhancing student academic achievement or that it was the more capable students who analysed them. The exemplars were also seen by students as forming a useful part of their revision and examination preparation.

In similar vein, Blair et al. (2014) asked students to evaluate three exemplar exam answers of different styles and qualities. Students then worked in groups to discuss the exemplars, followed by a whole-class discussion mediated by the teacher. Students reported finding these activities extremely valuable in demystifying the assessment criteria, as well as providing insight into good strategies for crafting responses to exam questions. The impact on lower-achieving students was particularly significant in clarifying some of their main misconceptions. Treating feedback as a collective dialogic activity also offers practical advantages through greater efficiency than individualised feedback (Blair, et al., 2014). As we illustrate in Chapter 6, purposeful teacher–student interaction is much more than one-to-one conversation.

Exemplars bring visibility into feedback processes. This resonates with the concept of 'on-display assignments' (Hounsell, 2003, p. 75) in which student work or performance is openly visible to students rather than being of a private nature, as is the case with most exam answers and essays. Oral presentations, online discussions, group projects and posters are examples of on-display assignments. Such modes of assessment may prompt students to reflect on what they and their peers have achieved, and make visible different ways in which quality can be manifested. This visibility can also encourage discussion, including providing or seeking feedback.

On-display assignments are a particular feature of certain disciplinary cultures, such as the creative arts, where completed or work in progress is frequently open to scrutiny and feedback of different forms can emerge (Orr, & Shreeve, 2018). Critical reviews or crits in Architecture open up possibilities rather than providing answers, and involve co-constructed feedback processes (Orr, Yorke, & Blair, 2014). These modes of feedback may also carry implications for other disciplines (Schrand, & Eliason, 2012) where old paradigm feedback practices are sometimes entrenched and fresh ways of thinking are needed. On-display forms of assessment where feedback processes are built into the assessment design might also be part of a suite of measures to minimise contract cheating (cf. Bretag, et al., 2019; Dawson, & Sutherland-Smith, 2018).

Conventional forms of writing are generally private so unless peer feedback is carried out, students often remain unaware of different approaches that could have been deployed. Written tasks that students work on over time provide opportunities for student internal feedback but student procrastination often impedes this kind of process unless staged submissions prevent it. Teacher feedback on drafts or work in progress is aimed at circumventing this phenomenon but represents a complex issue. Positive elements are that feedback on drafts is usually viewed favourably by students and there are opportunities for action on feedback. More negatively, there are risks of creating student dependency on the teacher and the workload implications for teachers need to be considered or resourced (Beaumont, O'Doherty, & Shannon, 2011).

There are also designs where, following feedback on a first submission, students are required to show how they have acted on teacher comments to improve the final version. This kind of process involves students in revising and resubmitting work in line with the norms of academic publishing. A useful example of this kind of design is that of Court (2014) where 70% of the grade was for the first submission and 30% for a revised version. The second submission was assessed on the basis of the extent to which students engaged with and acted upon comments on the first version. These kinds of design enable teachers to observe uptake of comments, reinforcing a key issue of when in a learning cycle it is most useful to provide feedback.

Portfolios and e-portfolios through their design are intended to encourage drafting, reworking, and uptake of feedback. They are generally designed to promote continuous engagement because they involve the collection, selection, and editing of material over time. When written work involves drafting and redrafting in this way, there are opportunities for peer feedback, internal feedback, and student uptake of feedback. Portfolios in digital environments have potential to enable providing, receiving, and working with feedback from teachers and peers as part of the curation process (Clarke & Boud, 2018). The portfolio is then positioned as a continuous work-in-progress containing curated collections that are mainly formative at earlier stages and can be presented summatively at a later date guided by the reflections of students. Fostering skills in curation of both content and feedback are necessary for manageability for staff and students (Clarke, & Boud, 2018).

In the "Connected Curriculum", Fung (2016) argues the case for a programme-long showcase e-portfolio of curated summative assessment as a means of allowing students to shape and edit their learning journey over a sustained period of time. Through this process students revisit feedback; set goals in line with self-regulated learning principles; and document progress and achievement. Multiple inputs from different sources can be managed digitally for the purposes of enabling an array of information to be recorded, revisited and used. Through reviewing and synthesising feedback messages in these ways, students are involved in planning for uptake of feedback and developing their feedback literacy. Digitally enabled feedback storage tackles a problem that students often find it difficult to track and act on the diverse feedback information that they receive (see also FEATS, Chapter 4).

Programme-based assessment (see also Box 5.4) is an attempt to minimise some of the compartmentalisation and discontinuities which are unwanted consequences of modularisation. Evidence from large-scale data collection via Transforming the Experience of Students Through Assessment (TESTA) suggests that a more connected flow of assessments across a programme might facilitate more effective cycles of feedback (Jessop, El Hakim, & Gibbs, 2014). Current practice, however, suggests a lack of overarching assessment and feedback designs across a whole programme and student difficulties in applying feedback from one module to another (Jessop, & Tomas, 2017). Although programme-wide assessment has been the topic of a number of papers (Gibbs, & Dunbar-Goddett, 2009; Jessop, McNab, & Guppy, 2012), the current research-base in major journals has yet to provide comprehensive examples of successful programme-wide approaches to feedback.

In summary, certain assessment tasks and designs seem to have more potential for iteration and cycles of feedback uptake. Figure 5.1 summarises some of the key points: a series of tasks can support student uptake of feedback; these can include two-part or multi-stage assessment tasks; draft-rework designs; and pre-task guidance through student engagement with rubrics, standards and exemplars.

Key examples from the literature

We now consider two examples from the literature that illustrate some of the possibilities and challenges in developing assessment designs to promote feedback.

1. Task series

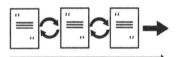

Students complete a series of similar tasks (for example, a series of lab reports), where each cycle of feedback enables them to apply comments to the next iteration of the task.

2. Two-part tasks

Students undertake a first task (for example, a presentation), followed by a feedback process whereby they use the feedback to inform a second, related task (for example, a written report).

3. Draft-plus-rework

Students receive detailed comments on a draft assignment. When students submit the final assignment, a portion of the grade is reserved for evidence that they have used the feedback from the draft (for example, by completing a written reflection on their feedback use).

4. Pre-task guidance

Students are given the opportunity to engage with rubrics, criteria, and/or exemplar assignments before completing their own assignment. This dialogue with peers and teachers serves as pre-task feedback that informs the approach they take.

Figure 5.1 Assessment task designs to facilitate uptake of feedback

The first was a design through which students were offered the opportunity to act on feedback by resubmitting an essay to obtain a higher grade (Prowse, Duncan, Hughes, & Burke, 2007). The second is a more process-oriented study of meaning-making during a group assessment involving multiple rounds of feedback (Esterhazy, & Damşa, 2019).

One way of designing for feedback is to involve students in drafting and redrafting over time so that students are engaged in using feedback. An interesting example of this kind of approach is described by Prowse et al. (2007) in the context of the first semester in a School of Education in a British post-1992 university. It contains both positive messages for feedback designs and also aspects that, as the researchers acknowledge, are potentially open to challenge.

Students submitted a written assignment in week 8 of a 15-week module. These were graded by the teacher with comments, and annotated essays were returned to students by email. Students were then required to attend a compulsory individual tutorial where they discussed their interpretations of the teacher feedback and explained to their teacher how they could improve the essay. This aspect permitted a dialogic exchange of ideas which was potentially beneficial for both students and teachers: there was negotiation of meaning; and students were providing 'feedback on feedback' to their teachers. At this point, students could choose between retaining the original grade for their essay or re-submitting it and trying to raise the grade; 22 out of 42 chose the latter option, using track changes or highlighting to indicate the modifications in order to make the marker's task easier. These 22 students then succeeded in achieving a higher grade for the course.

There are a number of positive elements in this case. There was a dialogue around feedback which enabled students' sense-making of comments; the important element of timeliness was well-managed; and students had opportunities to use feedback. This kind of recursive feedback promotes student engagement with feedback within the short timeframe of a single module. The processes were generally perceived positively by students which is important, given the widespread student frustration with assessment and feedback documented in Chapter 1.

Prowse et al. (2007) acknowledge, however, that there are a number of limitations inherent to this practice. The design is somewhat instrumental and teachers are, to some extent, pandering to student fixations with grades. This approach probably represents a pragmatic reality for contemporary higher education. There is some danger that the process inflates grades but this can also be seen as providing additional support to students in the first semester, a factor promoting retention. There is some risk that teacher marking workload increases through evaluating scripts twice rather than once although this is factored into the module planning and minimised by the highlighting and track changes requirements of the resubmission.

In our view, there is an additional danger that this kind of process aligns with old paradigm teacher-driven practices. The teacher tells the students what to revise and they go ahead with those revisions but they may not succeed in developing their evaluative judgement or becoming a more independent learner. In other words, feedback loops are closed but there are risks of reinforcing dependency on the teacher rather than ability to use internal feedback effectively (cf. Carless, 2019). Such processes are also not sustainable if they are dependent on teacher intervention to stimulate improvement. Students could, for example, have been encouraged to develop a more active role in self-evaluating their performance.

Turning to our second key example, processes of interactional meaning-making in relation to feedback comments are illustrated by Esterhazy and Damşa (2019) in the context of a class of 27 undergraduate biology students in a large Norwegian university. The assessment involved a portfolio task comprising three group assignments. As noted earlier in the chapter, a portfolio is itself an assessment design which through its drafting and redrafting process carries potential for the development of productive feedback processes.

The study describes how students carrying out group assessments made sense of and acted on teacher comments on drafts they produced. The findings demonstrated that students problematised teacher feedback comments and engaged in dialogue with the teacher and amongst themselves to co-construct understandings. In this way, feedback comments were not just messages transmitted from a teacher to students but opportunities for sense-making, negotiation, and subsequent action. Students construct meaning from the teacher comments and also of the underlying domain knowledge situated within a disciplinary culture. They develop strategies for working with these evolving understandings, for example, by finding ways to represent them in their assignment drafts. The process of drafting and redrafting involves social interaction, peer feedback, and sense-making within the group as they construct meanings together. Group assessment in itself encourages interaction between participants as their work evolves.

Methodologically, the study is also of interest for feedback research in that interactions within groups were recorded and analysed so that it was possible to investigate how meanings were constructed. There is a paucity of research that has actually analysed authentic feedback interactions, although this is beginning to be addressed (Ajjawi, & Boud, 2017; Steen-Utheim, & Hopfenbeck, 2019; Steen-Utheim, & Wittek, 2017). The data also provide insights into the co-construction of dialogues with the teacher instead of merely accepting what the teacher has said. When the teacher provided relatively minimal explanations within the dialogues, students were prompted to develop their own interpretations. This is an example of the subtle ways in which responsibilities are negotiated in feedback situations. A comment is not just a message transmitted from teacher to student but a resource that can expand or limit access to the knowledge space within which students operate (Esterhazy, & Damşa, 2019). This resonates with the ideas around interrogative feedback that are discussed in Chapter 6.

The study provides evidence that supports a case for conceptualising feedback as a process of student dialogue with peers and the teacher (Esterhazy, & Damşa, 2019). An important insight is that much depends on teachers' feedback literacy, including their approach to formulating comments; whether they are open to dialogue and facilitate meaning-making rather than dominating the process; and the depth of their understanding of students' prior knowledge and learning trajectories. Also pertinent is how students position themselves in the interaction with the teacher and with each other; and how proactive they are in exploring new meanings and their implications. These in turn relate to student feedback literacy (cf. Carless, & Boud, 2018).

Box 5.1 Key research findings

- Feedback needs to be seen as an integral part of curriculum and assessment design not merely isolated episodes of teacher comments (Boud, & Molloy, 2013).
- Guidance and anticipatory feedback are intertwined in that clarifying expectations is an important part of the assessment and feedback process (Hounsell, et al., 2008).
- By clarifying how quality is achieved, dialogic use of exemplars can facilitate student understanding of expectations and engagement with feedback (Carless, & Chan, 2017; To, & Carless, 2016).
- Staged assessment designs facilitate student uptake of feedback by providing motivation and opportunities for students to use comments (Zimbardi, et al., 2017).
- Principled assessment task design facilitates students' generation, processing, and use of feedback (Carless, et al., 2011).
- Assessment tasks such as group assessment and portfolios are natural sites for feedback dialogues (Esterhazy, & Damşa, 2019).

The case: Integrated assessment design for internal feedback

Context

The context for the case is a large second year class of around 250 students in the Faculty of Law at the University of Hong Kong. The teacher, Rick Glofcheski, has been teaching the course for more than 20 years and has placed particular emphasis on meaningful assessment design. Rick has won a number of awards for teaching based on his innovative assessment and feedback practice. David Carless researched his practices in 2013–2014 (Carless, 2015a, 2015b) and Rick has also written about his teaching (Glofcheski, 2017). What follows discusses recent refinements to his assessment and feedback designs, whilst also drawing on previous evidence. It exemplifies new paradigm feedback approaches by relocating much of the responsibility for generating and applying feedback from the teacher to students.

Undergraduate Law classes are often dominated by examinations with a not uncommon scenario being 100% of the assessment comprising an end of semester examination. Rick acknowledges that disciplinary cultures (cf. Chapter 1) necessitate examinations being part of the assessment design but he wishes to incorporate additional tasks to provide a more varied assessment diet. He wants students to be involved in assessment that relates to real-life uses of the discipline and designs feedback processes that capture students' attention. Rick believes strongly that learning should be based on authentic materials involving students in identifying and tackling complex and ill-defined problems: valued higher-order learning outcomes.

The course comprises Tort Law 1 and Tort Law 2 which run for an entire academic year from September to May, and is assessed as a single entity. In order to diversify the assessment for his Tort Law course, Rick has used since 2009 a reflective media diary (RMD) which in its 2017–18 version counted for 30% of the overall assessment weighting for the course. The RMD requires students to identify and analyse real-life Tort Law cases reported in the local media, and produce over time a reflective diary. The students also take a final, open-book examination which counts for 50% of the course grade. There is also a first semester test which counts for 20% or students can reduce this weighting to 10% by doing an additional coursework assessment. This element of choice and flexibility seeks to cater for student preferences and motivations. The assessment design is summarised in Box 5.2.

Box 5.2 Tort law assessment design

Reflective Media Diary		30%
1st semester test		20%
OR	1st semester test	10%
+	Coursework task	10%
Final Exam		50%

The feedback design

The main elements of the feedback design are detailed guidelines and exemplars to support students' appreciation of expectations; internally-generated feedback as students work on their RMD; coherence between the RMD and the exam; and same-day test and exam feedback. The teacher integrates guidance with anticipatory feedback. He does this through detailed guidelines stating expectations; rubrics indicating how performance relates to grades; and annotated exemplars posted on the LMS. Rick posts three samples of good RMD entries with brief teacher annotations and four samples of excellent exam answers. He supplements the exemplars with detailed guidelines on answering examination questions. These guidelines and exemplars are important ways of making assessment requirements clear from the outset.

A key design principle underpinning the case is that students should be involved in independent reflective learning by self-evaluating their ongoing work during the development of their RMD. The students are generating internal feedback as they monitor their selection and analysis of legal cases over a period of two semesters. For example, students reported identifying cases and then discarding them as more pertinent ones arose or when they could apply more insightful analysis to selected cases. A striking element is that there is little conventional teacher feedback as telling in that students are encouraged to take their own responsibility for their reflective diary. This is essential in a class of around 250 students.

An element of coherent assessment design is that the questions tackled in the examination are of a similar nature to those done in the RMD. In both tasks, authentic examples of legal cases are taken from local media and presented for analysis. The guidelines, exemplars, and students' own working processes for the RMD inform exam preparation because of the resonances between the two assessment tasks. In this way, the learning experience from the RMD prepares students for the exam and any internal or external feedback from the RMD carries forward into student exam preparation.

The teacher also uses an innovative approach to providing feedback on the test and exam. After the test or exam, students are invited on a voluntary basis to remain in the exam hall to discuss possible answers to the problems they have just been tackling. Rick believes that a key feedback principle should be for the timing of comments to come as close as possible to the submission. The immediate feedback aims at eliciting and responding to student views, so bringing dialogue into the process. If students make valid points that are not included in the provisional marking scheme, their insights can also contribute to a reshaping of the model examination answer. In view of the difficulties of enabling sustained oral dialogue within a large class, the dialogue around the examination answers is also continued on a voluntary basis through online discussion in the days following the final examination. This enables students to make more detailed and reasoned arguments, should they wish to do so.

Student response

The students generally responded positively to the RMD task. They are applying legal knowledge that they have learnt; they appreciate the linkages to real-life aspects of the law; they are putting in consistent effort over an extended period of time; and they see the ill-defined nature of problem identification and problem-solving as being a good preparation for the future workplace. The RMD also enables students to experience their own progress and perceive that they are producing more sophisticated analysis over time. Students also expressed appreciation for the commonalities between the RMD and the exam format, and offered the view that compiling the RMD was a form of training for the exam. This suggests that the students experience the assessment as a nested and iterative design.

Students reported finding the exemplars very useful in clarifying expectations for good assessment performance. A common concern about the use of exemplars is the risk of students copying them inappropriately. In this context, there is a design feature that prevents this because of the contemporaneity of the RMD so exemplars referring to legal cases from previous years are clearly not admissible. The main misgiving from students is that it represented a high workload for them. They have to do a lot of reading and synthesis for the RMD over a sustained period of time. They did not object to doing the extra work because it was a rich learning experience but some students pointed out that if multiple modules were arranged in such a way then their workload would have become excessive.

For the same day exam feedback, students were also positive and in fact so enthusiastic that they tried to persuade other teachers in the Law Faculty to adopt similar processes. Students voiced appreciation of the immediacy of comments whilst the issues are fresh in their minds. Some students expressed a concern about the emotional impact of realising immediately that wrong decisions or judgements had been made and avoided the post-exam dialogue on those grounds.

Enabling factors

Enablers include teacher, student, and programme factors. Rick has high credibility in terms of his popularity with students, his passion, and his status as a multiple award-winner. He has taught this course for more than 20 years and has carried out a sustained process of refinement. This continuity enables considerable workload efficiencies and deep understanding of student viewpoints. A further enabler is that the Law students form quite a close-knit disciplinary culture so the students are, to some extent, enculturated by their peers to the assessment and feedback procedures in the module so they do not experience too much anxiety or confusion at facing innovative practices.

The way the programme integrates Tort Law 1 and Tort Law 2 over an entire academic year is a facilitating factor for the coherent and iterative development of the RMD over an extended period. This design feature permits more time for student reflection and internal feedback than that afforded by a single module and allows students to develop their RMD progressively which then feeds into the final examination. The extended form of assessment minimises some of the unwanted consequences of modularisation.

Challenges

A major challenge is moving beyond disciplinary cultures which focus mainly on formal examinations. Rick makes the pragmatic compromise that he needs to retain examinations because of the conventions of the discipline but he tries to integrate them with other purposeful assessment tasks. Despite the limited feedback potential of an end-of-year examination, he innovates through the idea of same day oral and online exam feedback.

When implementing innovative assessment and feedback strategies, teachers need to obtain the trust and support of students and colleagues. One of the strategies Rick uses is to trial innovations and refinements, and to collect comments regularly from students. A challenge for many innovative assessment designs is students' potential unfamiliarity with what is required. Rick tackles this challenge by producing detailed guidelines and by posting annotated exemplars on the LMS.

Relationship to the literature

The practice illustrates many of the principles alluded to earlier in the chapter. The assessment design and feedback are interlinked in ways that encourage students to self-monitor their progress and generate internal feedback. The process of selection and organisation of the RMD lies firmly in students' hands in that they have freedom in selecting cases on which to focus and they are self-evaluating progress over time. In this way, the feedback processes are sustainable (cf. Carless, et al., 2011). The iterative nature of the task shares commonalities with portfolio-based assessment because learning materials are collected over time; the process is rich in internal feedback; and it leads to the development of a final product. Through a focus on authentic legal cases reported in the media, there is a direct relationship between assessment and real-life uses of the discipline (cf. Sambell, et al., 2013).

The attention to detailed guidelines for students resonates with the work of Hounsell et al. (2008) in relation to integrating guidance and feedback. The use of exemplars to clarify assessment requirements adds to the evidence from Hendry et al. (2012) and Carless (2017) that students find exemplars to be a useful means of illustrating what is required. The use of exemplars of exam performance also reinforces the work of Blair et al. (2014) and Scoles et al. (2013) in suggesting that sharing of exemplars is one of the most effective ways of developing anticipatory feedback processes for examinations.

Significance of this practice

This practice is highly sustainable in that feedback is almost entirely generated by the student. This makes the feedback processes quite subtle in that they are driven by the student and not the teacher. The contrast with feedback as telling is particularly significant and of course, feedback as individual telling is impossible with a class of 250 students. Rick facilitates student internal feedback by designing a rich authentic assessment task which promotes student engagement and requires iterative development over time. The provision of guidance and exemplars supports students in understanding expectations and the nature of quality, whilst not constraining them from developing their work in their own preferred directions.

The same day test and exam feedback scores highly on timeliness so its immediacy is a considerable strength. It enables students to receive feedback on examinations which is something that is not often available. It also involves interaction and dialogue orally and online. Students are involved in articulating their answers, receiving feedback from the teacher, and trying to justify their own particular stance with the possibility of contributing to shaping the marking scheme. From this, it is inferred that the main benefit of the immediate feedback session is not just the timing but the way that it engages the students in reflective discussion (Carless, 2015b). Same day exam feedback has elements of old paradigm practices, as students cannot readily apply it to a subsequent task. This does not imply that it is not a worthwhile practice in injecting some dialogue into the rather unpromising convention of an end of semester examination.

The RMD concept can be adapted to other disciplines which are frequently covered in the media, for example, Politics and International Relations, Economics, Medicine, Social Work, Science, or Education. In fact, several teachers in different disciplines at the university have adapted the RMD task for use with their own students. This is facilitated by Rick's active role as a local champion of innovative assessment and feedback practices.

Box 5.3 Implications for practice

- The design of assessments into sequences of interlinked tasks or stages facilitates the development of new paradigm feedback practices.
- Rich and engaging assessment tasks are a key catalyst for productive student learning and the development of internal feedback.
- Assessment design for feedback involves tasks in which students are encouraged to develop their academic judgement over time.
- Students often become more actively involved in feedback processes when working on assessment tasks that relate to real-life uses of the discipline.
- Guidance during the process of working on an assignment is invariably more useful for students than comments at its conclusion.
- Exemplars are tangible illustrations of quality criteria and are useful in clarifying expectations, producing guidance for students, and facilitating feedback processes.
- In the context of appropriate designs, less rather than more teacher feedback can be powerful in encouraging students to take responsibility for their learning and reduce dependency on the teacher.

Conclusion

The provision of feedback comments is not merely an isolated event that takes place after an assessment task has been completed. In a new paradigm feedback model, feedback involves ongoing cycles of learning through which students hone their skills, interrogate and crystallise their disciplinary knowledge, and develop the capacity to judge the quality of their work. In this chapter, we have emphasised the linkages between assessment and feedback designs and have explored the features of assessment tasks that open up or constrain possibilities for effective feedback processes. Our discussion has highlighted three interrelated elements of design: timing and alignment; authenticity; and guidance.

We have explored the role of iterative and aligned assessment designs in facilitating effective feedback processes. We have seen how the concept of timeliness in feedback does not simply represent a reasonable gap between completion of an assessment task and reception of comments. Instead, assessment designs enable effective feedback processes where tasks are sequenced to enable students to implement feedback from one task to the next. Beyond sequencing, sufficient overlap in task requirements or objectives facilitates transfer of feedback information.

We have also explored the concept of authenticity in assessment design, giving students the opportunity to engage with tasks that relate to real-life uses of their discipline. This notion of authenticity also extends to the feedback process itself; for example, on-display assignments, commonly used in the creative arts, provide students the opportunity to experience critical reviews or 'crits' which are a feature of feedback in professional life in many such disciplines. In the feedback design case, we saw how a rich authentic assessment task with clear guidance for students encouraged engagement. In the case, Rick's extended form of module assessment across two semesters resonates with the Integrated Programme Assessment of Brunel University, London (see Box 5.4). An implication for programme managers is to consider whether modules of longer duration can facilitate a less fragmented learning experience, and more co-ordinated assessment and feedback designs.

Finally, we have discussed the interplay between guidance and feedback, and have argued that in most cases pre-task guidance is more useful than post-task feedback. This is in line with new paradigm feedback principles of facilitating student uptake. Pre-task guidance can involve, for example, the sharing of rubrics and exemplars to clarify expectations, which can motivate and stimulate students to self-monitor their work in progress. A key way of designing effective feedback processes for large classes involves interplay between guidance, exemplars, and student self-evaluation. In fact, old paradigm feedback practices are unsustainable with large classes because it is impractical for teachers to deliver personalised feedback to multiple students.

If our aim is to empower students to engage with and implement feedback comments, then we need to consider how the design and sequencing of assessment tasks facilitates these outcomes. When designing assessment tasks, the capacity for student learning through feedback is a critical consideration. It is relatively simple to decide *how* to assess students' learning, but much harder to articulate *why* that particular task is the most effective way of enabling students not just to demonstrate prior learning through assessment, but to enhance their capacity for future learning and evaluative judgement. In a new paradigm approach to feedback, these considerations are inseparable.

Box 5.4 Key resources

- The Assessment design decisions website (www.assessmentdecisions.org) contains resources to support teachers in designing good assessment. Feedback processes are one of the key dimensions of the framework.
- Two-stage exams inject peer collaboration and dialogue into the usually private domain of examinations. www.cwsei.ubc.ca/resources/files/Two-stage_Exams.pdf
- Programme-based assessment carries significant potential to bring more continuity into assessment and feedback processes. Three good examples are TESTA, convened by the University of Winchester; Programme Assessment Strategies (PASS) at the University of Bradford and Integrated Programme Assessment at Brunel University, London.
  www.testa.ac.uk/
  www.brad.ac.uk/pass/
  www.brunel.ac.uk/about/awards/integrated-programme-assessment/About
- The Feedback for Learning Project involved the Digital Education Research Group at Monash University and Centre for Research in Assessment and Digital Learning (CRADLE), Deakin University. The project website contains a number of case studies of effective feedback, including the below focused on authentic feedback.
  http://newmediaresearch.educ.monash.edu.au/feedback/case-studies-of-effecti
  ve-feedback/case-study-4/
- Dai Hounsell compiled a number of assessment and feedback resources under the umbrella of 'Wise Assessment' during his one-year tenure as a Visiting Professor at the Centre for the Enhancement of Teaching and Learning, University of Hong Kong. The following entry discusses Flipping Feedback:
  www.cetl.hku.hk/teaching-learning-cop/wp-content/uploads/2015/08/wise-a
  ssessment-briefing12.pdf

Box 5.5 Questions for reflection and debate

- To what extent are assessment and feedback designs compromised by the need to cater for competing functions of assessment: grading, student learning, and accountability?
- To what extent are disciplinary cultures a barrier to staged assessment designs? What are the prospects for more imaginative uses of examinations, and how can these be promoted?

- Where does guidance end and feedback begin? In a new paradigm feedback approach, are they entwined and what are the implications?
- What are the main incentives for teachers to prepare good feedback designs when they are under pressure to perform on multiple fronts?
- Why is Integrated Programme Assessment not being taken up more vigorously and widely?
- To what extent can Programme-based feedback strategies be effectively integrated with programme-based approaches to assessment, and can these be scaled up?

Chapter 6

Enabling dialogue in feedback processes

Dialogue is at the heart of new paradigm feedback practices in aiming to move away from teacher-dominated forms of communication and enabling students to solicit and engage in feedback interactions. As argued by Nicol (2010, p. 503), "Feedback should be conceptualised as a dialogic and contingent two-way process that involves co-ordinated teacher-student and peer-to-peer interaction as well as active learner engagement". Involving students in dialogues is also an important aspect of good teaching enabled by questioning, sense-making, developing shared understandings, and clarifying ongoing thinking. When we talk about dialogic feedback we mean much more than a conversation between two people: it represents interactions between peers and in groups; it can occur during whole-class interactive teaching or through generic feedback; and it can occur through the medium of technology. One-to-one teacher-student oral dialogues are extremely resource-heavy so we do not view them as a major element of new paradigm feedback practices, more an occasional option.

Dialogic feedback can be defined as interactive exchanges related to the quality of student work in which interpretations are shared, meanings negotiated, and expectations clarified (Carless et al., 2011). The aim of this chapter is to discuss some ways in which dialogue can be embedded in feedback processes in practical user-friendly ways. A particular strategy that we highlight is the use of interactive coversheets to enable students to begin a dialogue with the marker of their work. The chapter also touches upon themes which occur elsewhere in the book: technology-enabled dialogue (Chapter 4), inner dialogue through self-regulated learning (Chapter 7), and peer feedback (Chapter 8).

Nicol (2010) points out that in mass higher education, interaction between teachers and students has been reduced and this lack of opportunity for sustained dialogue contributes to student dissatisfaction with how feedback is managed. The classic tutorial mode of oral discussion between teachers and individuals or small groups of students is probably an infrequent student experience outside the Oxbridge system. The lack of dialogue means that students rarely become fully aware of the contribution of feedback to their ongoing learning and teachers seldom see how their comments are being used (Orsmond, & Merry, 2011).

Since around 2010, a number of writers (e.g. Beaumont, O'Doherty, & Shannon, 2011; Nicol, 2010) have put forward the case for more dialogic approaches to feedback. Dialogue is an explicit attempt to circumvent the limitations of one-way transmission of teacher written comments on end-of-module assignments (Yang, & Carless, 2013). Dialogue has potential to reduce students' difficulties in understanding or appreciating feedback. It enables emerging interpretations to be communicated, shared, and interrogated so that students can construct individual and shared understandings of feedback for the purposes of ongoing development. Dialogue increases opportunities to engage with criteria and standards so that students are better placed to make sense of feedback.

Dialogue is positioned within a view of feedback as a communicative act and a social process in which power, emotion, and discourse impact on how messages are constructed, interpreted, and acted upon (Ajjawi, & Boud, 2017; 2018). When a safe and supportive atmosphere exists, dialogic feedback also plays a role in enhancing trust between participants in feedback processes (see also Chapter 9). Dialogue supports the relational dimension which is at the heart of successful feedback processes (Price, Handley, Millar, & O'Donovan, 2010). As a process, it also contributes to goal-setting, clarification and negotiation of expectations, the development of empathy, appreciation of alternative viewpoints, and relationship-building (Carless, 2013; Telio, Ajjawi, & Regehr, 2015).

An important role of dialogue is to narrow differing staff and student expectations and perceptions of feedback through communication and negotiation. Students seem to have rather different views of feedback to their teachers (Adcroft, 2011; Carless, 2006). For example, teachers report believing more strongly than their students that feedback is a crucial element of the student learning experience (Adcroft, 2011); and teachers perceive that their feedback is much more useful than their students do (Carless, 2006).

Through analysing feedback dialogues in the context of oral presentation tasks in a first-year international business communication course, Steen-Utheim and Wittek (2017) identify four potentialities for learning implicit in dialogic feedback. First, dialogic feedback involves affective factors which influence students' engagement with feedback and how they respond to emotional and relational support. Second, participants need strategies for maintaining and extending dialogue which can include initiating new topics and responding minimally to encourage elaboration or prolong dialogues. Third, students need opportunities for their voice to be heard in communication with others, so it is important for them to be enabled to develop an active presence in feedback dialogues. Fourth, creating opportunities for students to engage in dialogue with a competent other provides potential for individual cognitive development (Steen-Utheim, & Wittek, 2017).

As we signalled in Chapter 1, there are disciplinary differences in the potential for feedback dialogues; how they are likely to be managed; and the extent to which feedback is prioritised. There are disciplines in which discussion of work in progress is part of the signature pedagogies of the discipline. In Art and Design or Architecture, students are accustomed to receiving robust commentary on their designs during their production. In clinical practice, there may be opportunities for immediate oral feedback on diagnoses or interactions with patients. In the hard sciences, open-ended dialogues may be less common or may take the form of worked examples. The relational dynamics of different disciplinary learning activities provide various affordances and constraints for the emergence of productive feedback exchanges (Esterhazy, 2018).

Dialogues can also be broader in their focus than the specifics of particular pieces of work. Meta-dialogues discuss processes and strategies of assessment and feedback to demystify some of the 'rules of the game' (Carless, 2006, p. 230). Teachers and students can share their views of what feedback processes can and cannot achieve, and share their expectations of each other's contributions to feedback processes. These kinds of meta-dialogues facilitate students' appreciation of feedback and narrow gaps between teacher and student perceptions (Carless, & Boud, 2018).

Barriers to dialogic feedback

There are a number of barriers to the development of dialogic feedback processes. These are discussed below under the dimensions of teacher, student, and institutional barriers, although obviously they are not separate and there is interaction between them. We then discuss some of the main ways these challenges can be addressed.

Teacher-related barriers

For many academics, research and publication has to be a key imperative and this can sometimes act as a distraction from gaining a deep understanding of pedagogy. Within the multitude demands of academia, teachers may not prioritise feedback, appreciate or understand it fully, or they may perceive that dialogic feedback is impractical. The pervasive but limited image of dialogue as one-to-one conversation sounds unrealistic.

Teachers' primary academic identities are generally as members of disciplinary cultures. Accordingly, teachers may follow the norms of the discipline and these may not be conducive to dialogic feedback. Teachers with disciplinary knowledge but limited appreciation of varied teaching techniques may over-emphasise delivering content which sometimes results in one-way transmissive forms of instructional design. Ineffective assessment and feedback designs may compound these problems (see Chapter 5).

Teachers are not always skilful in implementing dialogic forms of feedback. The way teachers express comments may give the impression of a final judgement which closes down possibilities for further dialogue (Jolly, & Boud, 2013). Tensions arise when teachers dominate the discussion by communicating information in a relatively one-way authoritative tone as opposed to a more open dialogue that could involve questioning and challenging the teacher (Blair, & McGinty, 2013).

As the research of Steen-Utheim and Wittek (2017) exemplifies, teachers need to restrain themselves from dominating feedback dialogues.

In sum, teachers need to develop the pedagogic skills to organise curricula and assessment in ways which enable opportunities for effective dialogic feedback that develops students' feedback literacy.

Student-related barriers

Students may lack confidence, motivation, or opportunities to engage in dialogues with teachers or peers. In the context of history, politics and international relations undergraduates, Blair and McGinty (2013) collected evidence of students making efforts to engage in feedback dialogues by approaching their teachers to ask questions. Sometimes students were more focused on interpreting or challenging the grade awarded; not an unreasonable request but one that may not have a strong improvement orientation. Students also often found themselves positioned passively in dialogues without feeling much control over the discussion or their own ongoing learning. The quality of dialogic interaction is of central importance as unproductive dialogues can lead to misunderstandings or students' feelings of frustration or inadequacy (Steen-Utheim, & Hopfenbeck, 2019).

Convincing students that they want to engage in dialogue with their teachers is not always straightforward. Sometimes unequal power relations discourage students from entering into feedback dialogues with teachers for fear of exposing their weaknesses or suffering threats to their self-esteem (see Chapter 9). Dialogue and how it develops may be perceived as threatening to students and they may experience vulnerability (Steen-Utheim, & Wittek, 2017). For lower-achieving students, it can be particularly difficult to motivate them to engage in feedback dialogues because of concerns about being judged unfavourably. Lower-achieving students may also be unsure how to begin or maintain a dialogue if they do not understand comments or do not know how to respond to them.

Students sometimes do not recognise and appreciate opportunities for dialogues or may not fully understand what is expected of them. They may perceive teachers as unapproachable, intellectually intimidating, too busy, or pre-occupied with other priorities, such as their own research. For feedback dialogues to be realised, it is important for teachers to appear willing to help, demonstrate that they have students' best interests at heart, and for both parties to exhibit qualities such as open-mindedness and receptivity to each other's views. The timing of invitations for dialogue are important in that students are more likely to engage in dialogues if the process has potential to help them achieve higher grades.

Institutional barriers

Teachers and students operate within institutional and disciplinary environments which impact on the potential for meaningful dialogues to be enacted. University teaching is organised through modules of relatively short-term duration and assignments are usually end-loaded with comments often coming too late for students to benefit fully (Hounsell, 2003). Course designs are an important factor in facilitating or inhibiting dialogues, for example, in relation to assessment design (Chapter 5). There may not appear to be enough time and space in the curriculum for feedback dialogues to be engineered. Yang and Carless (2013) refer to these kinds of factors as the structural dimension of dialogic feedback to denote how universities generally organise and manage feedback processes. When modules seem like discrete entities and assignments are timed for obvious reasons towards the end of modules, it can be hard for students to engage in productive dialogues about their work. A further structural constraint relates to large class sizes and the sometimes distant relationships that are a by-product of massified higher education.

The multiple demands of academic life and the intensification of workloads are a further barrier that may impede dialogic feedback practices. Large course teams and pressures for standardisation may breed conservative and unimaginative approaches to assessment and feedback. The structural limitations of how feedback is generally organised in universities represent a genuine challenge which necessitates the kind of re-engineering of feedback processes envisaged by new paradigm practices.

Modes of facilitating dialogue

In this section, we discuss three main ways of engineering feedback dialogues centred on the roles of teachers, students, or technology as levers for dialogue. A number of them relate to themes also taken up elsewhere in the book.

Teacher-facilitated dialogue

There are a number of strategies through which teachers can facilitate dialogues in ways that are not excessively labour-intensive. This is important because our position on new paradigm feedback practices is that they should activate the student rather than lead to more work for teachers. Assessment designs (see Chapter 5) are a key means by which teachers enable different forms of dialogue: draft and re-draft designs enabling timely teacher input (e.g. Court, 2014); interaction around oral presentation tasks (e.g. Carless et al. 2011; Magin, & Helmore, 2001); or student-student dialogue within group projects (e.g. Esterhazy, & Damşa, 2019).

A useful and perhaps underplayed strategy is for teachers to provide more generic feedback that can either be applied to work in progress or be carried forward to future modules. Generic feedback is popular and useful in some of the hard disciplines, where worked examples or model answers are used to demonstrate how problems are solved or to model the process of designs or calculations. Timely generic feedback prior to submission is also likely to be more impactful than personalised feedback that is received too late for student action (O'Donovan, Rust, & Price, 2016).

Another way of facilitating teacher-student dialogue is through offering some flexibility and choice to students. In the context of a class of 84 first-year biological science students writing a 1,000-word essay, teachers offered students the option of either receiving written feedback in the normal way or attending a 15 minute tutorial where their assignment was marked in front of them (Chalmers, Mowat, & Chapman, 2018). The design was intended to be workload neutral in that 15 minutes was the estimate of the amount of time usually spent on marking. Out of the 84 students, 49 chose the tutorial and 35 opted for standard written feedback, perhaps partly because being present while your assignment is marked sounded potentially nerve-wracking. Both teachers and students found the experience of face-to-face marking positive in that it allowed for a feedback dialogue about the work, and was more valuable and satisfying to both parties than standard written feedback. This example shows how a modest design amendment can bring increased dialogue within written feedback processes.

There is also some evidence that students prefer oral feedback to written feedback (Mulliner, & Tucker, 2017; Steen-Utheim, & Hopfenbeck, 2019) but this is not always the case and may depend on disciplinary and interpersonal factors. Individual or small group tutorials could form part of oral feedback provision on work in progress. This process is analogous to postgraduate or doctoral forms of supervision where regular cycles of feedback are acted upon. One-to-one dialogues are resource intensive so need to be carefully planned and implemented. If managed effectively they carry a number of benefits, such as helping students improve their work and increased motivation when students feel that teachers care about them and their progress (Blair, & McGinty, 2013).

When implemented sensitively, dialogue also reduces the power differentials in teacher-dominated feedback and enables a shift in the relational power balance (Steen-Utheim, & Wittek, 2017; see also Chapter 9). Well-managed dialogues involve higher-order questioning and the use of 'wait time' whereby students are provided enough time to think and construct responses (Merisier, Larue, & Boyer, 2018). Teachers sometimes need to hold themselves back to allow time for the student voice to emerge, and to avoid dominating feedback exchanges. Many teachers find this hard to do because a natural teacher role is to share expertise or enthusiasm for the subject.

Interrogative feedback by raising questions to initiate a dialogue and invite response is a way of minimising teacher domination of feedback processes. A study in medical education found that when comments were posed as questions, they were more likely to stimulate students' reflections (Dekker et al., 2013). Questioning and response involve the making of judgements through which the quality of dialogue is developed and improved. In this way of thinking, commentary on students' work can play out as developing thinking rather than merely providing evaluation and instructions (Anderson, 2014). Research in online learning environments suggests that requests for explanation or clarification are aspects of new paradigm feedback practices and promote learning more effectively than corrective feedback (Guasch, Espasa, & Martinez-Melo, 2019). When feedback messages are corrective or express teacher opinion, they do not seem to generate much student response or action (Alvarez, Espasa, & Guasch, 2012). The points being made are that students need opportunities to take active roles in feedback dialogues through raising issues and questions themselves, negotiating meaning within dialogues, and reflecting for future action.

We have also demonstrated in Chapters 2, 4 and 5 that dialogic approaches to feedback are feasible with large classes. Effective feedback with large classes needs to be carefully designed and cannot be reliant on feedback as teacher-telling. In fact, a large class can act as a facilitator for new paradigm feedback practices because it can make teacher-dominated feedback approaches impossible. Dialogic feedback designs for large classes include embedding the development of student feedback literacy within the curriculum (Chapter 2), technology-enabled feedback processes (Chapter 4) and guidance integrated with internal feedback (Chapter 5).

Peer dialogue and inner dialogue

Peer dialogue is an important aspect of dialogic feedback and is more fully discussed in Chapter 8. For completeness, a few observations are introduced here. There are a number of potential advantages to peer dialogue. Peers are more plentiful than teachers so there are multiple opportunities to engage in interaction with them. Friendship is stronger and power differentials are less prominent, so it is sometimes easier or more comfortable for students to enter into dialogue with their peers rather than teachers. There is evidence that peer dialogue can be more accessible than teacher feedback and is helpful in the development of student understandings (Steen-Utheim, & Hopfenbeck, 2019). Peer dialogue and exposure to exemplars are useful for all students and may especially be a starting point for lower-achieving students to begin developing feedback literacy. Peer dialogue is also consistent with the social constructivist learning principles which we introduced in Chapter 1, given that social learning is an important way of developing and clarifying thinking.

Students also engage in internal feedback or inner dialogue when they are making decisions or adjustments when working on assignments. Internal feedback involves students self-monitoring as they evaluate performance or work in progress. The interplay between internal feedback from the self and external feedback from peers or teachers is a key feature of Chapter 7, hence we do not pursue those ideas further here.

Technology-enabled dialogue

There are various ways in which technology can be used to bring dialogue into feedback processes. Increasingly common trends that we discussed in Chapter 4 are audience response systems, such as clickers; and audiovisual forms of feedback, such as audio, video and screencasting feedback. There is evidence that students respond positively to these forms of feedback partly because they resemble a dialogue.

The interACT project (Interaction and Collaboration via Technology) at the University of Dundee is a useful example of technology-enabled feedback dialogues in the context of an online Masters in Medical Education (see also Chapter 4). Four principles guided the project: feedback is viewed as a dialogic process of communication; assessment design affords opportunities for feedback to be used in future assignments; students are empowered to seek feedback from different sources; and feedback should develop students' evaluative judgements (Barton et al., 2016). Interactive coversheets were used on assignments whereby students self-evaluated their submission against the stated criteria, summarised how previous feedback had informed their work, and requested specific feedback where needed (see sample prompts in Box 6.1).

Box 6.1 Sample dialogic prompts (Barton et al., 2016)

1 How well does the teacher feedback match your self-evaluation?
2 What did you learn from the feedback process?
3 What actions, if any, will you take in response to the feedback process?
4 What, if anything, is unclear about the teacher feedback?

Teachers responded to both student work and the related self-evaluation, and to promote student engagement with teacher feedback, students then responded to the prompts stored in a longitudinal feedback journal. The relevant teacher was automatically alerted via email when a student posted comments into their longitudinal feedback journal and they continued dialogue asynchronously as required (Ajjawi, & Boud, 2018).

Findings suggested that students needed to develop more sophisticated assessment and feedback literacy to make the most of the interactive coversheets; there was some need to simplify the longitudinal feedback journal in view of it increasing teachers' workloads; and enhanced teacher satisfaction emerged from seeing that students were using feedback (Barton et al., 2016). Although there are resource implications for the kind of curriculum redesign implicit in the approach, its value lies in promoting sense-making and action in response to feedback dialogues (Ajjawi, & Boud, 2018).

Key examples from the literature

We now discuss two key examples from the literature which illustrate some of the possibilities of injecting dialogue into feedback processes. A small-scale study with 23 first-year students from the School of Outdoor Studies at the University of Cumbria explored the use of interactive coversheets as part of assignment submission (Bloxham, & Campbell, 2010). The aim of the strategy is to shift the student role from a passive consumer of feedback to one in which they take some responsibility to interact with the marker. The technique can also narrow gaps between teacher and student thinking by providing teachers some insights into students' views about their assignments. A further pragmatic aim is augmenting the amount of dialogue without increasing the workload of staff. The strategy has the potential to decrease the time teachers spend on issues that students are less concerned with. One of the interactive coversheets was designed as per Box 6.2.

Box 6.2 Sample interactive coversheet (Bloxham, & Campbell, 2010)

First there were some tips on academic writing skills and referencing, then the following reflective prompts.

- What are the strengths of this essay?
- What are the weak points of this essay?
- The mark that this essay deserves is ___% because ... (relate to assessment criteria)
- If I wanted to increase my mark by 10%, I think I would need to ...
- What I would like your feedback on is ...

Through completion of the questions in Box 6.2, the student is beginning a dialogue with the teacher and is clarifying their own orientation to their work. This is important in developing an active student role in feedback exchanges congruent with new paradigm feedback practices. Of course, teachers are not obliged to respond only to students' requests and may raise other issues which they deem important.

The researchers collected interview data from students. Interactive coversheets were perceived as useful in prompting students to think about and reflect on their work. Students also appreciated the opportunity for dialogue and that their questions enabled them to begin a conversation with teachers. Some challenges were also reported. A reality was that students completed their assignments at the last minute before the deadline, so for some of them they then just wanted to submit it or were too tired or rushed to think immediately of reflective questions worth posing. Some students also found it hard to think of questions that they could usefully raise, and these difficulties were exacerbated by their limited understanding of expected standards. When students are unable to raise questions about complex elements of their work, they were more likely to ask questions about relatively superficial aspects, such as referencing. These challenges indicate the need for some scaffolding and strategies to develop student feedback literacy. A number of students expressed the view that what was important was guidance so that they had a better understanding of expectations. Teachers need to prepare the ground for dialogue by preparing students for such interaction. Peer discussion of assessment standards and assignment requirements could be a beneficial starting-point.

The completion of the interactive coversheet was also hampered by diversity of assessment tasks (essays, posters, projects) as this presented a further challenge for students in developing understanding of standards and criteria (see also Chapter 5). However, many students felt too embarrassed or intimidated to approach teachers for additional help. This is a common problem that can be tackled by teachers showing care, trust, and demonstrating that they have students' best interests at heart (Carless, 2013; Sutton, 2012). Repeated offers of encouragement and support may be ways of showing sincerity and commitment. This relational dimension is further explored in Chapter 9.

Teaching staff perceived some benefits. It sped up the marking process because reading a student request helped to focus the teacher's thinking and comments. The positive reaction of staff in terms of time saved and the focus on students' needs is important because teachers as well as students need to perceive benefits of feedback processes.

The second key article (Nicol, 2010) is an exemplary treatment of a range of practical ways in which dialogic feedback could be implemented. The article addresses the problem of written feedback being a mainly one-way form of communication. Nicol discusses five strategies to tackle this challenge so that the nature and quality of feedback dialogue can be enhanced even with large numbers of students and without adding significantly to demands on academic staff.

First, students need to be involved in dialogues which help them understand assessment task requirements. Students can discuss task demands in groups to clarify what is required and can be involved in generating criteria and applying them to exemplars of previous work. The more students actively engage with task goals, criteria, and exemplars, the more likely they are to internalise requirements. Subsequent teacher feedback that is focused on these criteria can build on these shared expectations and help students to make sense of comments. A further option is for students to be asked to produce a summary of their assignment when they submit it, in ways similar to an abstract. This abstract could clarify the wider message of the writing, help teachers to understand what a student was trying to accomplish, and so tailor their comments accordingly.

A second strategy described by Nicol, analogous to Bloxham and Campbell (2010) above, is to invite students to express their preference for the kind of feedback they would like to receive. Students reflect on the strengths and weaknesses of the submitted assignment and state the aspects on which they would like further support. Teachers can provide a framework to guide students using specific questions, such as "What was your main point?" "What questions do you have for me as a reader?" The dialogue can be extended by inviting or requiring students to respond to the teacher feedback. They could submit a note or action plan, outlining their response to comments and how they could use them to enhance future work. An alternative is for students to discuss comments in groups and make sense of them together.

Third, Nicol (2010) elaborates the merits of peer dialogue in enhancing feedback processes (cf. Chapter 8). When giving comments to peers, students are often exposed to student work of different levels and this can be a powerful way of enabling them to be more detached and critical about their own work. Being exposed to feedback from different sources mirrors typical feedback practices in the workplace and the peer review process in academia. Sometimes peers are able to make comments in student-centred discourse which is more readily understandable to students than teacher comments.

A fourth way of improving the richness of feedback dialogue is through assessment design (cf. Chapter 5), for example, collaborative assignments. Students can be involved in the co-authoring of essays with classmates providing peer feedback to each other. In collaborative authorship, students are both producing and receiving comments. They analyse each other's writing, detect problems, and make suggestions for improvement. This is beneficial for all students, and can be particularly helpful for those who may overestimate their capabilities or find it difficult to detect flaws in their own writing (Nicol, 2010).

A fifth strategy is to expose students to wider feedback dialogues. When students submit an assignment, they typically only see comments related to their own work. The process can be enriched by enabling exposure to a broader sample of comments. For example, students could be afforded access to the databank of comments for the whole class. Being exposed to the kinds of comments that teachers write on assignments provides a richer array of feedback. Students may pick up on areas of insight that were not addressed in their own specific assignment. They could be invited to select from the bank of comments those that they consider most relevant for further improvement.

The strategies elaborated by Nicol (2010) are part of wider goals of transforming feedback from models based on teacher delivery of comments to those based on co-construction with students. These kinds of changes in emphasis lie at the heart of new paradigm feedback practices. Enabling students to request feedback, respond to comments, and involve themselves actively in feedback dialogues are also fundamental to the development of student feedback literacy.

Box 6.3 Key research findings

- Dialogue can narrow misalignment between students' and teachers' perceptions of both broader feedback processes (Adcroft, 2011; Carless, 2006) and specific instances of feedback interaction (Esterhazy, & Damşa, 2019).
- By helping them to appreciate the nature of quality as well as their own strengths and weaknesses, dialogue can support students in self-regulating their own work (Carless, et al., 2011; Nicol, 2010).
- Dialogic feedback needs to be implemented in ways that avoid teachers dominating the discussion (Blair, & McGinty, 2013; Esterhazy, & Damşa, 2019; Steen-Utheim, & Wittek, 2017).
- There are various ways in which dialogue can be engineered without being labour-intensive for teachers (Nicol, 2010).
- Interactive coversheets are a practical means of bringing dialogue into written feedback processes (Barton, et al., 2016; Bloxham, & Campbell, 2010).
- Dialogue supports the relational elements of feedback processes (Price, et al., 2010; Steen-Utheim, & Wittek, 2017; Telio, Ajjawi, & Regehr, 2015).

The case: promoting dialogue through interactive coversheets with large classes

Context

The context for the case is the School of Psychology at Newcastle University. Dr Patrick Rosenkranz and Dr Amy Fielden are involved in the programme management of the undergraduate degree for Psychology. Patrick and Amy view feedback within a learning environment as those cues and processes that allow students to identify their current progress towards a learning goal and take steps towards furthering this progress. They see effective feedback as inherently reflective and metacognitive so that students derive insight into their own performance, and how it can be developed. This means that feedback is effective when students make sense of the cues and are actively involved in meaning-making.

In mass education, however, high student numbers and heavy workloads lead to a number of challenges. Feedback tends to take the form of written comments which are sometimes based on templates or rubrics with the consequence that feedback can end up as impersonal or too generic. This may be one reason that students do not engage with feedback as deeply as would be hoped (see also Chapter 3). The challenge Patrick and Amy are trying to address is to develop feedback processes that are meaningful for large groups of students. One way of doing this is to involve students more actively in the feedback process as part of new paradigm feedback practices. Professor Jarka Glassey, a National Teaching Fellow from the School of Engineering, has successfully used and promoted interactive coversheets to stimulate dialogue with students. She shared the strategy with the case teachers who decided to take it up.

The feedback design

The feedback design was focused on bringing increased dialogue into the processes of written assignments. The interactive coversheet strategy was introduced with undergraduate Psychology students in modules that focused on essay writing. As students were asked to submit a draft of their essay on which formative feedback was given, an opportunity presented itself to involve the students more actively in the feedback process. The teaching team designed a coversheet for each assignment that asked students to reflect on their work and to request specific aspects of feedback. The questions are presented in Box 6.4.

Box 6.4 Interactive coversheet questions

- What do you think is the strongest aspect of your assignment?
- What area of your assignment do you think needs improving?
- I would particularly like feedback on (list up to three specific areas):

These questions were introduced to encourage students to consider the strengths and weaknesses of the draft essay and to ask for specific feedback. If a student engages with these questions they are already reflecting on their own work in a constructive way. Asking the students what feedback they wish to receive begins a dialogue between the marker and the student. By requesting specific aspects of feedback, students can guide the marker to areas of interest or concern. This allows the marker to personalise the feedback they give. Ultimately, a goal is to enable students to determine and reflect upon their feedback in collaboration with teachers, rather than as passive recipients.

The feedback prompts can be easily implemented for individual assignments or more widely across a programme. In view of the purpose of beginning dialogues between teachers and students, the implementation should happen in the wider context of developing feedback practices that enable agency, ownership, and recipience. Students need to be supported in initiating and maintaining the dialogue.

This practice was later rolled out to essay assignments with other groups of students. Finally, these questions were embedded for all assignments in the undergraduate Psychology degree. In a later version of interactive coversheets, the teaching team sought to encourage students to incorporate feedback from various assignments into future work. To facilitate this, they decided to add a further prompt where students were asked to identify how they had used prior feedback on comparable work to inform their approach to the current assignment (see Box 6.5).

Box 6.5 Prompt for action

- Based on previous feedback, I have particularly focused on the following aspects of my assignment:

We view this prompt for action as a key element because it encourages students to make use of previous feedback to inform current action. One of the problems at present is that too much feedback is not engaged with or taken up. Box 6.5 and its implementation represent a useful reminder to students to make use of previous feedback that they have received.

Student response

Students responded well to being able to make requests for feedback. They generally appreciated the opportunity to reflect on the strengths and weaknesses of their assignments and felt that the feedback questions played a useful role in guiding their reflections. They liked being able to communicate with the marker and raise issues that they were finding challenging. Comments from students on standard teaching evaluation forms were also generally positive in relation to the feedback processes. Moreover, engagement with the process was high: on most iterations around 85–90% of students completed the stimulus questions on their assignment coversheet.

There was a recurrent student concern focused on the second question in Box 6.4 (i.e. "What needs improving?"). A number of students were hesitant to point out weaknesses or areas for improvement in their assignment out of fear that the marker would then focus on this to the detriment of their overall grade. This was an aspect of the process that the teaching team perceived as needing some further thought. To ensure students engage with this section rather than not complete it, in the next iteration the teaching team asked students to identify areas that 'they are confident about' rather than the strengths of their work, and 'areas they are unsure of' rather than areas of weakness.

Enabling factors

The main enabler was that the practice had already been used successfully in the university. The initial idea for this practice came from a senior colleague in another discipline and the conversation with her facilitated the initial use of interactive coversheets in the School of Psychology. An external examiner commended this as good practice which worked as a positive springboard for scaling-up. Positive external recognition of this kind can act as a stimulus for further implementation. The majority of colleagues in Psychology, as well as the Head of School, were supportive of the idea and while there were some reservations by colleagues who did not wish to adjust their normal feedback and marking practices, the interactive coversheet was adopted by all teachers.

Challenges

The success of interactive coversheets relies on teachers and students buying in to the process. It can be challenging to engage every marker sufficiently to change the way they give feedback and to adopt an approach that allows students to request specific feedback. A concern voiced by colleagues is that this might mean more work and teachers providing additional feedback. In practice, the feedback requests usually help teachers to focus their comments which means that composing feedback is not more time-consuming than it would normally be. In fact, it probably leads to modest time-savings in that redundant or unwanted feedback can be reduced.

A further challenge is to engage students with the process of reflecting on their assignments and articulating these reflections by initiating feedback dialogues. Feedback requests are sometimes fairly general, unspecific, and descriptive (e.g. 'structure', 'references') but with repeated usage, students learn to make more detailed and specific requests. It is important that students undergo repeated practice and receive coaching on how to make the most of opportunities for dialogue through the interactive coversheet. Accordingly, the strategy probably works best if it is integrated with attempts to develop student feedback literacy. Practice and guidance might aid this process, for instance by discussing and demonstrating prior to submitting assignments how to make the most of the possibilities afforded by the coversheet process. This may also go some way to alleviating the concerns mentioned by some students regarding highlighting the weaknesses of their work. Teachers could share their experiences on this issue by pointing out that in academic research, acknowledging the limitations of one's work is generally perceived positively rather than being seen as a weakness. Course climates need to make students feel that admitting doubts or weaknesses is normal and will not be held against them. This also reinforces the value of teachers sharing their academic and feedback-related experiences with students (see also modelling of peer review in Chapter 8).

Relationship to the literature

There is a strong resonance in this practice with other versions of interactive coversheets (Barton et al., 2016; Bloxham, & Campbell, 2010). There are two key points worth reiterating: supporting students in making the most of the process; and including a component of students stating previous feedback that has been acted upon. The practice also exemplifies the ideas of Nicol (2010) for developing user-friendly ways of promoting dialogue around written feedback processes in relation to students expressing preferences for what kind of feedback they would most like to receive. This form of dialogue is important because the literature (e.g. Adcroft, 2011; Carless, 2006) illustrates that there are dissonances between teacher and student views of feedback.

The practice also relates well to the framework for student feedback literacy developed by Carless and Boud (2018). Students are making initial judgements about the quality of their work and are becoming proactive in eliciting suggestions from teachers. Importantly, in the strategy showcased in Box 6.5, they are encouraged to show evidence of uptake.

Significance of this practice

The use of interactive coversheets is part of a repertoire of practices to promote feedback dialogue. Possibly its most powerful dimension is that it prompts students to reflect on their work and to consider what kinds of feedback might be beneficial to them. This is beginning to seed student feedback literacy in terms of making judgements and seeking feedback. The practice is also user-friendly for teachers and does not require additional resources or increase teacher workloads. The interactive coversheet strategy also begins the development of student–teacher partnerships in relation to feedback.

The success of this practice at Newcastle University led to rolling out an interactive coversheet to all assignments in the undergraduate Psychology degree with approximately 450 students. When developing the interactive coversheet for implementation across the programme, the teaching team reflected on how they could maximise its benefits. They felt that a key step was to encourage students to incorporate feedback from various assignments into future work and Box 6.5 illustrates this aspect. This element is congruent with our emphasis in this book on student action in response to feedback.

To enable scaling-up of the practice of student-initiated dialogue via interactive coversheets, it could become a departmental or institutional policy to bring some coherence and consistency to feedback processes. If the strategy is implemented on a larger scale, there is potential for students to become more sophisticated in their feedback requests. There is a danger, however, that with repeated use the strategy might become less fresh or novel and might become formulaic. To tackle this barrier, student experience in using interactive coversheets could be leveraged and appropriate student-initiated variations designed. The more students are involved in co-constructing feedback experiences, the greater the potential for new paradigm feedback practices.

Box 6.6 Implications for practice

- Teachers need to create some motivation and incentives for students to engage in dialogues, for example, through linking dialogues with ongoing assessment tasks and preparing the ground for student action.
- Teachers can prepare students for dialogue by inducting them into interpreting criteria and standards.
- Dialogue is about helping students to improve over the longer-term rather than justifying a mark.
- Teachers should provide multiple opportunities for dialogues of different forms: peer to peer; teacher to peer(s); technology-enabled dialogues; oral and written.
- Teachers should be careful not to dominate the dialogic feedback process by using strategies such as eliciting, wait-time and holding back commentary.
- Interactive coversheets can be used in different ways to promote dialogue within written feedback, including with large classes.
- Scaffolding ways to engage in and sustain dialogues support the development of student feedback literacy.

Conclusion

In this chapter, we have argued that developing user-friendly forms of dialogue is a fundamental part of new paradigm feedback practices. Dialogue is central to the social constructivist perspectives on feedback that we introduced in Chapter 1. The first half of the chapter reviewed some rationales for dialogic feedback, some challenges for implementation, and how they might be overcome. Benefits of feedback dialogues include cognitive ones in terms of developing shared under-standings of standards and criteria; metacognitive ones in terms of supporting self-regulation of learning; social and relational ones, including care and trust; and induction into disciplinary ways of knowing and being.

The second half of the chapter analysed the use of interactive coversheets as a means of beginning dialogues between students and teachers. This is a practical form of interaction which can be used for any written tasks whatever the class size. The strategy forms part of a repertoire of techniques for involving students actively in feedback processes. Interactive coversheets are a good example of empowering students to initiate feedback exchanges. In an old paradigm feedback model, teachers initiate the process by providing written or oral comments on students' work. In many cases, there is no further dialogue or student response. In new paradigm processes, students can make the first move by requesting feedback on specific elements of their work, or by seeking guidance on their work-in-progress. To use the analogy of a game of tennis, in this approach the student, rather than the teacher, is making the 'serve' in the feedback exchange. The teacher can then return the student's 'serve' by responding to the student's requests or queries. The student is then enabled to continue the 'rally' by providing evidence of how they have used prior feedback, or by engaging in further dialogue with teachers about their work.

High levels of teacher feedback literacy enhance the prospects for productive dialogues. Relevant aspects of teacher feedback literacy include a commitment to involve students actively in dialogues around the making of judgements; a willingness to restrain teacher interventions so as to open up rather than close down interaction; a sensitivity to relational and affective elements of a dialogue; and design elements of providing students opportunities to act on dialogic feedback in the context of ongoing or future assignments.

Box 6.7 Key resources

- The University of Edinburgh hosts a range of resources congruent with the thinking in this chapter.
  http://www.enhancingfeedback.ed.ac.uk/
  One of the strategies mentioned is 'elective feedback', essentially the same idea as interactive coversheets. Dai Hounsell includes the possibility of students requesting in what form they would like to receive feedback: handwritten, typed (e.g. using track changes and comments), emailed as a digital audio file, or spoken face-to-face.
  http://www.enhancingfeedback.ed.ac.uk/staff/resources/briefing.html#item3
- David Nicol's REAP (Re-engineering Assessment Practices in Higher Education) contains a number of useful papers and resources at www.reap.ac.uk. Congruent with new paradigm feedback practices is Nicol's Feedback as a dialogue campaign developed in association with the Student Union.
  http://repository.jisc.ac.uk/5596/3/interact.pdf
- Case study from the Y1Feedback Project: written feedback was provided after students submitted their reports, followed by oral exchanges in the next lab session to ensure students understood the feedback and had opportunities to raise questions.
  https://youtu.be/jq9pfUbCDc8

Box 6.8 Questions for reflection and debate

- How can dialogue be realistically promoted within massified higher education? What are effective ways of encouraging teachers and students to prioritise dialogues of various forms?
- Dialogue involves interaction between participants, but does the pervasive image of dialogue as an oral conversation between two people make it sound impractical? How can broader notions of dialogue be promoted or would an alternative term, such as interaction, be more useful?
- To what extent would long-term use of interactive coversheets be positive in developing student feedback literacy or might the novelty wear off and the exercise become formulaic?
- What would be effective balances between different forms of dialogue (face-to-face or technology-mediated; peer to peer, peer(s) to teacher)?
- What are effective or optimal ways of facilitating technology-enabled dialogues?

Chapter 7

Interweaving internal and external feedback

The position we have taken in this book is to place the student at the centre of feedback processes in that a key purpose of feedback is to promote student self-regulation. This way of thinking was persuasively brought to the scholarship of teaching and learning community in the influential work of Nicol and Macfarlane-Dick (2006). These authors drew heavily on a seminal paper by Butler and Winne (1995) which elaborated the links between feedback and self-regulated learning through their analysis of the interplay between internal and external feedback. Internal feedback refers to the metacognitive processes which students deploy when working on a task: it represents their self-monitoring whereby they evaluate their performance (Butler, & Winne, 1995). External feedback from peers or teachers guides and informs internal feedback. In the contemporary assessment in higher education literature, this has led to the inference that external teacher feedback can beneficially be focused on assisting students to refine their own internal feedback (McConlogue, 2015). This interplay is well represented by the view that "When students receive feedback from teachers, they must engage in self-assessment if they are to use that information to improve academic performance" (Nicol, 2009, p. 339).

Our orientation of new paradigm feedback practices resonates with this position in its emphasis on students taking responsibility for their own progress. An important role for students lies in the interplay between internal feedback through self-evaluation and external feedback from peers or teachers. The focus of this chapter is on examining student self-evaluation, self-regulated learning, and how students move between internal and external feedback when developing their assessed work. Students' capacities to self-evaluate their work effectively facilitates their involvement in feedback processes.

Student self-evaluation is defined as the involvement of learners in identifying and applying quality criteria to their own work and making judgements about the extent to which they have achieved these criteria (Boud, 1995b). Students are significant sources of feedback, given their constant and instant access to their own thoughts, actions, and work (Andrade, 2010). As indicated above, student self-evaluations are informed by feedback from teachers and peers because comments from others play a role in calibrating students' judgements about their own work.

There is a long-running strand of literature which argues that the systematic development of student capacities for self-evaluation should be a core element of university teaching and learning (Boud, & Falchikov, 2007; Sadler, 1989). University teachers need to do more to induct students into the process of becoming effective self-assessors (Sambell, McDowell, & Montgomery, 2013). Making complex judgements about their own work and that of others prepares students for lifelong learning in the uncertain and unpredictable circumstances in which they will operate (Boud, & Falchikov, 2006). Self-evaluation is also a key component of student autonomy in which individuals manage themselves sustainably without the need for frequent feedback. In this way of thinking, capacities for self-evaluation facilitate effective participation in a range of academic and professional practices (Bourke, 2014).

When self-evaluating, students are implicitly or explicitly engaging with criteria and standards to support the making of judgements. An early study in this area by Orsmond, Merry, and Reiling (2002) involved students in generating criteria for a poster assignment. Exemplars were also shared with students to illustrate different design styles without teacher comments as to their merits. Students used criteria co-constructed with the teacher to carry out peer- and self-evaluation of their own posters. These stages resulted in improved student understanding of assessment criteria and standards, and seemed to enable useful feedback processes.

Facilitating students' understanding of criteria and standards is also congruent with the social constructivist principles that we introduced in Chapter 1. Colleagues from Oxford Brookes University, most notably Price, Rust, and O'Donovan, have consistently argued for the application of social constructivism to feedback processes. For example, O'Donovan, Price, and Rust (2008) discuss how learning activities can be organised to support students in understanding how assessment judgements are constructed. When students are purposefully involved in discussions of criteria and standards, they develop their capacities to identify and use both prescribed and self-generated criteria to hone their evaluative judgement (Tai, et al., 2018).

Student capacities to self-monitor their performance during its production assist them in understanding and applying feedback (Sadler, 2010). Student self-evaluation is a core element of new paradigm feedback practices because it involves students actively in self-monitoring and reflecting on their performance. Making judgements about one's own work and that of others is also at the heart of student feedback literacy (Carless, & Boud, 2018). A pertinent question therefore concerns the extent to which university students are able to gauge their level of performance accurately. There is a wide range of evidence that lower-achievers tend to overestimate their performance and higher-achievers are more aligned with assessors or more critical of their own performance (Boud, Lawson, & Thompson, 2013; Falchikov, & Boud, 1989; Panadero, Brown, & Strijbos, 2016). This reinforces the need for teachers to provide multiple opportunities for students to be involved in making and refining their academic judgements.

When students are trained in making judgements about work, feedback plays a significant role in gauging the accuracy of their judgements and calibrating them in the light of evidence (Boud, & Molloy, 2013). Engaging students in improving their capacities to make sound judgements is difficult unless opportunities for comparison with the appraisals of experts are provided (Boud, Lawson, & Thompson, 2013). Recent studies suggest that students become more accurate in judging their work when afforded extended experiences of self-evaluation (Boud, Lawson, & Thompson, 2013; Boud, Lawson, & Thompson, 2015). Although students initially struggled to self-evaluate accurately, by comparing their judgements with criteria-based grades from their teachers and experiencing extended practice in self-evaluation over a number of years, students became more robust in their judgements (Boud, Lawson, & Thompson, 2015). Mid-performing students showed the most improvement in that they overestimated their performance at the outset but eventually became able to make judgements comparable to those of their teacher. High-performing students were already able to self-evaluate accurately. Low-performing students began with weak self-evaluation skills and evidenced modest improvements in making judgements over time (Boud, Lawson, & Thompson, 2015).

To sum up this section, a number of inferences arise. Whereas some students engage in self-evaluation activities irrespective of course interventions, there is merit in making this process a formal part of the curriculum. Engaging students systematically in self-evaluation over time provides them with opportunities to enhance their capacities to make judgements. Teacher feedback on students' self-evaluations plays a useful role in developing students' skills in making evaluative judgements (Boud, Lawson, & Thompson, 2015; Tai, et al., 2018).

Self-regulated learning

Student self-evaluation is a sub-process of the broader concept of self-regulation. A classic definition of self-regulation is "an active, constructive process whereby students set goals for their learning and then attempt to monitor, regulate and control their cognition, motivation and behavior" (Pintrich, 2000, p. 453). In other words, students devise goals and monitor progress towards them, with this taking place in a specific learning context. Students who are more effective at self-regulation are better placed to self-evaluate their work and to judge the usefulness and appropriateness of external feedback from peers, teachers and others.

In contemporary mass higher education, many students arrive insufficiently prepared for independent learning and so a goal of first-year feedback practices should be to develop students' capabilities for self-regulated learning (Beaumont, O'Doherty, & Shannon, 2011). Training in self-evaluation can increase the use of self-regulated learning strategies (Panadero, Jönsson, & Strijbos, 2016). An influential model of self-regulated learning is that of Zimmerman (2000), proposing a cycle of three stages: forethought, performance, and self-reflection. Forethought refers to processes that precede action, including task analysis, goal setting, and self-motivation beliefs, such as self-efficacy and outcome expectations. Performance or volitional control involves processes while carrying out the task, including attention-focusing and self-observation. Self-reflection involves processes that occur after performance and are focused on self-evaluation of the response; causal attributions evaluating factors such as effort or ability; and reactions of self-satisfaction or adaptive inferences about how self-regulatory approaches might be altered during subsequent learning (Zimmerman, 2000).

A comprehensive recent review of self-regulated learning highlights socio-cognitive, metacognitive, and collaborative models (Panadero, 2017). The latter aligns best with the social constructivist orientation of this book through the notion of co-regulation (Hadwin, Järvelä, & Miller, 2018; Hadwin, & Oshige, 2011). Co-regulation refers to a transitional process in self-regulation where self-regulated learning is gradually developed through interaction (Hadwin, & Oshige, 2011). Interaction with peers carries potential for students to develop self-regulation together through shared knowledge construction and collaboration. Co-regulation might involve a more capable partner, but it could also arise from a dynamic process distributed and shared across individuals involving scaffolding of metacognition. Co-regulation is seen as a temporary state or transition to individual self-regulation.

There is plenty of evidence that students who become proficient in self-regulation do well in their studies. It has long been known that effective students monitor and regulate their learning and as a result achieve greater academic success (Zimmerman, & Schunk, 2001; 2011). Research reviews and meta-analyses show that there are positive correlations between self-regulated learning and performance (Brown, & Harris, 2013; Panadero, Jönsson, & Botella, 2017; Sitzmann, & Ely, 2011). Students, however, sometimes have conceptions of teaching and learning which are not congruent with self-regulated learning or they are not willing to invest the time and energy in developing it (Vrieling, Stijnen, & Bastiaens, 2018). This kind of student thinking can be exacerbated by discourses of students as consumers which may inadvertently reinforce the notion that feedback is about telling students what to do to succeed. Students might be more motivated to engage in self-regulation if they had greater awareness that it was likely to improve their academic results.

A crucial point of relevance to this book is that student self-regulation is linked with the uptake of feedback. A recent study of university students in New Zealand, for example, evidenced positive correlations between using feedback and student self-regulation (Brown, Peterson, & Yao, 2016). Students are more likely to use comments from peers or teachers when their own self-evaluations suggest that it is necessary. Comments which do not fit with students' own belief systems or prior experiences are often downplayed or rejected. An implication is that increasing student awareness of alternative perspectives on quality work may enhance their appreciation of feedback messages and broader feedback literacy. Feedback-seeking behaviours, for example, both enhance academic achievement and inform student self-regulation (Crommelinck, & Anseel, 2013). Feedback-seeking, however, does not always come naturally because of the potential affective challenges, and there may also be cultural barriers to feedback-seeking in some contexts (MacDonald et al., 2013).

Internal feedback

Butler and Winne (1995) make the important point that research on feedback and research on self-regulated learning should be tightly coupled. In view of both its conceptual importance and its relevance to the discussion in this chapter, it is worth discussing what Butler and Winne (1995) have to say about internal feedback, its role, and functions.

Students develop their own individual cognitive routines for creating internal feedback. Their internal feedback also acts recursively in that monitoring of a current state in a task triggers adjustment that contributes to student self-regulation of subsequent cognitive engagement (Butler, & Winne, 1995). Students may modify their engagement by setting new goals or adjusting extant ones; they may re-examine tactics and strategies and select more productive approaches; adapt available skills; and sometimes even generate new procedures. When external feedback is provided, it offers additional information which may confirm, add to, or conflict with the student's interpretations of the task and the path of learning (Bounds, et al., 2013; Butler, & Winne, 1995). As a result of monitoring task engagement, students may alter knowledge and beliefs, which, in turn, might influence subsequent self-regulation (Butler, & Winne, 1995).

Internally generated feedback is inherent to task engagement. Such feedback has a tripartite nature consisting of (a) a judgement of task success in relation to multifaceted goals; (b) a judgement of the relative productivity of various tactics and strategies in relation to expected or desired rates of progress; and (c) affect associated with judgements about productivity (Butler, & Winne, 1995). If a student misinterprets a task and/or adopts inappropriate goals, not only is it likely that sub-optimal tactics will be adopted but internal feedback generated during monitoring will neither provide adequate information about task performance nor suggest tactics or strategies which adequately redress difficulties (Butler, & Winne, 1995). These points resonate with the notion of task compliance (Sadler 2010): the congruence between the type of response submitted by the student and the type of response stipulated in the task specifications.

Earlier in the chapter, we quoted Pintrich's definition of self-regulated learning as involving cognitive, motivational, and behavioural aspects, and these are also at the core of internal feedback. Cognitive aspects are exemplified by setting a plan for engaging in the task; generating criteria against which successive states of engagement can be monitored; or seeking feedback from external sources such as peers, teachers, or other resources (Butler, & Winne, 1995). Motivational elements include perceiving a need to work harder to achieve one's goals; the willingness to strive towards a specific goal; or investing effort in seeking and dealing with feedback information. Behavioural aspects could include how students arrange their study time or which classmates they choose to interact with. The motivational aspects relate to the discussion in Chapter 3 where it was noted that students are often unwilling to put in the hard graft needed to engage with and use feedback information effectively.

Nicol's work built successfully on that of Butler and Winne (1995) and related the ideas to assessment in higher education. Nicol and Macfarlane-Dick (2006) argue that feedback should be used to empower students as self-regulated learners and so good feedback practice is broadly defined as anything that might strengthen students' capacity to self-regulate their own performance. Feedback from teachers can help confirm or modify students' own judgements but too much external teacher feedback might inhibit students from deploying internal feedback (Nicol, & Macfarlane-Dick, 2006). These authors also reiterate that feedback is not just a cognitive process but one that interacts with motivation and beliefs. This is consistent with the view outlined earlier of internal feedback comprising cognitive, motivational, and behavioural dimensions. The influential seven principles of feedback for self-regulated learning (Nicol, & Macfarlane-Dick, 2006) are summarised in Box 7.1.

Box 7.1 Feedback for self-regulated learning (Nicol, & Macfarlane-Dick, 2006)

1   Clarifies good performance.
2   Facilitates self-evaluation.
3   Shares high quality feedback information.
4   Stimulates teacher and peer dialogues.
5   Encourages motivation and self-esteem.
6   Provides opportunities to close the gap.
7   Uses feedback processes to improve teaching.

Drawing on social constructivist learning theories, for feedback to be useful it needs to trigger inner dialogue in students' minds around disciplinary concepts and ideas (Nicol, 2010). This inner dialogue or internal feedback enables students to create meanings from feedback interactions, incorporate them into ongoing ways of thinking, and then use them in future actions. Internal feedback resonates with the arguments for sustainable feedback that we made in Chapter 1. Internal feedback may be stimulated by a number of sources: a peer, a teacher, an assessment result, some longer-term accumulation of evidence, or from self-reflection. For example, external feedback of success or failure generally leads to some kind of internal attribution of reasons for the outcome.

Once a student has received sufficient quantity and quality of external feedback, they are often better able to produce internal feedback for themselves. By developing satisfactory understandings of the standard being aimed for, they are equipped to self-monitor their progress towards that standard. Panadero, Brown, and Strijbos (2016) refer to this kind of process as private student self-evaluation as opposed to more public forms when evaluations are revealed to others.

In summary, internal feedback informs student self-regulation and is moderated by external feedback from other parties. These processes are fundamental to new paradigm feedback practices because they foreground the active student role in self-monitoring their work, evaluating feedback messages, and taking action.

Key examples from the literature

We now discuss two key examples from the literature which illustrate the potential to interweave internal and external feedback. The first involves work on peer review carried out with engineering students in Scotland (Nicol, Thomson, & Breslin, 2014). The second involves a study of the self-assessment practices of teacher education students in Hong Kong (Yan, & Brown, 2017).

The first example involves the interplay between external feedback from peers and internal feedback from the student in the context of peer review within a first-year engineering design class of 82 students at the University of Strathclyde (Nicol, Thomson, & Breslin, 2014). The major assignment was for each student to produce a product design specification, including layout drawings. Students received input on relevant design parameters and were provided with an exemplar product design specification from another topic area. Each student produced a draft product design specification and they then peer reviewed two draft designs of their peers. These peer reviews were conducted anonymously online using Peer-Mark within the Turnitin suite of applications (see also Chapter 8).

Marks were not specifically awarded for the peer review exercise, but students were strongly encouraged to take part. Participation in the peer review activities was high: 62 students completed two peer reviews and a self-review; 15 students completed two peer reviews without a self-review; and 5 students completed only one peer review. After carrying out peer review, students reviewed their own design using the same criteria as for the peer reviews. This stage prompted students to use their experience of the peer review to rethink their own assignment.

From survey and focus group interview data, a number of findings and inferences arose. Carrying out peer review can be effective in triggering powerful cognitive processes: critical thinking; application of assessment criteria; and learning transfer from peers' work to own work. Examining the work of peers can raise awareness of important issues that had not occurred to students. Receiving feedback on one's own work mainly addresses what has been done but analysing others' work can more readily raise awareness of aspects that have not been previously considered (Nicol, Thomson, & Breslin, 2014).

Students are producing peer reviews which are grounded in comparison with their own work. Interview data from students indicated that this interplay between the peer review and their own design triggers and strengthens internal feedback processes. Then they have opportunities for uptake of peer feedback and the closing of feedback loops through revising their design for the final assessment submission.

Although in this case teachers did not award a percentage of the overall grade for participation in the peer review process, we believe that this would be a pragmatic alternative option. It is often a fine judgement between worthwhile formative assessment and rewarding students via marks but student engagement in a task is often facilitated where there is some summative assessment weighting attached to it.

The study also carries significant implications for feedback practice. One of the barriers discussed in Chapter 1 is that feedback often does not connect with students because they do not understand the criteria or standards which markers are applying and so find it hard to relate to what teachers are saying. Learning activities which position students as peer reviewers help them to enter into the role of judging others' work. These processes prompt students to engage with criteria which helps them perceive the qualities exhibited in a piece of work. Student generation of feedback is also a core element of student feedback literacy (cf. Chapter 2).

We now turn to a valuable study by Yan and Brown (2017) who carried out qualitative research into the reported self-evaluation practices of 17 Hong Kong Chinese undergraduate teacher education students. The first author had taught the students on a previous module and so had established trusting relationships with the informants, and they could speak freely as he was no longer involved in teaching or assessing them. He carried out individual interviews to allow students to share their personal experiences in detail.

The major self-evaluation actions reported by students were feedback-seeking and self-reflection informed by criteria. Self-directed feedback-seeking behaviours included comparing their own performance with assignment criteria or previous examples, such as examination papers; seeking feedback from teachers on drafts; and a few students reported requesting advice from their parents. Student self-reflection involved evaluating the feedback that they had obtained, and using it to identify strengths and weaknesses for the purpose of improving a specific piece of work.

The interview data suggested that internal feedback could involve emotions, sensations and subjective personal feelings. These included personal intuitions about performance, such as a feeling that something was wrong or missing. This kind of internal feedback appears to be automatic, sub-conscious, and hard to articulate. The internal feedback is more frequent and regularly accessible so it may be more influential than episodes of external feedback. This could be positive in that the intuitions of the student may be valuable but there is also a risk that internal feedback may not always be accurate. External feedback can help to calibrate internal feedback when students weigh up both to make ongoing decisions. The students' accounts documented by Yan and Brown (2017) provide evidence of how students move between internal and external feedback. External feedback accrues through feedback-seeking behaviours and benchmarking work against samples and criteria.

The authors propose that student self-evaluation involves a cycle of determining relevant performance criteria, seeking feedback from various sources, self-reflection, and gradual calibration of judgements. Self-evaluation seems most meaningful and useful when feedback is available or sought by students, and self-reflection occurs based on those feedback processes (Yan, & Brown, 2017). It is also suggested that the interaction of both feedback and reflection are indispensable elements of student self-evaluation. The authors infer that either feedback or reflection on their own may lead to inaccurate self-evaluations, whereas the two of them together seem to promote effective self-regulation.

A key contribution of the study is to suggest that self-evaluation encompasses feedback-seeking. By eliciting feedback from others, it is likely that a more robust and useful self-evaluation can arise. Feedback-seeking behaviours are also viewed by Carless and Boud (2018) as representing an aspect of student feedback literacy (cf. Chapter 2). An unanswered question noted by the authors is how students reconcile internal and external feedback (Yan, & Brown, 2017). What sort of decision-making processes does this involve? How do students know when to trust their own evaluative judgements and when to place more weight on the views of others? These judgements and decisions form part of student self-regulated learning discussed earlier in the chapter.

Box 7.2 Key research findings

- An aim of feedback processes is to enable students to self-evaluate their work effectively (Butler, & Winne, 1995; Nicol, & Macfarlane-Dick, 2006).
- Students become more effective at self-evaluation when there are sustained opportunities to compare judgements with experts (Boud, Lawson, & Thompson, 2015).
- Internal feedback is generated by self-monitoring when working on a task (Butler, & Winne, 1995).
- External feedback from peers, teachers, or assessment results may confirm, override, or promote internal feedback (Bounds, et al., 2013; Butler, & Winne, 1995; Nicol, Thomson, & Breslin, 2014).
- Feedback-seeking and self-reflection together seem to promote self-regulated learning (Yan, & Brown, 2017).

The case: stimulating self-generated feedback

The context

The context for the case is a class of 25 students taking a double-degree program in Science and Education at the University of Hong Kong. The course is focused on preparing students to teach Biology in secondary schools. The teacher is Kennedy Chan who was awarded a University Early Career teaching award in 2017–2018. He was also the winner in the same year of an inaugural student-led Best Feedback award in recognition of his thoughtful feedback designs.

Kennedy is a student-centred and constructivist teacher whose aspiration is to support students to learn for themselves. He is familiar with the principles of formative assessment and is particularly influenced by the notion of gauging where the students are, where they are going, and how they are going to get there. Accordingly, he favours approaches which enable students to build a conception of the nature of quality work, so engages them in activities which prompt them to think about the criteria for good performance. He involves students actively in peer feedback and self-evaluation. He views internal feedback as being more important than teacher feedback or peer feedback because he believes it is mainly self-generated feedback which guides future development.

He believes that feedback needs to be tailored to the self and a student's own needs, capacities, and interests. Kennedy thinks that students will only act on comments that they believe are pertinent, so it can be more effective when students identify the areas they want to improve. Exposure to multiple voices helps students to consider the areas they would like to focus on to improve draft assignments. Seeking comments coupled with suggestions for actions from peers promotes the uptake of feedback.

The main assessment task for the course was a Video Production Task with an assessment weighting of 80%. This task involves students producing a short 5–10-minute video clip for the teaching of a chosen biology concept; students self-evaluating their video; students providing peer feedback on other students' videos; students revising and resubmitting their videos on the basis of peer feedback and self-evaluation; and writing a reflective essay based on this entire experience. The remaining 20% weighting is for some short writing tasks posted on the LMS. These involved both preparation tasks related to issues to be discussed in the next class and reflective thinking afterwards focused on what had been learnt and further issues for development.

The feedback design

Kennedy's main design principle is to create a carefully prepared learning environment for students to generate and use feedback. Accordingly, the feedback design involves the interweaving of student self-evaluation, peer review, and subsequent student action to close feedback loops. A summary of the main steps in the feedback design is presented in Box 7.3.

Box 7.3 Stages of feedback design

1. Draft video assignment
2. Student self-evaluation
3. Written peer feedback
4. Brainstorm and negotiate criteria
5. Oral peer feedback
6. Prioritise areas of concern
7. Develop action plan
8. Revise video assignment

A key design principle is for students to be actively involved in self-monitoring their work. Kennedy believes that it is important for the students to do this self-evaluation first. Then, when they carry out peer review, they can relate their own performance to that of their peers. Through receiving peer feedback, they can also discern insights that they were unable to generate on their own. The teacher wants students to notice gaps between what they know and what their classmates know. He believes that if students notice a peer can do something that they are not yet able to do, it can motivate them to perform better.

Students were invited to provide peer feedback through either audio feedback or written feedback; all students chose the latter because they perceived it as easier to do. Students also used tags to assign comments to specific parts of videos. Kennedy provided a structure for self-evaluation and peer review by asking students to provide at least five comments, including identifying areas for improvement. The students were asked to write a summary of their comments to clarify the main targets for improvement.

An important part of the feedback design was to involve students in co-creating criteria. Kennedy considered carefully when to implement this stage and believes that it is usefully done when students have engaged with the task by producing a draft and writing some peer feedback, but before they discuss that peer feedback orally. An obvious alternative would be to carry out this stage at the outset, but his view is that students are better placed to brainstorm criteria after they have some experience in making sense of and enacting task requirements. The criteria for evaluating the videos are generated first by groups of students and then through rich dialogues orally and using the audience response tool, Mentimeter. He incorporated these views into his draft rubric and after class posted a final version of the criteria on the LMS.

The next in-class stage involves students carrying out oral dialogues in which the receiver of peer feedback can comment on what they agree or disagree with. Sometimes when students receive feedback, they may not immediately unpack what it means. The students worked in a group of three so there was always a second opinion within the group. A further design feature is to ask students to prioritise areas of concern for discussion. Students were afforded the agency to focus on aspects that they would appreciate receiving advice on and identify areas for further development. A key focus was in turning the comments into actions. To facilitate this, Kennedy asked the students to complete an action plan outlining the aspects they would like to improve.

Kennedy believes that the process of talking and sharing ideas is important in peer feedback (see also Chapter 8). In written feedback, it is easy simply to reject or ignore what people say but through discussion there are opportunities to listen, interact, and defend a position. Students were encouraged to seek advice from the feedback composer about how they could turn the comments into actions. Kennedy was trying to prompt students to move beyond descriptive or evaluative comments to those that can lead to action. If students did not wish to act on feedback, he required them to give a reason why, adding a further level of engagement and dialogue.

Underpinning all of the above are two teacher goals. There is a short-term goal of promoting engagement with feedback in order to produce better videos for their assignment. There is also a longer-term goal of developing student feedback literacy: understanding better how to give thoughtful feedback; greater awareness of the need to seek feedback from peers; analysing feedback from multiple sources based on their own needs; and turning feedback into actions.

Student response

On the whole, the students appreciated the feedback practice they had experienced in this class. They described the feedback practice as collaborative and student-centred, and particularly valued the in-class dialogues where they were afforded plenty of opportunities for sharing of ideas. Peer discussion of comments and generation of evaluation criteria were perceived to be particularly influential stages of the learning process. One of the key perceived benefits was the opportunity to act on feedback on drafts in contrast to students' experiences in most modules where comments came too late for there to be subsequent action.

The students commented that it was rare in their undergraduate programme for them to experience systematic peer feedback processes. They generally appreciated taking control of feedback communication because dialogues were free from teacher intervention and they were given autonomy in directing the focus of discussion. They believed that this enabled them to understand the rationale behind peer comments, explain the design principles of their teaching video, clarify misunderstanding of concepts, and brainstorm improvement plans. The process of becoming more aware of positive and negative aspects of peers' work was seen by some students as helping them to reflect and improve the quality of their work.

Students expressed some concerns about workload, particularly when they had to take time to interpret peer feedback and revise their draft videos. Some students experienced frustration when the peer feedback processes revealed that they still needed to do a lot more to raise the standard of their work. The technical side of recording and editing videos was also quite time-consuming and sometimes stressful for those students who did not have prior experience in video production and editing. A viable alternative would be to provide students with choice of the medium through which to present their ideas.

Enabling factors

A major enabler is the teacher who has a high level of teaching expertise and related experience in carrying out pedagogic educational research. Kennedy is familiar with research on formative assessment and feedback in higher education, and thinks deeply on these topics. He is influenced by Royce Sadler's thinking that providing students with rubrics before they engage with a task may not be helpful in enabling them to develop a full-rounded sense of quality (see also Chapter 5). Another enabler is that he has plenty of autonomy to design the module in ways that suit him and his students. He also teaches more than once on the programme so he is able to build up relationships and trust with the students and they can come to appreciate his approach to teaching. A further potential enabler relates to the students who are based in a faculty of education. Because they are training to become teachers, they can both experience feedback as a learner and also consider how feedback processes can be designed for their future students. This form of dual learning has potential to increase their motivation to engage with feedback principles and their applications.

Challenges

The approach needs to demonstrate to students the value of self-evaluation, peer feedback, and dialogue around work in progress, and is facilitated if students appreciate the principles of self-regulated learning. One of the challenges noted by the teacher is that sometimes students lack the agency and willpower to think carefully and deeply about their academic work. They may have other competing priorities, such as social activities or part-time jobs, and they may be content to get by rather than reflecting deeply on learning. Kennedy is aware that not all students are eager to make extensive efforts in enhancing their work.

He tries to promote an orientation of continuous improvement by teaching in ways that encourage students to analyse and to think. He perceives that for those students who engage actively in peer review, drafting and revising the learning process is likely to be rewarding but there are still challenges. Even for those students who engaged actively, he found that peer feedback or self-evaluation was not always effective in identifying errors or misconceptions found in the draft videos.

Kennedy acknowledges that there are tensions between providing teacher guidance and encouraging students to self-evaluate for themselves. Not all the students know how to give peer feedback effectively, so some of the skills of composing peer feedback need to be scaffolded. His experience lends him to think that students are often more interested in teacher feedback than peer feedback. They also sometimes prefer comments which act as a definite answer rather than as something to trigger further thinking. Students also need some support and encouragement in acting on feedback. Kennedy perceives that these aspects take time which is sometimes hampered by relatively short modules. These factors can act as barriers to the active student roles envisaged by new paradigm feedback practices.

Kennedy noted affective challenges in relation to feedback; students often find it difficult to regulate their emotions when receiving negative or critical feedback (see also Chapter 9). In addition, he notes that students do not always have a naturally positive disposition towards feedback as they are not sure how it can directly lead to improvement. This carries implications for the development of student feedback literacy and assessment designs which enable students to gauge the progress they are making (see also Chapter 5).

Relationship to the literature

The practice illustrates a number of principles found in the literature. It involves both peer review and self-review as implemented in Nicol, Thomson, and Breslin (2014). There is an interweaving of internal feedback and external feedback from peers in alignment with the theoretical thinking informing the first half of this chapter (Butler, & Winne, 1995). Kennedy's practice also relates to emphasis in the literature on student agency in closing feedback loops (e.g. Boud, & Molloy, 2013).

Kennedy places himself in the role of designer and facilitator of feedback processes, so that feedback is co-constructed in line with social constructivist principles. He purposefully defers the stage of generating criteria until students have produced their own draft work, in line with the position of Sadler (2015) discussed in Chapter 5. The implementation is carefully designed through stages which include oral discussion of peer feedback to negotiate meaning, and action plans for uptake to improve their draft videos. The teacher prioritises students' seeking of information for improvement and self-monitoring of progress over time. The practice is well-aligned with the framework for student feedback literacy proposed by Carless and Boud (2018) in that it encourages students to appreciate feedback, make academic judgements, manage affect, and use feedback for ongoing improvement.

Significance of the practice

The case is significant for a number of reasons. It is based on a careful and principled feedback design with a series of well-designed stages, including self-evaluation; peer review; co-generation of criteria; and the closing of feedback loops. It involves students actively in the feedback process through peer review and student self-evaluation, and interweaves the two. It aims to develop student feedback literacy so that students can appreciate their active role in feedback processes. As the students are training to become teachers in schools, there is also an additional dimension of teaching them how to become facilitators of feedback processes with their future school-age learners.

Box 7.4 Implications for practice

- Peer review and student self-evaluation can be profitably integrated in that both involve the making of judgements.
- The development of student self-evaluation carries potential to inform the broader goal of enabling self-regulated learning.

- A promising feedback design involves student self-evaluation, peer review, and the closing of feedback loops.
- Involving students in co-creating criteria enables them to take some ownership of standards and supports their involvement in self-evaluation.
- Principled feedback designs develop student feedback literacy by enabling students to make judgements and use feedback to revise work.

Conclusion

In this chapter, we have discussed the interplay between several key concepts. Student self-evaluation is an important sub-process of the broader notion of self-regulation. Internal feedback is an inner self-evaluation process which can be informed by external feedback from peers or teachers. These concepts are in line with a key purpose of new paradigm feedback practices being to enable students to self-evaluate their own performance effectively.

In the case which was the focal point of the second half of the chapter, there is an interweaving of internal feedback from the student and external feedback from peers in the context of drafting and revising a video assignment. The key points from the case reiterate the importance of thoughtful feedback designs. The approach involved self-evaluation; generating criteria; peer feedback; and action plans to promote the closing of feedback loops. A central aim was to promote active student involvement in feedback processes and stimulate the development of student feedback literacy.

In this example, the class size was small but as most of the feedback is student-generated it would be relatively straightforward to carry out analogous practices with a larger class. The teacher places himself in the role of designer and facilitator of feedback processes, so that feedback is co-constructed. He evidences awareness of the limitations of old paradigm feedback practices of teacher telling as these may not make sense to students and are often ineffective. These factors enabled him to develop a feedback design congruent with new paradigm feedback practices.

When evaluating the quality of feedback processes in higher education, we typically ask students to consider the feedback they have 'received'. It is perhaps not surprising that students commonly report less than optimal satisfaction when emphasis is placed on only the comments that they have been given by someone else. Truly effective feedback processes lead to the student being less reliant on others for feedback; by honing their understanding and analysis of quality work, students become empowered to generate feedback for themselves. This opens up a whole new realm of feedback information to which students have access. New paradigm feedback processes look beyond passive reception of feedback to its active construction.

Box 7.5 Key resources

- The Assessment Futures website based on a project led by David Boud focuses on how assessment and learning can equip students for life after graduation. This approach is congruent with the self-regulated learning approach of this chapter.
  https://www.uts.edu.au/research-and-teaching/learning-and-teaching/assessm ent-futures/overview
- In the context of a Year 1 Medieval History course at Monash University, learners are involved in an interweaving of peer feedback, teacher feedback, and their own self-evaluation:
  http://newmediaresearch.educ.monash.edu.au/feedback/case-studies-of-effecti ve-feedback/case-study-1/
- Students in the Y1Feedback Project used VoiceThread to create conversations with image, text and voice for their presentations in an engineering course, enabling self-evaluation along with peer feedback by sharing the recordings with other students:
  https://youtu.be/JdQAGUh9I0M
- A useful guide to self-assessment in higher education drawing on key strands of relevant literature is compiled by Mike Wride, Trinity College Dublin:
  https://www.tcd.ie/CAPSL/assets/pdf/Academic%20Practice%20Resources/ Guide%20to%20Student%20Self%20Assessment.pdf
- A resource from the Yale University Center for Teaching and Learning recommends pedagogic practices for enhancing university students' meta-cognition:
  https://ctl.yale.edu/sites/default/files/basic-page-supplementary-materials-files/m etacognition_handout.pdf

Box 7.6 Questions for reflection and debate

- What are effective ways of teaching or scaffolding the development of students' self-evaluation skills?
- Are students aware of the correlations between self-regulated learning and achievement, and could this inter-relationship be leveraged as an incentive for them to engage more in enhancing their self-regulated learning capacities?
- At what stage of an assessment and feedback cycle can students most usefully be encouraged to co-construct and deploy criteria?
- How can lower-achieving students be supported to develop capacities in making sound academic judgements? What are effective feedback processes in support of lower-achieving students?

- How effective are learners in generating accurate internal feedback as they work on their assessment tasks? How could educators help them to become more effective? What are the facilitators and barriers?
- Under what circumstances does external feedback override internal feedback? What are the characteristics of students (ability, personality, motivation, feedback literacy) who are likely to prioritise internal or external feedback respectively? To what extent do different sources of external feedback impact on students' internal feedback?

Chapter 8

Implementing peer feedback

Peer feedback is at the heart of new paradigm feedback practices. Peer feedback or peer review involves students commenting on each other's work thereby developing capacities in making academic judgements. A useful definition of peer feedback congruent with the position we take in this book is "a communication process through which learners enter into dialogues related to performance and standards" (Liu, & Carless, 2006, p. 280). This definition reinforces that feedback is a process; involves dialogic interaction; and is based on implicit or explicit standards and criteria. Sadler (2010, p. 542) argues that we should "Provide students with substantial evaluative experience not as an extra but as a strategic part of the teaching design".

Peer assessment involves similar processes to peer feedback, and we distinguish them through suggesting that the former includes a grading element, whereas the latter focuses on making comments only. This distinction can be slippery in that some forms of peer feedback might also generate grades and some writers use the terms interchangeably. An important consideration is that students often resist peer assessment using marks because they do not feel comfortable awarding grades to their friends and classmates (Boud, Cohen, & Sampson, 1999; Liu, & Carless, 2006; Patton, 2012). In the context of peer assessment with grades, students expressed frustration at markedly different views of multiple peer assessors (McConlogue, 2012). These are some of the reasons why peer assessment usually generates more student concerns than peer feedback.

Theoretical underpinnings for peer feedback arise from aspects flagged earlier in the book: social constructivism and self-regulated learning. Collaborating with peers aligns with the social constructivist views of learning that we introduced in Chapter 1. Peer feedback informs self-evaluation and self-regulated learning as discussed in Chapter 7. In this chapter, we review the rationale and potentials for peer feedback, discuss how some of the challenges can be tackled, and discuss a case which involved exemplary practices of training and coaching students to do peer feedback well.

Peer feedback rationale, benefits and implementation

Students gain a lot from examining their peers' assignments, identifying strengths, weaknesses and areas for improvement. Such processes begin to sensitise students to what good performance looks like and differences between their work and that of others. Peer feedback helps students develop the self-review strategies found in expert writers so that they can detect, diagnose, and solve writing problems (Cho, & MacArthur, 2011). There is also potential for peer feedback to be available more quickly and in greater quantity, in comparison with more authoritative but slower teacher input. Additionally, it is sometimes easier for students to accept critiques from their peers than their teachers (Nicol, & Macfarlane-Dick, 2006).

The more complex learning is, the less likely that it can be accomplished in isolation from others (Boud, 2000). Collaborative forms of learning carry potential to expose students to different ideas and increase the development of higher-order thinking. As these goals match with the aspirations of higher education, frequent opportunities for student involvement in peer review should be a core component of assessment and curriculum design rather than being of a one-off nature (Sadler, 2010). Increasing the frequency of peer feedback practice is also helpful because greater experience of peer feedback has similar positive influences to training (Van Zundert, Sluijsmans, & Van Merriënboer, 2010). Repeated peer feedback enhances teamwork skills and longitudinal research suggests that these skills are also transferred into the workplace (Doria, O'Neill, & Brutus, 2018).

A common peer feedback sequence is that students produce a draft assignment, receive feedback from peers, and then revise the same assignment (Nicol, Thomson, & Breslin, 2014). One of the benefits of such a sequence is the potential for timely feedback that students can act upon (Cartney, 2010). This aligns with a key element of new paradigm feedback practices: student uptake of feedback.

A key research finding is that the giving of peer feedback is often more beneficial than receiving comments because it is more cognitively-engaging, involving higher-order processes such as application of criteria, diagnosing problems and suggesting solutions (Nicol, Thomson, & Breslin, 2014). The gains from providing peer feedback are an important part of its rationale which needs to be communicated with students so that they are clear about the benefits of productive involvement in peer feedback. Generating, clarifying, and applying criteria also emanate from peer feedback processes.

As we discussed in Chapter 7, engaging with the work of peers is helpful in enabling students to self-regulate their own work. When receivers of peer feedback were requested to give written feedback to the providers, it enabled them to gain greater metacognitive awareness of the process and enhanced their performance (Kim, 2009). A pertinent feature of Kim's quasi-experimental study is that the process of 'feedback on peer feedback' promotes active engagement by the recipient of comments, although in this case the interaction was through completing a form rather than oral dialogue.

This element of dialogue is an important facet of peer feedback (see also Chapter 6). Feedback is usefully explained orally and discussed with the receiver as the peer interaction allows students to clarify writing issues and potential revisions (Van den Berg, Admiraal, & Pilot, 2006a). If students feel excluded from dialogue

about an assessment judgement, they may be less able or less willing to take subsequent action (Cartney, 2010).

One of the ways in which dialogue can be enriched is through receiving comments from a variety of peers rather than just one (Villamil, & de Guerrero,
2006). Peer feedback trios involve students in receiving comments from two
classmates instead of just one (Ballantyne, Hughes, & Mylonas, 2002). In a study
of seven peer feedback designs in the context of undergraduate history courses,
Van den Berg, Admiraal, and Pilot (2006b) identified groups of three to four as
being an optimal design feature in that receivers had opportunities to compare two
to three sets of comments. Students receiving feedback from multiple peers performed complex revisions of their work and produced higher quality products
(Cho, & MacArthur, 2010). Engagement with multiple peers carries potential to
maximise possibilities for self-regulation or co-regulation.

Peer feedback challenges and possible solutions

There are considerable challenges in implementing peer feedback and these are
evident in the literature and in anecdotal accounts from colleagues. In this section,
we discuss some of the main challenges for peer feedback and propose some ways
of tackling them. Students may lack the competence or expertise to carry out peer
feedback effectively or their classmates may perceive, rightly or wrongly, that they
lack this expertise (Panadero, 2016). Students may be concerned about inaccuracy
in peer feedback or the fairness of their classmates' judgements. There is sometimes student resistance to receiving comments from peers because they are disappointed by classmates' failure to commit to the process seriously (e.g. Patton,
2012) or have insufficient understanding of the potential benefits (Yucel, et al.,
2014). Students may prefer more authoritative teacher feedback, and in particular
high-achievers may not believe that they can learn much from low-achievers. Discourses of students as consumers may reinforce this kind of view.

Better appreciation of the benefits of generating peer feedback comments can
address these challenges. Diagnosing their partners' problems and suggesting
solutions is a rich cognitive process and can also promote better awareness of
strengths and weaknesses of one's own writing. Peer review opens our horizons to
different ways of doing things and enables us to compare our approach to that of
others, and sensitises us to key areas for improvement. Even if high-achievers do
not receive much insight from a peer, they can still learn from explaining to their
peers, resonating with the adage that to teach is to learn twice. Partnership
approaches congruent with the 'students as partners' movement are a persuasive
rejoinder to views of students as consumers (Bovill, et al., 2016).

There are social-affective challenges emanating from the relational elements of
feedback (see also Chapter 9). Sometimes students may experience anxiety about
evaluating or being evaluated by others (Cartney, 2010). Other times, input from
peers can strengthen the social-relational aspects of feedback and reduce the power
differentials and defensive reactions which can arise from teacher feedback (Yang,

& Carless, 2013). Social-affective support involves actions that build students' trust in the teacher and peers so that an open and critical classroom culture can be cultivated (Carless, 2013; Xu, & Carless, 2017).

One of the ways to manage social-affective challenges is for peer feedback to be designed in motivating and non-threatening ways. Students are sometimes concerned that other students may steal their ideas (Beaumont, O'Doherty, & Shannon, 2011). This is partly an assessment task design issue, so if students are all doing exactly the same assignment individually then peer feedback may not always be appropriate. It often works best when peers are carrying out parallel tasks but with different content, for example, an individual project on a topic of their own choice.

There are some cultural issues that might play a role in peer feedback. Students from collectivist cultures may be more naturally inclined to engage in peer support than those from individualistic cultures. Desires for face-saving and harmony may discourage students from offering critical commentary and this may be particularly prominent in certain cultures (Hu, 2005). Chinese students' respect or even reverence for the teacher may accentuate preference for teacher feedback over peer feedback (Hu, & Lam, 2010). Peer feedback is, however, situated within students' contexts and varied learning histories, so there are individual variations that are not easily explained by cultural differences (Yu, & Hu, 2017).

It is sometimes difficult to stimulate student action in response to peer feedback. In the context of an Open University draft assignment (Walker, 2015), students were trained in using prescribed criteria to evaluate samples and it was found that even when peer feedback comments were timely, accurate, and of good quality, students often still failed to act. It seems that reasons for not acting on feedback lie with the recipient not the feedback itself, with some students unwilling to accept that a shortcoming identified by a peer was indeed a weakness (Walker, 2015). Receivers of peer feedback need more support to interpret, evaluate, and act on feedback. This again reinforces the core theme of student feedback literacy and emphasises the importance of coaching students to make use of feedback (see Chapter 3).

Although it is desirable for students to see the benefits of peer feedback and be willing to carry it out, a pragmatic option is to hold them accountable for producing satisfactory peer feedback. A way of motivating students to engage seriously with the work of their peers is through awarding marks for the quality of peer assessment comments (Bloxham, & West, 2004). In that study, 25% of the module grade was awarded for the quality of peer marking and the researchers inferred that this had a positive impact on the seriousness with which the students approached the task. Recent studies also suggest that grading students' peer assessment improves effort and quality of reviews (Kearney, Perkins, & Kennedy-Clark, 2016; Liu, & Li, 2014). It should be acknowledged, however, that with large classes grading students' peer feedback may not be feasible or even desirable. After all, one of the aims of peer feedback is to seed student autonomy and accountability.

Training, modelling and coaching

Many of the challenges alluded to in the previous section can be alleviated by training and supporting students in how to do peer feedback well. The importance of training students prior to carrying out peer feedback is well-documented in the literature but not always heeded in practice. Teachers may assume that students know how to do peer feedback or have been trained previously but this is often not the case. Training is important because providing effective peer feedback is a cognitively complex process requiring understanding of the task, application of criteria, judgements about performance, and suggestions for improvement (Topping, 2009). Training generally improves feedback quality, evaluative skills, and student attitudes (Van Zundert, Sluijsmans, & Van Merriënboer, 2010). Beginning training in the first year of an undergraduate program could have a number of benefits in developing student confidence in judgements of themselves and peers (Sluijsmans, Brand-Gruwel, & Van Merriënboer, 2002). Training can also address students' beliefs or doubts about the value of peer feedback (Evans, 2013).

In the context of a teacher education program, Sluijsmans, Brand-Gruwel, and Van Merriënboer (2002) reported a four-stage training process for an experimental group of students. First, students were introduced to the meaning of peer assessment and the product that they were going to evaluate and then implement themselves: a creative lesson. Students observed a video of the creative lesson and drafted criteria to evaluate it. Second, criteria were further defined and negotiated between groups of students and the teacher. Third, the teacher provided input on the purpose and guidelines for providing constructive feedback and shared an example of an expert report giving feedback on the lesson video that the students had observed. Students discussed the expert feedback and developed a list of characteristics of constructive feedback: specific, direct, accurate, achievable, practical, and comprehensible. Fourth, students were trained further in judging performance by analysing the language and content of the expert report and comparing it with novice evaluations. A finding of the study was that the experimental group used the criteria more effectively and produced more constructive comments than those in the control group. Students in the experimental group also scored significantly higher grades on the course. Implicit in the above is that student understanding of criteria is an important element of the training process for peer feedback. Students can be involved in drafting what they think are the important elements of good performance for a specific task. Students are most likely to engage with and understand criteria if they have played some role in generating them (Boud, 1995b).

Because doing peer feedback well needs practice and experience, it is generally the case that support needs to be extended rather than short one-off input. So, in addition to training at the outset, students need teachers to model for them the processes of peer feedback and coach them in doing it more effectively. Modelling how to give and receive constructive feedback is an important but sometimes underplayed aspect of the teacher role in supporting peer feedback processes. Modelling peer feedback is also part of student induction into assessment processes as they transition from school to university (Beaumont, O'Doherty, & Shannon, 2011). In a study in China, the teacher modelled for first year English language students how they could move beyond peer feedback correcting linguistic errors to develop deeper insight into a key criterion of content (Xu, & Carless, 2017). With scaffolding and support, this message was gradually taken up by the students in developing their peer feedback. Through modelling, teachers can demonstrate how to give effective feedback or scaffold and enrich students' own attempts at feedback.

Another useful form of modelling would be for teachers to share with students the ubiquity of peer review processes in higher education and how they contribute to improvements. Peer review is a central part of academic publishing as well as in programme reviews for quality enhancement. Teachers could discuss with students how they are exposed to feedback from peer review on a regular basis, model some of their responses to critique, and share some of the emotional challenges that are faced and how they can be tackled (Carless, & Boud, 2018; see also Chapter 9). Academics could also share some of the challenges of handling multiple, and often contradictory, reviews. Importantly, peer review in academia usually necessitates action on feedback which is received.

In addition to training and modelling, students also need coaching. Students are primed to develop their feedback literacy through peer feedback when they receive effective coaching on how to do it better (Carless, & Boud, 2018). Enabling students to develop better understandings of criteria and standards is an element of the coaching process. Teachers can also discuss with students useful and not so useful examples of peer feedback. Peer feedback comments focused on the bigger picture of writer intentions, argumentation, and organisation are generally much more useful than surface comments on spelling or grammar. Students can be coached on different aspects of peer feedback, including encouragement, critical feedback, specific and generic feedback (Xu, & Carless, 2017).

The need for coaching is reinforced by the fact that the benefits of peer feedback may not be immediately apparent (Evans, 2013). It is preferable if students have positive early experiences of peer feedback as this can help them see its benefits and encourage them to engage actively in its practice. There is also evidence that student engagement and satisfaction with peer feedback improves over time (Dochy, Segers, & Sluijsmans, 1999; van Gennip, Segers, & Tillema, 2010), although presumably this is dependent, to some extent, on skilful implementation. Peer feedback seeds the long-term development of feedback literacy by encouraging students to take responsibility for generating feedback. The long-term element underscores the need for sustained implementation and coaching of peer feedback.

Technology-enabled peer feedback

Technology-enabled feedback is analysed in Chapter 4 and for completeness a few points related specifically to peer feedback are discussed here (see also Box 8.4). Peer collaborative learning can profitably be integrated with technology-enabled approaches to feedback. Nicol (2007) describes students responding to multiple-choice questions through an electronic voting system and then carrying out peer teaching to explain their answers to classmates, stimulating dialogue and potential re-appraisals as students revise their thinking when the correct answer is revealed. A similar strategy uses Peer-Wise, an open access software that enables students to construct, share and answer multiple-choice questions. A recent study of second-year psychology students found that PeerWise appeared to be a useful learning tool and contributed to significantly increased examination scores (Howe et al., 2018). Composing and completing multiple-choice questions aided review and self-assessment processes, and the extent of student engagement with PeerWise was positively correlated with exam performance.

Digital affordances can support students to generate feedback and engage in peer review. A useful recent example is a study by Hung (2016) which involved students in producing video feedback for each other, thereby combining student generation of feedback with digital facilitation and avoiding modes of feedback dominated by teacher-telling. This represents a useful variation on teacher video feedback and avoids perpetuating the kind of information transmission approach noted in a recent review of audio, video, and screencast feedback (Mahoney, Macfarlane, & Ajjawi, 2019; see also Chapter 4).

The seminal Nicol, Thomson, & Breslin (2014) study used PeerMark within the Turnitin suite of applications to enable students to read, review, and evaluate submissions anonymously. Moodle Workshop for peer assessment allows anonymising of student submissions, automatic allocation of peer assessors, teacher review of grades, and features that support students in evaluating the work of their peers. In a large class of 800 first years studying macro-economics, Mostert and Snowball (2013) facilitated peer assessment through Moodle Workshop with students finding that providing peer feedback was the most useful part of the process. The open-access online peer review system Aropa can also be used to enable anonymous, randomly-allocated peer feedback based on teacher-designed rubrics (Purchase, & Hamer, 2018). There are probably administrative efficiencies in handling large-scale peer feedback with this kind of technology (Debuse, & Lawley, 2016). Anonymity is, however, a complex issue. It has the advantage of encouraging frank feedback, but it restrains dialogue and may reduce accountability for the comments one produces.

Key examples from the literature

We now consider two examples from the literature which illustrate some of the possibilities and challenges in designing effective peer feedback processes. The first illustrates composing and receiving peer feedback drawing on a case study of a student (McConlogue, 2015). The second example illustrates some key implementation issues from a study of peer feedback at a university in China (Zhu, & Carless, 2018).

The setting for the study conducted by McConlogue (2015) was a large class of Engineering students involved in writing a laboratory report. The process began with online submissions of assignments followed by a training session focused on rehearsal marking as recommended by Falchikov (2003). The training involved students reading, commenting, and grading three sample reports of differing qualities. Students compared comments and grades in groups which led to a discussion of the meanings of the assessment criteria and the broader notion of academic standards. The teacher then led a discussion explaining how she had made evaluative judgements and responded to questions. Following the training, students were allocated four to six reports for peer marking representing a range of standards. This exposure to diverse standards could be an important step that is less evident in forms of peer feedback that only involve one or two samples of work.

In order to probe more deeply into these processes, the researcher investigated a single volunteer student through analysing her peer feedback comments and notes, her own laboratory report, and carrying out repeated interviews. This focal student found the process of composing peer feedback comments engaging and devoted a number of hours to analysing her classmates' reports. From this experience, she identified that there is no single correct way of writing a laboratory report and even in weak reports she felt that there was something she could learn. She seemed to be involved in a process of comparing her peers' reports to her own (cf. Chapter 7) and through this benchmarking process, she sought ways in which she could develop her own understanding of what makes a good Engineering report. When she received peer comments on her own report, she experienced disappointment. Classmates had not invested as much time and effort as she had, and she did not feel that their feedback provided her with much insight. She also reported a loss of trust in her peers to reciprocate her efforts.

McConlogue (2015) draws a number of conclusions. Supporting students to make judgements about their own work and that of their peers may have more impact on student learning than conventional teacher written feedback when there is deep student engagement in these processes. Enabling students to become competent peer assessors does, however, seem to be a long-term endeavour. For peer feedback to be fully successful, all students involved need to appreciate its value and the process is facilitated when trust is developed between participants. For students distrustful of peer feedback, training them first in how to compose peer feedback might be a positive first step. An implication is that teachers need to convince students of the value of composing peer feedback and alert them to the possibility that they may not always receive insightful peer feedback from classmates. Even then, they can still derive useful learning from what they invest in the process.

In the second example (Zhu, & Carless, 2018), the first author researched five teachers implementing peer feedback in an English writing course at a university in southern China. The research methods involved classroom observations, interviews with the teachers, and data collection from students: individual and focus group interviews and reflective journals (Zhu, 2018). The main focus was on student perceptions of the processes of providing and receiving peer feedback.

The main way of providing peer feedback was that students drafted a piece of writing and then collected feedback from peers before re-submitting it to the teacher for grading. Classroom observations of ten sessions in which peer feedback was carried out was a significant feature of the research because few studies have conducted in-depth observation of the implementation of peer feedback. It was observed that the students received little guidance or training about peer feedback at the outset. Two of the teachers provided an introduction of about ten minutes concerning the procedures and criteria, whereas the other three hardly provided any guidance at all. Three groups used a peer review form comprising evaluation criteria (organisation and focus; elaboration and style; grammar, usage and mechanics) and space for making comments, whereas the other two groups were provided with guiding questions related to these same evaluation criteria.

The interview data revealed that the students were quite critical of the lack of teacher guidance. Without sufficient training and support about peer feedback, students' initial experiences were mixed. Some found discussing with their peers to be valuable in exchanging ideas, while others expressed disappointment about the quality of peer feedback or lack of serious engagement from peers.

The teachers were able to ascertain that some students were having difficulty in providing useful feedback in that some comments were quite superficial, focusing just on grammatical accuracy or typos. Facing these challenges, two of the teachers sought to scaffold effective peer feedback practice. One of the teachers provided guidance by using good examples of peer comments on organisation and argument. Students reported finding this useful and journal entries revealed that reviewers began to concentrate on structure or reasoning rather than just language. Another teacher modelled how to complete the peer review form by sharing a sample annotated student draft with teacher feedback alongside a completed peer review form. Student journal entries evidenced positive student perceptions of this kind of guidance. So, in those classes where teachers provided coaching, the student experience of peer feedback became more fruitful.

Students identified that an important part of the peer feedback process was oral dialogue between participants and reported two key inter-related benefits. The provider of written comments obtains feedback on their feedback (cf. Kim, 2009). In other words, they can see how their partner is responding which enables them to reflect on their evaluative skills. The receiver has the opportunity to clarify or negotiate meaning with the feedback provider by explaining their original intentions or asking peers to elaborate or justify comments. Negotiating feedback messages can enable students to think more deeply about the nature of quality work. Iterative peer feedback dialogues enhance opportunities for co-regulation of learning (Zhu, 2018). The findings also suggest that dialogue around peer feedback increases cognitive engagement and the potential for student uptake of feedback messages because information is less likely to be rejected out of hand.

Some key messages from this study are to reinforce the need for initial training of students in peer feedback as well as the need for coaching and guidance during the process. Wherever possible, peer feedback should involve both written and oral elements to enable mutual clarification and negotiation of meaning. Students could be advised that they may sometimes experience some disappointment concerning the quality of their peers' comments but in that case they can still gain from what they invest in the process.

Box 8.1 Key research findings

- Peer feedback enhances learner self-regulation (Cho, & MacArthur, 2011; Nicol, Thomson, & Breslin, 2014).
- Composing peer feedback is often even more beneficial than receiving peer feedback (McConlogue, 2015; Nicol, Thomson, & Breslin, 2014).
- Peer feedback can fruitfully involve both written and oral elements (Van den Berg, Admiraal, & Pilot, 2006a; Zhu, & Carless, 2018).
- Students need training and coaching in carrying out peer feedback (Sluijsmans, Brand-Gruwel, & Van Merriënboer, 2002; Van Zundert, Sluijsmans, & Van Merriënboer, 2010).
- Peer feedback trios are a useful design feature because they facilitate composing and receiving more than one peer review (Ballantyne, Hughes, & Mylonas, 2002; Van den Berg, Admiraal, & Pilot, 2006b; Villamil, & de Guerrero, 2006).
- There are a number of useful digitally-enabled approaches to peer feedback (Howe, et al., 2018; Hung, 2016; Purchase, & Hamer, 2018).

The case: Training and coaching students to do peer feedback well

Context

The teacher, Professor Min Hui-Tzu, works in the Department of Foreign Languages and Literature at National Cheng Kung University in Taiwan. She has won numerous outstanding teaching awards from her university and has also gained awards for research achievements and outstanding research performance. One of her key teaching duties is to teach English language writing to undergraduate classes of around 25–30 students specialising in English. This small class size is a facilitating factor and within the case we suggest variations that would enable some of the practices to be scaled up. The implementation of peer feedback is a central part of her teaching philosophy; she has been documenting and writing about her experiences in implementing peer feedback for around 15 years (e.g. Min, 2005; 2006; 2008; 2013; 2016).

The teacher believes that feedback is important because it provides students and teachers with opportunities to interact with one another to enhance teaching and learning effectiveness. Through this interaction, students understand how teachers and peers perceive their work, what criteria are used in judging it, and they can develop capacities in monitoring their own performance using these criteria. Professor Min implements peer feedback systematically. Through her early experiences in her teaching career, she came to a realisation that students need training and support in how to use peer feedback.

The feedback design

The first stage of the feedback design is for students to receive training in how to carry out peer feedback effectively. Professor Min prepares students through a two-hour training session using a sample student essay from a previous cohort to model four different types of feedback: clarifying the writer's intention; identifying potential problems; explaining the nature of these problems; and making specific suggestions (see also Min, 2005; 2006). This four-step procedure was based on her initial analysis that two major factors impeding peer feedback are the peer reviewer not understanding the writer's intentions and the peer reviewer failing to provide clear suggestions.

In terms of the writing task, the students are producing work of the same genre but on different topics. This enables them to have some autonomy in selecting topics and because they are working on different topics, concerns about possible stealing of good ideas are minimised. The next stage of the design is for students to produce peer feedback on work in progress and then revise their draft. The teacher wants students to appreciate the value of composing and receiving peer feedback, developing their evaluative judgement, and using comments to improve their drafts.

Peer reviewers work in randomly-assigned trios so that all three give and receive two peer reviews. She prefers random allocation to avoid friendship groups or cliques, and to provide a variety of perspectives with students working in different trios on each cycle of peer review. The design is based on a process writing sequence of multiple stages as summarised in Box 8.2.

Box 8.2 Stages of peer feedback

Brainstorming → 1st draft → face-to-face reciprocal peer review in class in trios → 2nd draft → oral presentation and peer oral response in small groups to encourage additional peer feedback → individual teacher-student conferences → 3rd draft → teacher written comments (often posed as questions) posted on LMS to assist preparation and then discussed orally in tutorial → final submission which is just graded as feedback has already been provided.

This design enables plentiful iterative peer feedback, dialogues to negotiate meaning, and opportunities for uptake of feedback. There is, of course, flexibility in the design so that the process could also be simplified for other contexts. For example, there is the possibility of omitting the teacher comments and tutorial after the third draft on the grounds that peer feedback has already been provided.

After students have produced two rounds of peer feedback, students are coached to improve their commentaries on the academic writing of their peers. Professor Min schedules a 30-minute conference with each reviewer evaluating the quality of their feedback and suggesting how to refine the comments so that they are better focused on the four-step procedure. With a large class, this procedure would not be feasible and could, for example, be substituted by some whole-class teacher guidance on peer feedback practices.

After the coaching, reviewers evidenced improvement in composing specific and relevant feedback, and receivers showed widespread uptake of the peer feedback implying that comments from classmates were useful and pertinent (Min, 2006). Common changes that students make to their revised texts included: enriching the content and development of ideas; argumentation and elaboration; and improving the cohesiveness of texts. The emphasis on uptake of feedback comments is congruent with new paradigm feedback practices.

Student response

Based on Professor Min's long-term experience of researching and implementing peer feedback, she perceives the student response as generally positive. Students appreciate playing roles as both receivers and givers of feedback as this enables them to gain different perspectives and make comparisons between their work and that of others. Students found that effective peer review was helpful in focusing their ideas and enriching the content of their work. They particularly appreciated opportunities for oral feedback from peers including explanation and elaboration, so the receiver can appreciate how and why judgements are reached.

Lower-achieving students felt that they could gain a lot from peer review as it was sometimes easier to receive suggestions from peers rather than teachers. When they invested effort in the process, lower-achievers also gained from exposure to higher quality work of their peers. Seeing how their classmates wrote could support the development of their own writing skills. Relational aspects were particularly important for the lower-achievers, and they gained most when they felt comfortable with their randomly-assigned teammates. High-achievers also gained confidence and metacognitive insights from composing feedback and making comparisons with their own work. Not surprisingly, higher-achievers also tended to write the most detailed and insightful peer reviews.

Some students expressed frustration that the peer review they received was not correct or insightful, an experience that academics can also empathise with! Implementation of peer review underscores the importance of students appreciating the value of giving peer feedback. When feedback is incorrect or when peer reviewers provide mixed messages, there are still opportunities for students to develop evaluative judgement. There are also some students who do not immediately appreciate the benefits of peer feedback processes but over time they often improve their attitude and implementation. The training and coaching aspects were viewed positively by students because without this kind of support, they may not have known how to produce useful feedback.

Enabling factors

A major enabler is the teacher who has deep knowledge and experience of conducting peer feedback effectively. Her role as a teacher-researcher is particularly focused on the implementation of peer feedback and she is well-published in the area. She has a combination of practical experience, research experience and familiarity with the literature.

The course meets twice a week for 18 weeks which affords sufficient time to build relationships and for students to appreciate what the teacher is doing, and practice some of the peer feedback skills they are being taught. One of the special features of the case is that the teacher is willing to invest time for the preparation and implementation of peer feedback. The small class size is a further facilitating factor, although the teacher has also implemented peer feedback successfully with larger classes and over shorter time-frames. There is a high degree of mutual trust between the teacher and the students, and between students themselves. Professor Min believes that trusting and harmonious relationships are more important than cultural issues in relation to peer feedback. She provides an incentive for students to engage fully in peer feedback processes by grading student peer review responses which count for 15% of the overall grade. This has the advantage of motivating and rewarding students for good peer review but might need to be omitted in the case of large classes because of the workload implications for teachers.

Challenges

Professor Min believes that the main challenges to the implementation of peer feedback are threefold: teachers' beliefs; time available; and insufficient training of students. First in relation to beliefs, some teachers have doubts about students' ability to provide quality feedback and thus do not want to learn more about it or include it in their practice. Knowledge about peer feedback is sometimes limited, and attitudes towards peer feedback may not be positive. In relation to concerns that Chinese students may prefer to hear the teachers' views rather than those of their peers, the teacher tackles this challenge by being cautious in intervening during classroom peer dialogues so as to avoid curtailing student voice.

Second, sometimes teachers prioritise other activities, such as delivering content or covering the syllabus. This may prompt them to feel that they do not wish to devote time to peer feedback and it is indeed the case that training students to do peer feedback well is quite time-consuming. Third, and relatedly, some teachers try out peer feedback but do not train students properly, thus resulting in low-quality peer feedback. If rushed implementation is ineffective or results are mixed, then teachers might in turn abandon carrying out peer feedback.

Relationship to the literature

The case speaks well to the issues and challenges for peer feedback discussed earlier in the chapter. The practice reinforces key literature (e.g. Sluijsmans, Brand-Gruwel, & Van Merriënboer, 2002; Van Zundert, Sluijsmans, & Van Merriënboer, 2010) in emphasising the importance of training students to carry our peer feedback. The systematic training, modelling and coaching processes in the case add to the literature by detailing carefully-designed stages in supporting students for peer feedback. The practice of supporting students in carrying out peer feedback also contributes to the development of their feedback literacy (Carless, & Boud, 2018).

The practice reinforces some of the thinking on peer feedback designs reviewed earlier in the chapter: working in randomly-allocated and varying trios (Van den Berg, Admiraal, & Pilot, 2006b); and written feedback supplemented by oral dialogue (Zhu, & Carless, 2018). The reported benefits of lower-achievers are also significant in that feedback research and practice often fails to suggest strategies which help less competent students (cf. Orsmond, & Merry, 2013). This practice also reinforces other studies (e.g. Xu, & Carless, 2017) in highlighting the role of trust in facilitating productive peer feedback processes.

Significance of this practice

The significance of the practice lies in reinforcing the importance of training and coaching students in carrying out peer feedback. Students need training at the outset, and also coaching after they have tried it out. The practice also exemplifies that there is a need to devote time to setting up and preparing students for peer feedback. One of the limitations of much current peer feedback practice is that teachers seem to assume that students know how to do it well, or do not devote time to supporting them in doing it better.

There is also evidence of student development of feedback literacy as well as indicators that this is a long-term endeavour. Students are being inducted into all four of elements of the student feedback literacy framework developed by Carless and Boud (2018). They are learning to appreciate and understand the value of peer feedback, and they are gaining experience in making evaluative judgements. When comments are critical, they are learning to manage the emotional side of feedback. Most crucially, they have opportunities to use feedback to improve their work.

Box 8.3 Implications for practice

- The rationale for peer feedback needs to be persuasively shared with students so that they are aware of its potential benefits.
- It is important to train and prepare students for peer feedback at the outset and provide coaching in how to do it more effectively, including sharing examples of useful feedback.
- There should be opportunities for students to air their experiences and concerns about peer feedback and it is useful to discuss strategies for tackling or reducing some of the challenges.
- Peer feedback trios might be an optimal arrangement so that multiple peer reviews are generated.
- Grading the quality of students' peer reviews can enhance motivation and provide incentives for students to invest in the process.

Conclusion

The first half of the chapter reviewed some key ideas on peer feedback. These include the important but sometimes underestimated value of composing peer feedback so as to trigger the deployment of criteria, problem-detection, and suggestion of solutions. Peer feedback also plays a role in enabling students to experience different perspectives and through comparing their work with that of others to enable self-regulation.

A key point of emphasis is on the need to train and coach students in how to carry out peer feedback. The effective implementation of peer feedback is dependent on a number of factors: teachers' commitment and skill in training students, setting up and supporting peer feedback; the class atmosphere and the relationships between participants; the student response; and the way peer feedback is designed.

The second half of the chapter discussed some exemplary practices of training and coaching for peer feedback at a university in Taiwan. Based on her long-term experience, the teacher-researcher scaffolds students' peer feedback through systematic processes of preparation and training; practice in carrying out peer feedback and coaching on how to do it better; and using feedback to enhance work. Professor Min has made efforts at transferring her ideas to colleagues. For example, in 2013 she carried out a workshop to demonstrate how to train students to do peer review. After the workshop a number of colleagues interacted with her informally for further discussion of implementation strategies. She is aware that at least four teachers in her department have been carrying out her ideas, and one colleague duplicated the entire peer feedback training programme with her students. The anecdotal evidence from colleagues is that the students appreciate the explicit procedures for peer review.

A crucial issue is how the practice could be embedded within large classes. The training elements can be done in analogous ways with a large class but the individual coaching elements would be impractical at scale, and would probably need to have an online component or be integrated within whole-class instruction. In a co-ordinated, programme-based approach to peer feedback students could be trained in peer review in the first year, and then afterwards teachers could build on that starting-point. The technology-enabled peer feedback strategies reviewed earlier in the chapter are an important means of designing for scaling-up of peer feedback.

Peer feedback should be embedded cumulatively and at increasingly higher levels of sophistication throughout the curriculum. The systematic training and support for student implementation of peer feedback is an important strand of this goal. Students who are trained in peer feedback carry it out more successfully and become more aware of its benefits. If peer feedback is well-established in the first year and more teachers implement it effectively then teacher scaffolding can be reduced, and it can become a core element of the undergraduate curriculum. For these aspirations to be fulfilled, it is necessary to create course climates in which the giving and receiving of peer feedback is a regular occurrence and its implementation becomes sustainable over the longer-term (Boud, 2000). Accordingly, peer feedback research which adopts a longitudinal approach may be particularly beneficial (Huisman et al., 2018).

In line with the embedding of peer feedback within the curriculum, teachers need training and support in implementing it, in particular how to involve students effectively in feedback processes and how to coach students in providing good quality and useful peer feedback (Wanner, & Palmer, 2018). In the same way that teacher feedback literacy is needed to develop student feedback literacy, teachers need skills in implementing peer feedback in order to enable students to carry it out. For the successful adoption of new paradigm feedback practices, the co-ordinated development of staff and student feedback literacy is necessary.

Box 8.4 Key Resources

- The Teaching Center of Washington University at St Louis contains a practical guide to in-class peer review of writing:
  https://teachingcenter.wustl.edu/resources/writing-assignments-feedback/using-peer-review-to-help-students-improve-their-writing/
- The JISC-funded PEER (Peer Evaluation in Education Review) Project led by David Nicol built on the REAP project and contains a number of useful resources:
  https://www.reap.ac.uk/PEER.aspx
- The HEA (Advance HE) has a number of practical resources for enabling feedback through technology with a number of the practices focused on peer feedback:
  https://www.heacademy.ac.uk/system/files/resources/10_ideas_for_enhancing_feedback_with_technology.pdf
- This example from the Y1 Feedback project includes peer feedback with a large class:
  http://y1feedback.ie/wp-content/uploads/2017/01/MU-1-Tatiana-Olga-2.pdf

Box 8.5 Questions for reflection and debate

- What are effective ways to convince students of the value of peer feedback?
- Whilst training students in peer feedback is essential, how much time should be devoted to it? What is the appropriate balance between training and coaching? If peer feedback is embedded more fully within a programme-based approach can efficiencies be gained?
- What are effective ways of supporting students to make sense of, evaluate, and use peer feedback appropriately?
- How can the interpersonal, dialogic strengths of feedback be maintained within technology-enabled peer feedback?
- Is the most pragmatic option to allocate marks for peer feedback or is it preferable for students to appreciate the value of the activity in its own right?
- How can both lower-achievers and higher-achievers maximise the potential benefits from peer feedback processes?
- Would an optimal means of implementing peer feedback involve a cumulative long-term approach within a programme-based feedback strategy? Are teaching teams co-ordinated and committed enough to make this happen?

Chapter 9

The relational dimension of feedback

The somewhat hidden nature of much assessment and feedback practice can make it easy to forget that the process involves people, not just pieces of work. Students may submit an assignment through the LMS, identified only by their student registration number. The marker may read this student's work as one out of a large number of assignments and might type comments onto an electronic version of the student's assignment. The marked work might then be made available to the student via the LMS, with the marker's identity perhaps also being hidden. Crucially, the marker may never see that student's work again, so has little opportunity to see the impact of their feedback on students' subsequent learning.

The Latin roots of the word 'assessment', *ad sedere*, translates as 'to sit beside'. Thus, it is rather worrying that in many contemporary higher education environments, the whole process could take place without any interpersonal interaction whatsoever. Within the current climate of contemporary higher education, paying attention to the relational dimension of the feedback process is perhaps even more important, given recent changes to staff-student ratios and class sizes, and increasing diversity in student demographics (Rowe, 2011). It is not just students who can find the assessment process disheartening; many teachers report feelings of anxiety and frustration in response to assessment and feedback processes (Molloy, Borrell-Carrió, & Epstein, 2013). Because so many elements of higher education have become depersonalised, recognition of human relations within the feedback process is arguably more important than ever. The relational dimension of feedback is an important part of new paradigm feedback approaches, because emotions influence students' reception and processing of feedback, and their motivation to take subsequent action (Värlander, 2008). As argued by Watling and Ginsburg (2019, p. 79), "Teacher-learner relationships based on trust create safety for learners to engage with feedback". Furthermore, the relational dynamics within feedback process provide the context in which students' sense-making of feedback information takes place (Esterhazy, 2018).

The complex relationships between emotion and response to feedback

The primary focus of this book is the creation of environments that facilitate students' uptake of and learning through feedback. In this context, it is essential for us to understand emotional barriers, defences, and threats to self-efficacy in the feedback process. Emotional responses can prevent the educational benefit of feedback from being realised (Carless, 2006), where feedback can be "obscured by emotional static" (Chanock, 2000, p. 95). Students in a study by Ferguson (2011) reported that overly critical feedback was too upsetting to look at; such reactions can lead to what has been termed "academic paralysis" (Nash, Crimmins, & Oprescu, 2016, p. 596), whereby negative emotion has a detrimental impact on academic motivation. Many experienced academics report a similar feeling when receiving critical comments through peer review; sometimes, they report a need to put them to one side until the initial emotional reaction has subsided. Crucially, students may be less likely to use comments if they have a negative emotional impact or are demotivating (e.g. Poulos, & Mahony, 2008), and this effect can be exacerbated for international students who are entering a new academic culture (e. g. Tian, & Lowe, 2013). Indeed, international students are more likely than home students to find feedback critical and upsetting (Ryan, & Henderson, 2018). Beyond the motivational effect, emotion can also have a direct impact on cognitive processing of feedback. For example, positive emotions can broaden the focus of attention, whilst limited attention can result from negative emotion (Huntsinger, 2013). However, the broader literature on emotion and learning tells us that the distinction between positive and negative emotions, where negative emotions lead to detrimental outcomes, is far too simplistic to account for the impact of emotions on behaviour in the context of feedback.

The relationship between emotion and feedback is complex; for example, while praise can elicit positive emotions, it can concurrently undermine motivation to invest future effort (e.g. Cassidy et al., 2003). Pekrun's Control-Value Theory (CVT) offers some indication of why these complex interactions between emotion and response to feedback might occur. This theory identifies a suite of 'achievement emotions' which can be elicited in the context of assessment, defined as "emotions that are directly linked to achievement activities or achievement outcomes" (Pekrun et al., 2011, p. 37). Pekrun (2006) suggests that emotions differ not only according to valence (positive/negative), but also their activation potential (whether they are 'activating', in terms of initiating action or effort; or 'deactivating', in terms of inhibiting action or effort). For example, enjoyment and pride are emotions that are positive in valence and activating in effect. In contrast, contentment and relief are also positive in valence, but deactivating in their effect as they often do not promote further action (Pekrun, et al., 2007). Similarly, shame and anxiety are negative in valence and activating in effect, whereas hopelessness and disappointment are negative deactivating emotions (Pekrun, Elliot, & Maier, 2006).

The crucial contribution of CVT to our understanding of the impact of emotion within assessment contexts is the recognition that the outcome of achievement emotions interacts with emotional valence. Thus, whilst it might be perceived that positive emotions are motivationally beneficial, positive emotions such as relief can actually discourage further effort and learning. This distinction is crucial for our exploration of the influence of relational factors on students' uptake of feedback because it leads us to expect that two students may display a similar behaviour (limited engagement with feedback) on the basis of polarised emotional experiences (e.g. one student may be relieved, a positive deactivating emotion; and one student may be disappointed, a negative deactivating emotion).

Also within the framework of CVT, Peterson, Brown, and Jun (2015) used a diary method to track which achievement emotions were commonly experienced within an assessment cycle. Those students who performed better on the assessment reported a higher level of positive emotions and lower levels of negative emotions, with the opposite being true for more poorly-performing students. Importantly, many students who had performed well reported feeling 'chilled', which, as a positive deactivating emotion, might limit engagement with feedback. In another study, 'feedback-seekers' (those who positively anticipate performance feedback), demonstrated fewer negative and more positive emotions in response to negative feedback, and greater hope in response to constructive criticism (Fong et al., 2016). Thus, one recommendation for supporting students' uptake of feedback is to support cognitive reframing as a way of managing the emotional response to feedback, hopefully leading to superior cognitive processing of feedback (Raftery, & Bizer, 2009).

The influence of feedback on identity and self-efficacy

The impact on emotion is just one part of the relational dimension of feedback. Feedback can also influence the way in which a student views themselves as a learner, and their own levels of confidence and self-belief. As argued by Lave and Wenger (1999, p. 31), "learning and a sense of identity are inseparable. They are aspects of the same phenomenon". As well as feedback having the potential to threaten self-esteem (Mutch, 2003), a student's level of self-esteem can also influence the ways in which they respond to feedback. In particular, findings from a study of mature students by Young (2000) suggest that students with high and medium levels of self-esteem respond to feedback with a sense of agency to act upon it; in contrast, the impact of feedback on students with low self-esteem is more negative, leading some students to question whether they should be at university at all.

Students' beliefs about their own ability are also likely to influence their preconceptions of what grade they expect to achieve on their work. If students hold an expectation of what they expect to achieve, there is clear potential for discrepancy between expectation and reality (see Chapter 7). If expectations are met, then positive emotions such as pride are likely to be experienced; in contrast, doing worse than one expects is likely to lead to feelings of disappointment and shame (e.g. Kahu, et al., 2015). For example, Ryan and Henderson (2018) reported that students who had received a grade lower than expected were more likely to experience sadness, anger, and shame than students who had achieved a grade that was higher than expected. These differential emotional reactions can lead to differential behavioural responses to feedback. In a study where physicians were presented with multi-source feedback, they exhibited a positive emotional response when the feedback aligned with their own self-perceptions of their competence, and a negative emotional response when there was misalignment (Sargeant, et al., 2008). Importantly, alignment between feedback and self-perceptions resulted in constructive engagement with and use of feedback. In contrast, where misalignment occurred, there was evidence of less adaptive responses to feedback. For example, one physician who received feedback that did not align with his own self-perception remarked that: "I did not get a good report … I didn't sleep for several nights after that" (Sargeant, et al., 2008, p. 280).

In the context of our relational focus, receiving feedback that is discrepant with one's own self-concept is not just important because it can lead to negative emotions; this mismatch between one's own self-concept and the evaluation of another can result in the student adjusting their beliefs in their own capability to succeed in future. Albert Bandura (1997, p. 3) described "beliefs in one's capabilities to organize and execute the course of action required to produce given attainments" as their level of self-efficacy. Evidence attests that self-efficacy is positively related to academic attainment (e.g. Honicke, & Broadbent, 2016), and feedback itself is an important influence on raising self-efficacy, if encouraging, and especially if from key figures such as teachers and lecturers (Bandura, 1997). In contrast, negative feedback can lower self-efficacy, leading to "debilitating effects on future performance on similar tasks" (Ilgen, & Davis, 2000, p. 562). Another important influence on self-efficacy is the experience of mastery: achieving and doing well in a particular task. This suggests that encouraging students to feel that they can improve through feedback is facilitated where they have experienced low-stakes opportunities to receive formative feedback (van Dinther, et al., 2014). It also suggests that the student–teacher relationship is crucial to the formation of positive beliefs in one's ability that are not detrimentally affected by feedback experiences. Whereas some students, particularly in the early stages of their university experience, crave encouraging comments, it is important to recognise that in some contexts, individuals desire critical feedback (see, for example, Fishbach, & Finkelstein, 2012). Just as interactive cover sheets can be used for students to request feedback on specific elements of their work (see Chapter 6), they could also enable students to request comments of a preferred tone.

Power relations in the feedback process

Boud and Molloy (2013) identified as one challenge with feedback the process of students and their work being judged by their teachers, whereby comments perceived to be judgemental and not with students' best interests at heart do not inspire action on the part of students. This process of casting judgement on students' work from a position of authority, that may ultimately influence a student's overall performance, places teachers in a position of power, with assessment being "a primary location for power relations" (Reynolds, & Trehan, 2000, p. 267). The power asymmetry between teacher and student is exacerbated by the fact that the former occupies a dual role, as facilitator of learning, whilst also passing judgement on the quality of students' work (Higgins, Hartley, & Skelton, 2001). The power differential can exacerbate the emotional impact of teachers' judgements (Carless, 2015a). Of course, this position of expertise can give the marker credibility in the eyes of students, leading to them valuing the judgements they might give on their work. For example, a student participating in a qualitative study conducted by Small and Attree (2016, p. 2089) reported that:

> ... it's when you get feedback from the likes of, you know, this person who is a University Masters Professor person. You know? ... and it's someone you hold a lot of respect for ... and they're highly qualified to comment. And when you get a good comment from someone like that, you're like, wow. They said the word good. So, yeah, it really invigorates you to go again to try again for your next blog and try to work out what is required so that you can get those extra marks.

Conversely, the power imbalance between teacher and student can detrimentally affect students' uptake of feedback, if students feel reticent to ask for further discussion to understand feedback, because they perceive academics to be too busy and with much more important work to do (Small, & Attree, 2016).

Furthermore, international students may feel that it is disrespectful to engage in dialogue about feedback which might be perceived as challenging academic authority (e.g. Tweed, & Lehman, 2002). Where emotional and relational factors can limit dialogue in the feedback process, this may act as an impediment to a new paradigm approach to feedback where student involvement is critical. Where dialogue is such an important part of the feedback process (see Chapter 6), how might we facilitate the development of positive student-teacher relationships that overcome the challenges inherent to this power imbalance?

We're in this together: building trust and relationships through feedback

Opening up one's work to evaluation by another person, particularly someone held in a position of esteem or authority, opens up oneself to judgement and hopefully constructive criticism. This process has the potential to be particularly problematic if the feedback process is characterised by feedback as 'telling' (Sadler, 2010). This model results in the student receiving a unilateral declaration, without any opportunity for dialogue to co-construct meaning of the teacher's thoughts about the work.

Building strong relationships within the feedback process is important because it can support students to feel confident to engage in meaningful dialogue with their teachers, through which they can learn more from the feedback, by unpacking its meaning and discussing future actions. Students often report that they wish to engage in one-to-one dialogue with their teachers (Blair, & McGinty, 2013), but relationships need to be established in order for students to feel confident to do so (Poulos, & Mahony, 2008). A student in Sutton and Gill's (2010) study reported that: "We know we need to approach this tutor to get help but we cannot because we are all scared" (Sutton, & Gill, 2010, p. 9). In contrast, where students do feel that they have a strong relationship with their teacher, they describe a sense of agency and volition to engage with and use feedback (Rowe, Fitness, & Wood, 2014).

High quality relationships between students and teachers can also buffer against the negative emotional impact of receiving critical comments on one's work, and lead to greater acceptance of the developmental advice (e.g. Lizzio, & Wilson, 2008). A feedback culture characterised by trust, empathy, and authentic guidance can enable students to overcome inhibiting emotional reactions in response to feedback, resulting in more meaningful uptake of the advice (Carless, 2013). Creating such a culture is not easy, particularly when, as disciplinary experts, it can be difficult for teachers to place themselves in the position of novice students experiencing inculcation into the conventions of an academic discipline (Vär-lander, 2008). One way to develop a feedback culture involving mutual perspec-tive-taking between teachers and students is through 'feedback preparation activities' (Värlander, 2008), whereby students can explore through dialogue the processes of giving and receiving feedback, which also affords staff insight into students' concerns about receiving feedback. These processes are fundamental to the development of feedback literacy, and the *Developing Engagement with Feed-back Toolkit* (Winstone, & Nash, 2016), discussed in Chapter 2, contains activities that serve this function.

A further reason why relationships are important in the feedback process is that the massification of higher education is limiting opportunities for personalised and sustained dialogue with teachers (Nicol, 2010). Placing focus on the relational dimension of feedback has the potential to support students to feel that they are an individual, not just a registration number or a face within a large cohort of students. While many universities worldwide have moved towards anonymous marking, such practices can prevent teachers from providing personalised com-ments to students (Forsythe, & Johnson, 2017). It is also evident that the provi-sion of anonymous feedback limits students' perceptions of their relationship with their teacher and leads them to perceive the feedback as being less useful (Pitt, & Winstone, 2018). It is beneficial for students to feel that their teacher genuinely cares for them as an individual. In a series of focus groups to explore students' experiences of receiving constructive criticism, Fong et al. (2018) reported that students perceive feedback as constructive rather than critical if they perceive that the teacher cares about their work and their progress, and that the teacher is perceived to hold authority and expertise. However, if unnecessarily harsh, the authority is counterproductive.

A recent meta-analysis of 78 studies by Fong et al. (2019) suggests that if negative feedback is delivered in person, intrinsic motivation is enhanced relative to neutral feedback, whereas negative feedback that is not delivered in person reduces intrinsic motivation. The authors argue that this reflects the fact that, in person, care can be expressed more easily, and that the critique is perceived to be less threatening. This important meta-analysis reminds us that the affective and motivational impact of feedback is dependent on the relational features of the feedback environment. As we shall see later in the chapter, the beneficial characteristics of in-person feedback do not necessarily require meeting face-to-face. We now turn to explore two examples from the literature which demonstrate how the relationship between emotional responses to feedback and uptake of the feedback are influenced by relational factors.

Key examples from the literature

The two examples we have selected from the literature illustrate through the voices of students the issues of emotion, power, and self-efficacy that we have explored thus far. The first (Shields, 2015) provides insight into the affective impact of feedback on first-year undergraduate students. The second (Pitt, & Norton, 2017) has implications for managing the 'emotional backwash' of feedback.

Shields (2015) approached the relational dimension of feedback from the perspective of students' transition to university, and the processes through which students come to develop a sense of belonging in their new academic environment. She deliberately avoids a deficit approach, where students are seen as unable to 'cope' with negative feedback; instead, the focus is on the role of feedback in fostering 'belongingness' and a sense of competence.

To this end, Shields interviewed 24 first-year undergraduate students from a post-1992 University in the UK studying on one of two modules: an optional study skills module available to all Humanities and Social Science students, and a Psychology module. The assessment for the former module involved a portfolio, and for the latter, two research reports. The students were interviewed at the start of their second semester, and were invited to discuss their experiences of the feedback they had received during their first semester at university. Students were invited to bring that feedback to the interview, as a stimulus for discussion. This study is of particular value because building relationships in the feedback process is likely to be enhanced by understanding the lived experience and 'social reality' of students. Such an approach may have a positive impact on student retention.

The analysis revealed that students can hold quite fragile academic identities, and that the assessment process is a strong influence on their developing identity as a learner. The students revealed that waiting for their first piece of feedback at university is a particularly anxiety-provoking time, as illustrated by this participant:

> I think feedback is important if you can get it as soon as possible because you're already anxious as to how good the work is and the longer it takes to get feedback you start thinking of all sorts of things like maybe I didn't do it quite well and then you have got other things that you are working on.
>
> (Shields, 2015, p. 618)

If the first feedback that students receive is on a high-stakes piece of summative work, then they may be waiting a long time for some information that might help them to benchmark their work, and the approach they might be taking for other assignments, against expected standards and assessment criteria. When feedback does come, it can create anxiety, meaning that "it takes students a long time to engage with feedback when it has a detrimental impact on their confidence, particularly on their first assignments" (Shields, 2015, p. 620). Thus, here we can see that assessment design is important not just in facilitating opportunities to act upon feedback (see Chapter 5), but also in ensuring that students can gain confidence early on in their programme of study. For this reason, Shields (2015) suggests that it is likely to be highly beneficial for new students to get feedback early on, as a result of completing low-stakes tasks, as "the finality of submitting assignments without any chance to improve or with little sense of being able to evaluate your own assignments is likely to increase anxiety and lessen confidence" (p. 622). This serves to illustrate the value of staged assessment designs which are discussed in more depth in Chapter 5.

Students in this study also revealed how feedback can influence their self-esteem and associated feelings of competence. Crucially, it is not simply the case that negative feedback can lead to them feeling they lack the necessary academic competence; additionally, the difficulties they might experience understanding what feedback is asking them to do can also diminish their self-esteem, as revealed by a student who, in not being able to understand the meaning of the marker's feedback comments, asked "is she saying I'm being stupid?" (p. 619). In supporting students' uptake of feedback, learner identity is a critical factor.

A striking feature of the findings reported by Shields is the extent to which students experience the power differential between teacher and student. It appears that part of the fragile learner identity in students comes from the power that teachers have in pointing out what is wrong in students' work, where students find it difficult to see the distinction between themselves 'being wrong', and an aspect of their work that is 'wrong'. The 'red pen' effect is a further example of the power exerted over students by those marking their work, as described by this student:

> They are writing all over my work and it is like mangled up and most of the lecturers use red pen and I don't know it kind of gets to me if I open it up and it's covered in red crosses and marks and it's horrible. It's like my work is bleeding.
>
> (Shields, 2015, p. 620)

Particularly in the early stages of a university course, the importance of building relationships between markers and students cannot be underestimated. As students' identities as learners influence their engagement with feedback (Shields, 2015), the relational dimension is important in developing new paradigm approaches to feedback.

Our second example extends the work of Shields by shifting the focus from first-year to final-year undergraduates, demonstrating how emotional responses to feedback can influence student uptake at a later stage of the academic journey. Pitt and Norton (2017) explored the experiences of final-year undergraduates when receiving feedback on their work. The study is built on a recognition that the learning potential of feedback can only be realised if students engage with and act upon comments, thus situating this work firmly within a new paradigm approach. The first author interviewed 14 final-year undergraduate students on a Sports Studies programme, using a phenomenographic approach. Students were invited to bring examples of feedback on what they perceived to be a 'good' and a 'bad' piece of work that they had completed at any stage of their programme. The interviews began by discussing the 'good' piece of work, followed by discussion of the 'bad' piece of work. In each case, students were invited to summarise the marker's feedback and to identify the suggested directions for improvement. Next, they were asked to discuss how the feedback made them feel, how they reacted, and how they implemented the feedback.

Pitt and Norton (2017) identified three patterns of emotional response to feedback: motivating positive feedback, motivating negative feedback, and demotivating negative feedback. These categories resonate with the distinction between activating and deactivating emotions in CVT, discussed earlier in the chapter (Pekrun, 2006). There was evidence in Pitt and Norton's analysis of negative emotion being both activating and deactivating, as these student responses serve to illustrate:

> Saying I didn't do so well makes me feel bad and spurs me onto wanting to get a better mark next time.
>
> (Pitt, & Norton, 2017, p. 504)

> If I see a negative comment I blank it out of my mind instead of maybe looking over it and going right, that's what I actually needed to do.
>
> (Pitt, & Norton, 2017, p. 504)

In this sense, Pitt and Norton's study is a good example of the complex relationship between emotion and response to feedback.

The influence of feedback on students' competence beliefs and self-efficacy was also evident in Pitt and Norton's findings. The final-year undergraduates in this study showed a similar response to the first-year undergraduates in Shields' (2015) study, whereby the judgements of markers can be internalised as representing stable features of their own competence, rather than of the work itself; one student expressed that "if I've got bad feedback I think I'm obviously not good at the subject. Basically if the tutor's saying I'm no good at it then obviously I think I'm not" (Pitt, & Norton, 2017, p. 506). This illustrates how feedback can have a direct impact on students' self-worth and self-efficacy; however, Pitt and Norton's analysis also revealed that comments can have a positive impact on raising students' self-efficacy, if they communicate a belief that students are very much capable of making the recommended improvements, as illustrated by these student narratives:

> The feedback made me realise my weakness but also the fact that with the right preparation I could do it right.
>
> (Pitt, & Norton, 2017, p. 508)

> It actually made me think 'actually I can do this', instead of thinking 'I did all right'. I need good support, someone to tell me 'yes you can do it'. They obviously believe that I can do it, which is kind of pleasing for me.
>
> (Pitt, & Norton, 2017, p. 507)

Pitt and Norton (2017) introduce the concept of 'emotional backwash' to represent students' affective responses to feedback. Their analysis illustrates that feedback can be motivating or demotivating, and that markers hold the power to influence students' self-efficacy and competence beliefs in both positive and negative ways. It is likely that facial expressions and verbal cues can enhance the communication of markers' perceptions; such cues are likely to be harder to convey through written feedback. We now turn to examine a case study of practice where these interpersonal factors enhance the relational dimension of feedback.

Box 9.1 Key research findings

- The relationship between emotional responses to feedback and subsequent uptake is complex (Pekrun, 2006).
- The power imbalance between teachers and students can lead to a sense of distance, where students are reluctant to engage in dialogue with teachers (Small, & Attree, 2016).
- It is important to build relationships between teachers and students so that students feel comfortable approaching teachers for guidance and further feedback (Sutton, & Gill, 2010).
- Receiving feedback in person may minimise the negative effects of critical feedback on intrinsic motivation (Fong, et al., 2019).

- Students can find it difficult to differentiate between critical feedback on their work, and on themselves as a learner (Pitt, & Norton, 2017; Shields, 2015).
- If students do not understand how to enact feedback, this can have a negative impact on their self-esteem and self-efficacy. Conversely, where markers express a belief that students can improve, students' self-efficacy can grow (Shields, 2015).

The case: Putting a face to the name through video feedback

Context

This case focuses on the work of Dr Emma Mayhew, an Associate Professor in the Department of Politics and International Relations at the University of Reading, UK. In her third-year undergraduate British Foreign and Defence Policy module, Emma introduced video/screencast feedback to two different cohorts: those taking the module in 2013–2014 and those taking the module in 2014–2015. Each year around 30 students were enrolled on the module. Emma recognises the powerful learning potential of feedback, viewing timely, constructive, and motivating feedback as central to the facilitation of student engagement, learning, and attainment.

The feedback design

The assessment for the module involved students writing two 3,000–3,500-word essays. Emma wanted to personalise the feedback process by having a more direct link with her students than could be provided by text-based feedback, and wanted her students to get a better sense of the feedback process, and how she was constructing her feedback to them. Emma decided to introduce video feedback on students' first essays each year. In order to capture the video, she used Camtasia, an inexpensive piece of screen capture software. The student saw their essay on the left-hand side of the screen, and Emma's face on the right-hand side of the screen. The student followed Emma through the process of providing the feedback as she scrolled down. Each recording lasted for between five and ten minutes, and was saved as a simple MP4 file which was released to students via the LMS.

Student response

Emma used an anonymous questionnaire to explore the student response to video feedback. She asked students to respond to a series of statements using a simple five-point Likert scale with additional open-ended questions. In total, 50 out of a possible 60 students completed the questionnaire, with their responses providing insight into their experience of the process (see Box 9.2).

Box 9.2 Student responses to video feedback

- 90% said that they preferred video to written feedback.
- 81% said that they would prefer video feedback than written feedback on their next essays.
- 100% thought that they should receive at least one piece of video feedback at university.
- 72% of students reported that being able to see the marker's face made the feedback feel more personal.
- 86% said that the video feedback helped them to clarify areas they did not understand and 84% said that there was less scope for misunderstanding in comparison to written feedback.
- 88% of students felt that they received more detailed comments on their work than they might have done with written feedback. Video feedback contained an average of 1,360 words in a typical eight-minute video, three or four times more than the amount of words students would typically get in a word-processing document.
- 78% of students felt that video feedback prompted them to look back over the subject matter more than written feedback.
- 87% felt that they would perform better in subsequent work following video feedback, in comparison to written feedback.

While these findings are promising, it is not clear whether students' beliefs about the impact of video feedback actually translated into behaviour. Such insight could have been achieved by building into the process an opportunity for students to respond to the feedback.

Enabling factors

Emma worked in a department that fosters innovation in learning and teaching, with particular encouragement for innovations in the electronic management of assessment. Thus, the departmental feedback culture was supportive of experimentation, favouring innovation rather than adherence to the status quo. Emma was already familiar with the use of the technology supporting screen capture. The Camtasia platform is simple to use and has been widely deployed for the delivery of screencast feedback.

Emma's values were also an enabling factor in this case; she recognised that the provision of screencast feedback did not necessarily reduce the amount of time spent marking students' work, yet saw that this was still a highly beneficial strategy in terms of building a stronger relationship with her students in the marking process, and providing clearer and richer feedback information. In this sense, the practice neither increases nor decreases workload, but results in a more satisfying process. Emma also made the process more personal through her creativity; when recording her feedback, she sat in front of her Christmas tree during December marking and her Easter display during March marking. Emma decided that she would not attempt to create perfect video files. In one instance, her cat jumped up in front of the camera, and Emma resisted the temptation to edit interruptions to the dialogue. Students valued a human approach over a tightly-controlled formal delivery of feedback.

Challenges

Not all students show a preference for video feedback; some of Emma's students asked for written feedback in addition to video feedback so that they could more easily refer back to it. Emma suggested that they could transcribe her words if they felt that this was important because that process in itself supports greater engagement with the content of the feedback. Emma's response is important in emphasising the importance of students rather than their teachers doing more to realise the impact of feedback.

There are also challenges relating to the process of video feedback. Emma cautions that given the natural dialogic feel of audio feedback, it is easy to give too much! Indeed, less can be more in feedback (Boud, & Molloy, 2013), and students might be more likely to revisit shorter, more focused comments. The moderation process also requires internal and external moderators to watch the feedback videos, so mechanisms need to be in place to ensure that they have access to the video files.

Relationship to the literature

Emma's experience, and that of her students, aligns with other reports in the literature whereby students experience video feedback to be more personalised than written feedback (see Chapter 4). There is also evidence that being able to demonstrate empathy and respect through facial expressions and tone of voice can help mitigate against the common power imbalance inherent to the marker–student relationship (Ryan, & Henderson, 2018). Reducing the perceived distance between assessor and student is likely to facilitate more meaningful communication in feedback exchanges, because assessment relationships are commonly characterised by power asymmetry (Värlander, 2008). The nuanced communication afforded by facial expressions and hand gestures, for example, may convey to students their teachers' investment in their learning (Mahoney, Macfarlane, & Ajjawi, 2019). One of the aspects that students really liked was Emma's use of nonverbal communication and the way she used her voice to soften criticism. Video feedback affords this kind of communication in ways that text-based feedback does not.

However, while we can speculate that such affordances of video feedback might positively influence students' uptake of feedback, it is uncommon for this practice to actually go one step further and build into the process opportunities for students to respond to the feedback (Mahoney, Macfarlane, & Ajjawi, 2019). This leads us to question the extent to which audiovisual approaches to feedback embody new paradigm principles, or whether they are mainly rooted in old paradigm approaches, due to emphasis on the delivery of feedback (see Pitt, & Winstone, 2019). As discussed in Chapter 4, if audiovisual approaches to feedback merely replicate the transmission of comments through a different medium, then they remain aligned with old paradigm principles. While students often perceive audiovisual feedback to feel more dialogic than written feedback, this dialogue is somewhat illusory (Mahoney, Macfarlane, & Ajjawi, 2019), unless students have the opportunity to respond to the feedback. It is relatively easy to facilitate students' response to the feedback; Henderson and Phillips (2015) conclude each video feedback recording with a direct invitation to continue the feedback exchange with the marker, and, as discussed in Chapter 4, screencast technology could be utilised for students to submit a recording of their response to the feedback (Fernández-Toro, & Furnborough, 2014).

Despite the presence of some old paradigm features, this does not mean that audiovisual feedback is not effective, nor that it cannot concurrently embody new paradigm principles. By adopting a relational approach, Emma is able to minimise the power asymmetry between herself and her students (Värlander, 2008), and by pinpointing within students' work where and how they can improve, this approach is likely to facilitate student uptake. This is where Emma's approach illustrates core features of new paradigm approaches. Managing affect in the feedback process is an important component of student feedback literacy (Carless, & Boud, 2018), and feedback literate teachers will be aware of the potential impact of their students' emotional responses to feedback. By recognising and seeking to overcome these challenges, Emma is demonstrating her own feedback literacy as a teacher.

Significance of this practice

This case is a good example of how individual students can experience a stronger connection to the marker through quite a simple change to the feedback process. The response of Emma's students demonstrates that as well as preferring video feedback, they reported that this practice would facilitate greater uptake of feedback in comparison to their experience of written feedback. One potential reason for this belief is that the video format leads students to perceive markers to have a genuine interest in supporting their improvement. This creates the conditions for the development of a strong 'educational alliance', which further facilitates a belief that they are more likely to engage and to partake in further dialogue (Telio, Regehr, & Ajjawi, 2016). A strong and authentic educational alliance is indicative of a feedback culture characterised by trust and mutual value placed on students' development. Emma is also frank in sharing that this approach did not necessarily save her any time in the assessment process. This is an important reminder that innovation in feedback processes is not always about saving time, but seeking to repurpose and reinvest time to make the process more meaningful and impactful for teachers and students.

Emma's approach has opened up a critical discussion about the value of old and new paradigm approaches to feedback. While the delivery of comments through audio-visual media could be seen as embodying old paradigm features, this does not mean that the practice does not have promise. We have seen how students value this approach and perceive that their uptake of feedback will be enhanced, and with minimal adjustment, student response could be built into the process. By gaining a more nuanced understanding of teachers' comments on their work, students are likely to develop their feedback literacy. Furthermore, by removing many of the barriers to the use of feedback that stem from power differentials, this practice is also likely to enable students to better manage affect in the feedback process, also a key dimension of student feedback literacy (Carless, & Boud, 2018).

Box 9.3 Implications for practice

- Supporting students' uptake of feedback is likely to benefit from building strong relationships between students and their teachers, so that they feel comfortable to engage in further dialogue about their work.
- In the early stages of their programmes, low-stakes tasks with feedback are likely to give students more confidence in their ability to meet degree-level standards in their work.
- Students and teachers are likely to benefit from activities that prepare students to give and receive feedback, and to manage emotional reactions to the feedback process.
- Improving the level of personalisation in the feedback process does not necessarily require feedback to be given face-to-face. Using technology whereby students can see the marker's face, or hear their voice, can lead to a greater sense of personalisation.
- Markers can raise students' self-efficacy to improve by framing comments in such a way that communicates their belief that improvement is something that the student can achieve.
- Teachers can model to students how to handle critical feedback and emotional responses to feedback, as part of supporting students to manage affect in the feedback process.

Conclusion

Very few of us would claim that we enjoy receiving critical feedback. We can often find ourselves feeling defensive in response to others' critique, and often try to protect our own self-esteem as a result. Our students are also at the mercy of their emotions during feedback processes. In most cases, they will have submitted work that they are proud of, and as a result, the critical judgements passed by their teachers can often be unexpected and can lead to students feeling anxious, frustrated, despondent, and even angry. In this chapter, we have discussed how the relationship between emotion and response to feedback is a complex one; it is not simply the case that negative emotions lead to resistance to take action in response to feedback. In fact, it may well be the case that in some cases, experiencing negative affect in response to feedback may lead to stronger motivation to act than experiencing positive affect (Pekrun, 2006). We have also seen that feedback can have a real impact upon students' sense of competence and identity as a learner.

If, as part of a new paradigm feedback approach, we wish to provide an environment that facilitates students' uptake of feedback, then we cannot ignore the motivational, emotional, and interpersonal dimensions of the feedback culture. Teachers occupy a position of power over students: holding students' academic performance and progress within their hands. Perhaps more importantly, students can internalise the judgements of their teachers, and can often see comments on their work as comments on themselves as a learner. However, central to a new paradigm approach to feedback is facilitating student advancement; thus, sometimes feedback needs to be frank and critical, as well as being sensitive to students' likely emotional responses. Indeed, attempts to avoid being too critical in feedback exchanges through the use of language, sometimes referred to as 'hedging' (Ginsburg, et al., 2016), can obscure the message of the feedback, thus impeding student uptake.

A new paradigm feedback culture requires us to invest effort in ensuring that students and teachers develop relationships characterised by willingness to engage in dialogue. Students are often portrayed as being primarily interested in grades, rather than feedback. While this may be true, it is often the words of their teachers that have a stronger and more lasting effect on students' self-esteem than a numerical or alphabetical grade. If we can motivate students by conveying our interest and belief in their improvement through ongoing dialogue, they may well engage more meaningfully with feedback processes.

Box 9.4 Key resources

- A summary of the common emotional and defensive reactions to feedback: http://www.bbc.com/future/story/20170308-why-even-the-best-feedback-can- bring-out-the-worst-in-us
- How staff-student relationships might influence engagement with critical feedback: http://www.learningscientists.org/blog/2016/11/1-1
- How neuroscience can help us give and receive critical feedback – a post from Monash University: https://www2.monash.edu/impact/articles/how-neuroscience-can-help-us-give-and-receive-critical-feedback/
- Developing assessment and feedback processes in partnership with students: a case study from University College London: https://www.ucl.ac.uk/teaching-learning/case-studies/2018/feb/how-ucl-department-improved-assessment-and-feedback-partnership-students

Box 9.5 Questions for reflection and debate

- Reflect on a recent experience of receiving feedback, perhaps as part of the peer review process, or from a teaching evaluation. What emotions did you experience, and in this situation, were they 'activating' or 'deactivating' in their effect?
- Take a piece of feedback you have received and look at the language used by the feedback-giver. What elements of their feedback make you feel uncomfortable? How could the comments be reframed?
- How can you empower your students to use emotions to support positive engagement with feedback?
- How could you reduce the power asymmetry in your feedback exchanges with students?
- How can teachers provide honest, constructive feedback without risking upsetting students? Is there a risk that supportive feedback becomes anodyne? How are these tensions managed? Is greater partnership between teachers and students a possible way forward?

Chapter 10

Moving feedback forwards

The central theme of this book is the active involvement of students in feedback processes, such that feedback is not something done *to* students, but a process through which their agentic engagement is central to its impact. Drawing upon the Feedback Cultures project, we have explored elements of the feedback process that align in a specific way with a new paradigm approach to feedback. Through analysis of the cases we have seen how various intrapersonal and situational factors facilitate the adoption of such practices. In this final chapter we draw together these insights, chart some possible ways forward, and offer some practical tools to enable individual teachers and course teams to evaluate and develop their practice in line with a new paradigm focus. In so doing, we echo Boud's (2000, p. 158) exhortation that "Changing feedback is at the heart of pedagogy – it is never marginal".

Metrics such as the UK National Student Survey and the Australian Course Experience Questionnaire place emphasis on the quality of feedback transmission. As a result, in contemporary higher education much focus has been placed upon surface technicalities of the feedback process, such as the turnaround time and the detail and consistency of comments, at the expense of considering how feedback facilitates students' learning. The quality of feedback processes in higher education does not rest upon the format or detail of written comments provided to students. Hence, when students are asked to evaluate the extent to which they have received helpful and timely comments on their work, they are rating the quality of old paradigm, rather than new paradigm, approaches to feedback (Winstone, & Pitt, 2017). If staff and students agree that the purpose of feedback is to facilitate improvement (e.g. Dawson, et al., 2019; Mulliner, & Tucker, 2017), why isn't the quality of feedback processes evaluated in terms of the impact on student behaviour and learning, rather than the quality of what, until translated into student action, is merely "dangling data" (Sadler, 1989, p. 121)?

The tides are beginning to turn; key scholars in the area of assessment and feedback have been calling for a shift away from viewing feedback as transmission and towards feedback as a tool for learning that has an impact on what students do next. We have also seen evidence of this shift within the cases presented in this book. In each case, the teacher has considered how they can involve students more significantly in the feedback process, supporting them to understand, apply, and generate feedback. Realising a shift towards the new paradigm does not in many cases require large or time-consuming changes, nor complete abandonment of old paradigm features; rather, simple shifts in the ways in which feedback is discussed and enacted can resituate practice away from transmission and towards learning (see Figure 10.1).

For example, many attempts to improve feedback processes involve the setting of arbitrary turnaround times within which marked work accompanied by feedback comments should be returned to students. Focusing on this element of the timing of feedback processes places emphasis on what the educator does; a simple shift towards a new paradigm approach can be achieved by viewing timely feedback as that which occurs in time for feedback exchanges to have an impact on students and what they might do next.

Perhaps because of the common wording of items through which students evaluate their experiences of assessment and feedback, in many discourses around feedback high quality feedback has become synonymous with detailed feedback, as if providing a high volume of feedback on students' work means that it will automatically be useful for students. Of course, for some highly-motivated students this might be the case but again this focus places emphasis on what the educator, not the student, does within the feedback process. In fact, the important feature of comments on students' work is not that they are detailed, but that they are actionable; that is, they identify something concrete that students can use to develop their skills, thinking, or conceptual understanding.

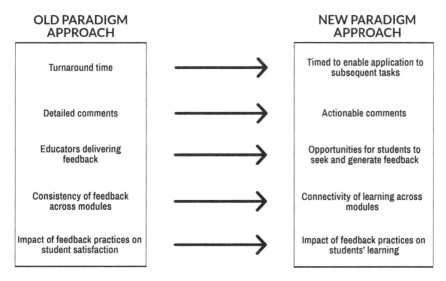

Figure 10.1 Resituating practice towards a new paradigm perspective

A risk in teacher-driven old paradigm approaches is that emphasis is placed on the delivery of information from expert to novice. It is not that teachers providing information to students is necessarily unwise, it is that unless it is done carefully or designed skilfully it risks reducing the students to passive receivers of information, or making them become dependent on the teacher. As we have explored in this book, part of a shift towards a new paradigm perspective on feedback is to recognise that feedback exchanges can involve peers, family members, or learning advisors, for example, as well as stemming from students' own evaluative judgement and reflective activities. In this sense, new paradigm feedback practices are congruent with the social constructivist underpinnings of feedback that we introduced in Chapter 1. New paradigm approaches involve students in co-constructing meanings with peers and teachers. They promote the development of shared and individual interpretations of feedback messages, promoting different forms of dialogues between participants through face-to-face, whole class, group, and technology-mediated interactions. These are interpersonal co-constructions which build upon students' prior experiences, understanding, goals, and motivations.

When responding to students' apparent dissatisfaction with feedback, many well-meaning responses are firmly aligned with an old paradigm perspective which, while possessing some merit, are not necessarily most beneficial for students' learning. For example, many such responses focus on maximising the consistency of the feedback experience across units and programmes, perhaps using common feedback templates, or recommending that markers write at least five points of feedback on students' work. Even more useful than consistency is connectivity, such that students can apply their learning from one task to the next. Shifting towards a new paradigm focus requires us to look beyond the impact of feedback practices on student satisfaction to the impact on student learning. This is not to say that student satisfaction is unimportant; we have a duty to pay heed to feedback from our students, and metrics are undoubtedly important from institutional perspectives. However, placing student learning through feedback at the centre of improvement endeavours will likely lead to gains in student satisfaction. For example, many common action plans in response to student (dis)satisfaction with feedback incorporate knee-jerk, superficial reactions that aim to make students happy, regardless of whether this represents best practice from an evidence-based perspective. Furthermore, a heavy focus on enhancement aligned with student satisfaction metrics can lead to the emphasis being placed on enhancing the experience of cohorts who complete student satisfaction surveys (final-year undergraduates in the case of the UK NSS), rather than working with all students to transform the overall feedback culture and ethos within a School, Department, Faculty, or Institution.

Transforming assessment and feedback practices can seem like a daunting task, involving significant time and effort to change the culture. In fact, it is often not substantial changes that facilitate positive outcomes, but the combined effect of lots of small changes. The aggregation of marginal gains is well-illustrated through the approach of Sir David Brailsford, the performance director for British Cycling.

By making multiple small changes to training and athlete care, the combination of 1% improvements in different elements of performance aggregated to form a significant overall improvement, through which 70% of all the Gold medals for track cycling at the London 2012 Olympic Games were won by the British team (Clear, 2018). These impressive performance gains were not brought about by dramatic changes, but by seeking ways to enhance performance through multiple small changes. A similar approach can facilitate the shift towards a new paradigm approach to feedback. Within the chapters of this book we have discussed many different strategies for developing new paradigm feedback practices, some of which involve more significant change than others. With the aggregation of marginal gains in mind, in Table 10.1 we suggest some small changes that could be enacted in order to involve students more significantly in feedback processes, in relation to the topic of each of the chapters in this book. Together, these small changes can add up to an overall shift in the direction of a new paradigm feedback culture.

Resituating practice towards a model embodying new paradigm principles is likely to involve encountering various barriers, perceived or real. In the Feedback Cultures project, we chose not to ignore potential barriers, but through dialogue with teachers to explore how to overcome them. Our engagement with teachers also revealed many facilitators of new paradigm approaches to feedback, both intrapersonal and situational. In the following two sections, we synthesise what we have learned through the project about barriers and facilitators to new paradigm feedback approaches.

Tackling perceived barriers to new paradigm feedback practices

As discussed in Chapter 1, many participants in the Feedback Cultures project expressed concerns about their agency to implement learning-focused feedback practices. Such concerns related to their perceived expertise in the domain of feedback, the constraints of their workload and cohort sizes, and the challenges inherent to their discipline. We now turn to a consideration of how these barriers can be tackled at individual, departmental, and institutional levels, recognising that there are interrelationships between these barriers, and the levels at which they operate.

Teacher expertise

While courses for new lecturers (e.g. Post-Graduate Certificates, or PGCerts, in Learning and Teaching or in Academic Practice) may cover elements of assessment and feedback, it is unlikely that such programmes can equip teachers with knowledge and skills in all dimensions of feedback processes. Questions have been raised about the limited impact of formal training courses on practice (e.g. Ginns, Kitay, & Prosser, 2010), while informal learning from others through 'corridor conversations' is likely to have a stronger impact on practice (e.g. Boud, & Brew, 2013; Thomson, & Trigwell, 2018). Similarly, Winstone and Boud (2019)

Table 10.1 Marginal gains in feedback processes

Dimension of feedback processes	*Suggested practices*
Developing students' feedback literacy	• Engage in dialogue with students to discuss the purpose and process of feedback. • Use dialogue with personal tutors as a way for students to connect feedback processes across a programme.
Developing students' engagement with feedback processes	• Discuss with students the importance of their active involvement with feedback processes. • Encourage students to complete feedback journals or collate reflection sheets to consider how they plan to take action on feedback comments.
Using technology to facilitate feedback processes	• Use web-based student response systems to facilitate 'just in time' feedback during class time. • Use the analytics function within a LMS to gain insight into students' engagement with feedback.
Assessment and feedback design	• Consider where within the assessment cycle the provision of detailed feedback is best placed. • Break down larger assessment tasks into a two-stage design where students have the opportunity to apply feedback from one component to the next.
Bringing dialogue into feedback processes	• Invite students, when submitting assignments, to request feedback on specific elements of their work. • Ask students to comment on how they have used feedback from previous assessments in carrying out the current task.
Interweaving internal and external feedback	• Give students the opportunity to engage with exemplars. • Stimulate students' self-evaluative capacity by inviting them to reflect on the strengths and weaknesses of their assignment in relation to the stated criteria.
Effective peer feedback and peer mentoring processes	• Opportunities for peer feedback processes could be built into existing peer mentoring schemes. Peers have insight into the programme-level assessment experience in a way that staff teaching on a particular module may not. • Many LMSs have features that facilitate peer review processes.
The relational dimension of feedback	• Discuss with students your own experience of peer review processes, sharing how you felt and how you acted. • Share strategies for harnessing emotions to facilitate, rather than inhibit, development in response to feedback.

demonstrated that formal training has less of an influence on feedback practice than informal learning and development such as that which occurs through engagement with the literature and discussions at departmental meetings. Thus, overcoming the barrier of perceived expertise to innovate in feedback practice on an individual level is likely to benefit from exposing individuals to informal learning opportunities, and through facilitating discussions with others.

It is also noteworthy that may of our case practitioners are the recipients of teaching awards. While occupying the status of an award-winning teacher is not a prerequisite for the development of innovative approaches to feedback, being the recipient of an award provides a platform for acting as a 'champion' of innovative practice. For example, Kennedy (Chapter 7) was the recipient of an institutional student-led 'Best Feedback' award, specifically recognising his impactful feedback approach. Feedback awards surface and reward good practice, and encourage others to explore similar approaches. Student-led feedback awards are increasingly being offered by a variety of higher education institutions e.g. Hull University, Queen Margaret University Edinburgh, Staffordshire University, University of Central Lancashire and Aberystwyth University. The Stanford University Medical School, Department of Paediatrics also has an award to recognise a faculty member who provides effective oral feedback. We hope this trend will continue and expand further as it can play a role in spreading and encouraging good feedback practice.

On a departmental level, fostering and rewarding a mindset of experimentation in feedback practice is important, as often it is not extensive expertise but a willingness to try something new that can open up opportunities for innovation in feedback processes. Those who lead learning and teaching within departments can also help colleagues to feel equipped to engage in new approaches to feedback by facilitating discussion around what 'effective' feedback processes might look like within the context of the discipline. In addition, fostering a departmental culture that resists adherence to the status quo, and encourages change and innovation, is also likely to facilitate development in practice (Winstone, 2017).

Moving to the institutional level, concerns over the transfer of learning from formal programmes could be facilitated by ensuring that they cover practices such as assessment and feedback in a context-specific rather than generalised way, such that participants can explore the direct application of theory to their own contextualised practice. Central Technology-Enhanced Learning departments also have a crucial role to play in developing the self-efficacy of teaching staff to use media such as audio or video technology to support feedback processes. In reality, many such tools are simple to use but staff are likely to benefit from demonstration and implementation support. Technology-Enhanced Learning departments can also facilitate the sharing of practice within the institution so that staff can hear about successful implementation of new approaches to feedback in other parts of the campus.

Time and workload

Time pressures are perceived as one of the most significant barriers to innovation in feedback processes; this was the most common area of discussion in the Feedback Cultures interviews, as presented in Chapter 1. However, this can result in time and workload being seen as a convenient excuse for maintaining the status quo in feedback practices. When only old paradigm feedback practices are envisaged, time seems an insuperable barrier. In fact, a new paradigm approach to feedback seeks to minimise time spent on unproductive marking and feedback practices that, due to their timing or format, do not have a strong impact on student learning. Thus, on an individual level, overcoming this barrier requires teaching staff to be open to consideration that they could enhance feedback processes in such a way that repurposes their time spent on feedback, rather than adding to it.

This shift in mindset can be supported at the departmental level, through the voices of 'champions' or 'opinion leaders' that emphasise this message. This was evident in the cases of Claire (Chapter 3), Rick (Chapter 5) and Emma (Chapter 9). Claire recognised that providing individual oral feedback would be challenging in terms of time, but created a similar dialogic process though repurposing class time. Emma expressed that while screencast feedback did not save time, it enabled her to craft it in ways that had greater impact on her students.

Moving to the institutional level, processes such as the UK Teaching Excellence Framework have the potential to place greater focus on quality teaching, including assessment and feedback processes. Crucially, then, workload planning models at an institutional level should allocate realistic amounts of time to assessment and feedback activities, such that a 'tick box' culture of feedback is not inadvertently promoted through the message that feedback is something that can be done quickly, and in a set amount of time.

Student numbers

Student numbers seem like an unsurmountable obstacle if old paradigm feedback practices of feedback as telling are envisaged. Within new paradigm feedback practices a different picture emerges. On an individual level, overcoming the perception of cohort sizes as a barrier to innovation is again likely to depend on the individual's mindset, and a willingness to consider different ways of enacting feedback processes. The cases in Chapters 2, 4, 5 and 6 illustrated how new paradigm approaches can be adopted with large cohorts. For example, in Chapter 2, we saw how Robert enabled a formative feedback process not by reading every student's portfolio, but by reading a sample and providing cohort-level feedback on key themes, and facilitating an activity where students could consider the extent to which this feedback applied to their own work. In Chapter 5, Rick provides anticipatory feedback to classes of 250 students through detailed guidelines and annotated exemplars. In that case, a rich authentic task motivates students to produce positive learning outcomes in which they generate internal feedback as they work on it over time.

Overcoming barriers arising from large cohort sizes can be facilitated on a departmental level by encouraging team-based approaches to feedback processes. As we saw in Chapter 1, many teachers expressed hesitation to carry out audio feedback as they were concerned about technical and workload implications. In Chapter 4, we illustrated how Jaclyn led a team of up to 30 markers to carry out audio feedback at scale. In this case, Jaclyn led, modelled, and supported implementation of technology-enabled feedback approaches through carefully-designed feedback stages.

Teaching in teams is a way of scaling-up good practice. Scaling-up involves the spread of good practices to larger groups of colleagues and across disciplines. Individual 'champions' or teams such as academic development units may be able to share tried and tested models for scaling-up practices developed with smaller groups to much larger class sizes. Would-be innovators need some combination of motivation to change, awareness of worthwhile practices, taking ownership of ideas, and support in carrying them out. Projects which involve larger groups of colleagues working collaboratively can be a breeding ground for scaling-up practice.

Nature of discipline

In our discussion of the Feedback Cultures interviews in Chapter 1, we saw how some respondents felt that innovative feedback processes were easier to enact in some disciplines than others. While it may well be the case that some disciplines rely on 'signature' assessment and feedback processes, this does not mean that other approaches are not valid, nor necessarily prohibited by accrediting bodies. Overcoming this barrier on an individual level requires a willingness to look beyond the boundaries of one's own discipline and to be open to learning from colleagues working in other areas. Rick (Chapter 5) is a good example as he is open to learning from the literature and picking up practical ideas on assessment and feedback. Exams are firmly entrenched as a disciplinary practice in Law Schools but he is willing to move beyond them to other coursework tasks and also carry out anticipatory feedback and same day feedback for examinations.

On a departmental level, innovation in feedback processes can be fostered where spaces are created for discussion about creativity in assessment design for learning-focused feedback processes. Similarly, breaking down disciplinary boundaries on an institutional level can be facilitated through events that foster interdisciplinary discussions about different approaches to assessment and feedback, and that provide a forum for sharing and exploring practice. In Chapter 6, we saw how Amy and Patrick's use of interactive cover sheets was transported from the discipline of Engineering to their own discipline of Psychology.

Enablers to the adoption of new paradigm feedback practices

In each of Chapters 2–9, we have explored cases of practice in which individual teachers have in some way demonstrated a new paradigm approach to feedback. These cases have served as a rich source of learning about the characteristics of the teachers and the environments in which they work that foster and enable such innovative approaches to thrive. We now synthesise what we have learned from these cases about individual and contextual enablers to the adoption of new paradigm feedback practices. As discussed in Chapter 1, these influences can operate at the level of the individual and their local setting, the policies and regulations that guide an individual's practice, as well as features of the dominant disciplinary culture. We further contextualise these enablers through quotations from the Feedback Cultures interviews, where respondents also identified similar enablers as important influences on innovation in feedback processes.

Individual enablers

Within the cases that we have discussed, we have seen evidence of the influence of dispositional characteristics that act as enablers on an individual level. For example, Claire (Chapter 3) and Kennedy (Chapter 7) exemplified enthusiasm in teaching; being at relatively early stage of their careers, they showed commitment to place student learning at the heart of their practice. In Chapter 4, we saw how Jaclyn's reflective approach to practice, alongside her vision and leadership, enabled herself and her team to develop an effective approach to feedback processes with large cohorts. The evidence from Chapter 5 illustrates how Rick's passion for teaching drives him to re-engineer assessment and feedback practices to focus on a rich student learning experience. His sustained involvement in the course he teaches has facilitated a deep understanding of students' needs and how assessment can be engineered to promote effective student learning processes. The cases of Rick and Min (Chapters 5 and 8) are also illustrative of the value of ongoing refinement of practice. It is often the case that pedagogical trends and the quest for innovation seem to encourage teachers to be innovating relentlessly. Both Rick and Min have been refining their practices in conversation with their students for more than a decade. Working within cultures that value the slow accumulation of experience and expertise support these developments. Several of our case practitioners showed strong levels of engagement with the literature on learning-focused approaches to feedback, including contributing to that evidence base through their own research. Robert Nash (Chapter 2) and Kennedy Chan (Chapter 7) have both worked collaboratively with the co-authors and this enables mutually beneficial insights to evolve.

Teacher feedback literacy is central to the possibilities for new paradigm feedback practices: without teacher feedback literacy, it is unlikely that student feedback literacy will develop. Our inductive analysis of the practice of the eight teachers featured in Chapters 2–9 leads us to infer a series of characteristics of feedback literate teachers (see Box 10.1). Crucially, the practices of feedback literate teachers implicitly or explicitly develop aspects of student feedback literacy: they encourage students to see the value of feedback processes; they involve students in making judgements about their own work and that of others; and they strive to design their courses in ways that encourage student action in response to feedback.

Box 10.1 Characteristics of teacher feedback literacy

Feedback literate teachers:

- Possess many of the attributes of effective teachers. Good teaching correlates with effective feedback practices.
- Are receptive to pedagogic and feedback ideas from various sources. They adapt their ideas for use with their students, and they reflect upon and refine these strategies over time.
- Involve students in a range of practices congruent with new paradigm thinking: the development of students' feedback literacy; student engagement with feedback; technology-enabled feedback; assessment designs for feedback; dialogic feedback; internal feedback and self-regulated learning; and peer feedback.
- Are sensitive to the relational elements within a supportive feedback culture. They seek to develop open and trusting relationships with students' best interests at heart.
- Place student progress and improvement at the core of their practice. They design feedback processes in ways that promote student uptake.
- Develop strategies to overcome institutional and contextual challenges, such as disciplinary conventions or large class sizes.
- Collaborate with colleagues at a team, project, programme, or institutional level to share and promote good feedback practice; are pro-active in discussing feedback ideas formally or informally.

Contextual enablers

We have also seen how dimensions of the context in which the practitioners work can serve as enablers to innovation. Claire's case (Chapter 3) demonstrates that engagement in courses such as PGCert programmes can provide not just training but a space to reflect and engage in dialogue with peers and share ideas. For Claire, her engagement with this programme was a source of empowerment, facilitating her development of innovative approaches to practice. The influence of CPD can be enhanced where engagement with such opportunities is encouraged at a departmental level.

A departmental or institutional commitment towards student-staff partnerships is also a strong enabler to new paradigm approaches to feedback. Partnerships exemplify that feedback is not something done *to* students but an ongoing process in which they participate fully. This should include an active role in design, for example by co-designing assessment tasks, co-creating rubrics, and having input into the nature and timing of feedback processes. This ethos of student-staff partnerships also relates to maximising the impact of feedback. If we see feedback as a two-way process, then students' actions in response to feedback serve as an important source of information to staff about the efficacy and utility of their assessment and feedback designs. Creating a feedback culture predicated on student-staff partnerships also sends a powerful message about the importance of dialogue in feedback processes. In addition, valuing student input into the development of feedback practice is also likely to foster innovation as it is the students who are driving the change process.

Partnership could extend to the idea of students as co-researchers, whereby staff and students collaborate on research and development projects seeking to enhance feedback processes. We provided an example of this kind of partnership in Chapter 4 by discussing the FEATS project at the University of Surrey, where students worked with academic staff and learning technologists to design a feedback e-portfolio. This approach grew out of research exploring the challenges students faced in the feedback process, and students created design briefs for the e-portfolio, considering what would work to make the feedback process more impactful for themselves and other students.

Examination of the cases and discussions in the Feedback Cultures interviews reveals that a highly significant enabler to the development of new paradigm feedback practices is working within a departmental or institutional culture that promotes and rewards innovation; for example, where "*innovation is part of our progression criteria for all that concern teaching*" (Participant 8). Both Claire (Chapter 3) and Emma (Chapter 9) described how they perceived their departments to value and encourage experimentation in feedback processes; these views were also expressed by many participants in the Feedback Cultures interviews. For example, one participant spoke of moving to a new institution, characterised by "*an environment where innovation, creative strategies … were much more part of the culture of the institution. The debates on innovative practices have really flourished*" (Participant 8). In contrast, cultures where maintenance of the status quo is the norm can lead to a risk averse approach, where innovation is less likely to flourish (Winstone, 2017). Leaders and managers working at the cross-institutional level also hold considerable power in facilitating the development and embedding of innovative approaches to feedback. In the FEATS project, leverage at the institutional level, in the form of strong support from senior management, facilitated the promotion of this new paradigm approach to feedback processes.

It is through the creation of a climate where innovation is valued that feedback cultures that promote and normalise new paradigm thinking can thrive. In the Feedback Cultures interviews, it was clear that some respondents were seeking a 'champion' of certain approaches in order to encourage them to innovate: "*It's not within our culture. I think what it needs is someone to start it and to champion it*" (Participant 27). Others explained that they would be more likely to try something new if it were perceived to be the norm rather than the exception: "*it's an institutional culture thing as well. I think if everyone was doing audio feedback then I'd join in*" (Participant 14).

Sometimes, it takes a shift in departmental or institutional cultures to open up dialogue around new paradigm feedback processes, raising their status and encouraging innovation: "*there's been a real emphasis on the assessment process, particularly within the last five years. I think we're seeing quite a shift at the moment in terms of the use of formative feedback*" (Participant 22). Change can be facilitated where a different emphasis on feedback is seen as "*the done thing*" (Participant 7), for example where across an institution there is a shift resulting in "*more attention being paid to students understanding the feedback*" (Participant 20).

There is also potential for enhancement of feedback practice to be stimulated by quality assurance and quality enhancement processes. By identifying areas of practice that might benefit from enhancement, programme reviews, stakeholder input, or external examiner reports can act as a stimulus for renewal. Quality enhancement agendas can provide opportunities for academic developers or managers overseeing teaching and learning to work with colleagues in developing action plans. When these are handled well, they sometimes involve a wider sample of colleagues than those who would be typical innovators or natural participants in teaching and learning development activities.

Thus, feedback cultures where innovation is encouraged and rewarded, where students play a fundamental role in feedback design, and where dialogue around feedback practice is commonplace, may enable the development of new paradigm feedback approaches. In contrast, feedback cultures focused on adherence to the status quo may inhibit the development of new paradigm approaches to feedback. Nevertheless, these broader, contextual features can be influenced by individual and team approaches to feedback practice. We now consider ways through which individuals, teams, departments, and institutions can critically evaluate their own approaches to feedback.

Evaluating and developing practice

As discussed in the Introduction to this book, the Feedback Cultures project comprised three strands of work: seeking to understand practice pertinent to new paradigm feedback approaches; to understand drivers of practice; and to consider how practice might be advanced in directions aligned with new paradigm thinking. In this next section, we present modified versions of some of the tools used within the project that can be used by individuals, course teams, and academic developers to facilitate reflection, examination, and development of practice. These tools can be used as a basis for discussion, to identify priorities for development, or to track change in beliefs and practices over time.

The first tool (Box 10.2) provides an opportunity to take a snapshot of current practice, either at the level of an individual unit/module, a programme, or within the context of an individual's practice.

Box 10.2 Evaluating your practice

How often do you use the following in your own practice?
(1 = Never; 2 = Sometimes; 3 = Regularly; 4 = Always)

		Never	*Sometimes*	*Regularly*	*Always*
		1	*2*	*3*	*4*
1	Discuss with students the purpose and meaning of feedback				
2	Encourage students to recognise feedback exchanges beyond summative feedback on written work				
3	Support students to develop a range of strategies to implement their feedback				
4	Consider the emotional impact of feedback on students				
5	Invite students to request feedback on specific elements of their work				
6	Support students to develop the skills to evaluate their own work				
7	Provide opportunities for students to engage in peer feedback exchanges				
8	Provide opportunities for students to contribute to the design of assessment criteria/ rubrics				
9	Consider opportunities for implementation of feedback at the point of assessment design				
10	Relate feedback to programme learning outcomes/graduate attributes as well as module/ unit learning outcomes				
11	Use technology to facilitate student uptake of feedback				
12	Seek evidence of the impact of your feedback on students' learning				

Scoring:
Totalling your scores for items 1, 2, 3 and 4 provides a self-evaluation of your orientation to students' feedback literacy.
Totalling your scores for items 5, 6, 7 and 8 provides a self-evaluation of the extent to which you involve students actively in feedback processes.
Totalling your scores for items 9, 10, 11 and 12 provides a self-evaluation of the quality of your feedback designs.
There are no reverse-coded items.

On the basis of the scores on this tool, it is possible to explore where practice is more or less closely aligned with new paradigm approaches to feedback. These questions might also help course teams to identify priorities for development in a programmatic approach to assessment and feedback.

The next tool (Box 10.3) facilitates reflection on one's own fundamental beliefs about the importance of feedback, and the role it plays in student learning.

Box 10.3 Evaluating your beliefs about feedback

Please rate your agreement with the following statements on the following scale:
(1 = Strongly disagree; 2 = Disagree; 3 = Neutral; 4 = Agree; 5 = Strongly agree)

		Strongly disagree	Disagree	Neutral	Agree	Strongly agree
		1	2	3	4	5
1	Feedback is a powerful influence on learning					
2	Feedback is designed to convey to the student their level of performance					
3	Feedback is important in conveying to students how much their effort is valued					
4	Feedback is important in justifying the grade that has been awarded					
5	Feedback helps students to judge their own performance					
6	Feedback is important in demonstrating that assessment procedures are transparent					

		Strongly disagree	Disagree	Neutral	Agree	Strongly agree
		1	2	3	4	5
7	Feedback is important in meeting quality assurance requirements					
8	Feedback is important in helping students to manage their own learning					
9	Feedback from peers is effective in developing students' learning					
10	Effective feedback is important in ensuring high levels of student satisfaction					

Scoring:

Summing your scores for items 2, 4, 6, 7 and 10 will inform you how strongly you align with the principles underpinning a transmission-focused (old paradigm) approach to feedback.

Summing your scores for items 1, 3, 5, 8 and 9 will inform you how strongly you align with the principles underpinning a learning-focused (new paradigm) approach to feedback.

There are no reverse-coded items.

It may well be that an individual finds that it is difficult to disagree with any of these statements. It is not the case that beliefs aligned with an old paradigm approach are 'wrong', just as beliefs representing new paradigm thinking are not automatically 'right'. It is reflection on the *relative* importance of the statements that can provide insight into where practice can be developed. For example, just because an individual believes feedback to be important in justifying grades, this does not mean that they cannot also adopt learning-focused practices. However, if they believe that the grade justification function of feedback is more important than its learning function, then this might illustrate that their beliefs align more strongly with an old rather than new paradigm approach to feedback. This tool could also be used to open up discussions with students about the purpose of feedback, if given to students to complete. It may also help to surface misalignments in the perceptions of staff and students, or between staff teaching on the same unit/module or programme.

In Chapter 2, we argued that all of the approaches to feedback discussed in this book are in some way related to the development of students' feedback literacy. The final tool uses the framework of feedback literacy proposed by

Carless and Boud (2018) as a way of evaluating existing practices that support students' involvement in feedback processes, and as a way of considering potential areas for innovation (Box 10.4).

Box 10.4 Developing your practice

For each element of Carless and Boud's (2018) framework of feedback literacy, consider what you already do in your practice to helps students develop each area of competence. Next, consider how you could develop your practice to incorporate further opportunities for students to develop these attributes and skills.

	Feedback literate students:	*What you do/could do in your practice?*
Appreciating feedback	Understand and appreciate the role of feedback in improving work and the active learner role in these processes	
	Recognise that feedback information comes in different forms and from different sources	
	Use technology to access, store, and revisit feedback	
Making judgements	Develop capacities to make sound academic judgements about their own work and the work of others	
	Participate productively in peer feedback processes	
	Refine self-evaluative capacities over time in order to make more robust judgements	
Managing affect	Maintain emotional equilibrium and avoid defensiveness when receiving critical feedback	
	Are proactive in eliciting suggestions from peers or teachers and continuing dialogue with them as needed	
	Develop habits of striving for continuous improvement on the basis of internal and external feedback	
Taking action	Are aware of the imperative to take action in response to feedback information	
	Draw inferences from a range of feedback experiences for the purpose of continuous improvement	
	Develop a repertoire of strategies for acting on feedback	

Future directions for research and practice

Through listening to the voices of teachers, synthesising evidence from the literature, and exploring cases of practice as part of the Feedback Cultures project, we have identified a number of good practices and inspiring examples of thoughtful feedback designs. There are many ongoing challenges in the enactment of feedback processes and we have also discussed many limitations of the current evidence base. We now consider some key priorities for the development of research and practice (see Figure 10.2). We see the development of research and practice as inherently interlinked, as represented in Figure 10.2. Research should respond to issues identified in practice and the changing landscape of higher education, just as practice should draw upon the research literature.

In setting a research agenda to inform our understanding of feedback processes that facilitate student learning, a key priority is to seek evidence of the effects of feedback on measures other than student perceptions as gathered using self-report instruments. The field needs to move beyond the dominance of survey methods, towards research designs that collect behavioural data, and even physiological and neurophysiological measures of the processing and outcomes of feedback. Longitudinal work is also essential, if we are to understand the impact of feedback on students' cognitive, motivational, and behavioural landscapes over the course of their programmes. If our focus on a new paradigm approach to feedback is to place emphasis on student involvement and use of feedback, and the impact of feedback on students' learning, then the field needs to shift towards the dominant use of research methods that enable us to answer the research questions that really matter.

The Feedback Cultures project has revealed how individual, departmental, and institutional characteristics interact to create an environment in which learning-focused feedback processes either thrive or are inhibited in their growth. There is great potential to understand better not only how such cultures develop and are maintained, but how they change over time in response to ever-changing policy

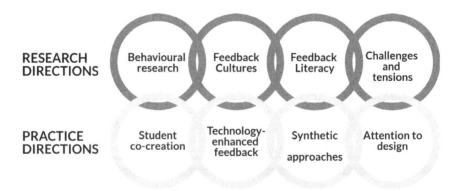

Figure 10.2 Future directions for feedback research and practice

drivers (such as national frameworks that evaluate 'excellence' in research and teaching), the shifting role of the student in higher education (for example due to the prominence of metrics such as the National Student Survey and the rise in tuition fees), and the financial and political climates.

The publication of Carless and Boud's (2018) paper on feedback literacy has itself posed a number of important directions for future research. In the context of a new paradigm approach to feedback, the development of staff and student feedback literacy is essential to the sustainability of processes where teachers and their students assume joint responsibility for ensuring that feedback is impactful. A key endeavour is to establish the efficacy of different instructional approaches that aim to facilitate the development of feedback literacy, and to chart how feedback literacy develops over time and in response to growing experience with feedback processes. The relationships between staff and student feedback literacy are also an important avenue of enquiry.

Central to any future research agenda is gaining a strong appreciation of the challenges and tensions inherent to the enactment of feedback processes 'on the ground'. It is only when armed with this knowledge that we can begin to create environments where practice can meaningfully develop towards new paradigm principles. In this chapter we have made some tentative suggestions as to how particular barriers might be tackled, but these suggestions merely represent empirical questions that require testing through rigorous research programmes.

Moving to consideration of future practice directions, our first suggestion is that in a new paradigm feedback culture we will need to place greater emphasis on student co-creation. By this, we mean that if students are to play a more significant role in feedback processes, this should involve not just engagement and action after work has been completed, but involvement in the development of criteria, rubrics, and feedback at earlier stages of the cycle. In this book, we have presented many ideas as to how students can become more involved in feedback processes, and we argue that if meaningful partnerships are to be created, students need to have ownership of key feedback-related artefacts.

Technology can be used to facilitate developments in feedback processes away from transmission and towards student involvement. Thus, we see much promise for future practice developments involving different technological approaches, but here we re-emphasise our argument in Chapter 4 regarding the importance of specific affordances of technology in the feedback process. Many different tools already exist, and we predict that many more will come to the market in future years. If such tools are to facilitate student learning through feedback processes, then decision-making should be driven by a specific vision where the technology affords a beneficial outcome that meets new paradigm principles, not just a time-saving gain for teachers. We also believe that digital tools are more likely to benefit students, and that students are more likely to 'buy-in' to the use of these tools, if they themselves are involved in the co-design of technological solutions to common feedback challenges.

The development of feedback practice away from a transmission focus is likely to require us to look beyond individual feedback events or instances, to a synthetic perspective where the learning potential of feedback is realised through looking at the bigger picture. Too much focus on individual modules or units limits the learning potential of feedback because the transfer of learning through feedback is less apparent to students, and the impact of feedback on students' learning is often invisible to teachers. Programmatic approaches to assessment and feedback (as discussed in Chapter 5) focus on a student's overall learning journey, and practices that support students to synthesise feedback from multiple assignments (as discussed in Chapter 4) also hold promise in maximising the impact of feedback.

Finally, we propose that the starting point for practice that facilitates student learning through feedback has to be assessment and feedback design. Opportunities for students to learn through feedback need to be designed into assessment cycles from the outset. Designing into curricula prospects for the development of student feedback literacy is likely to be more effective than delivering one-off sessions, and opportunities for peer feedback and self-evaluation also need careful planning.

Conclusion

What we are seeing in the research literature and in pockets of good practice are the beginnings of a paradigm shift away from an approach to feedback characterised by the transmission of comments from expert to novice, to a learning-focused model characterised by student engagement and action. In this book, we have argued that fully realising this paradigm shift requires us to look beyond student satisfaction to student learning, beyond comments to opportunities to implement feedback, and beyond feedback-related artefacts such as standardised proformas to meaningful dialogue in the feedback process. However, we have also suggested that small shifts in practice can add up to create more significant changes in culture. In Box 10.6, we summarise the key ideas presented throughout the book regarding the design of effective feedback processes. As with any key development, a crucial enabler is a critical mass of individuals working towards the goal. With that in mind, we invite readers to consider what small changes you will now make to your own practice, and how you will share your learning with your colleagues and your students. Perhaps you will become a 'champion' of new paradigm practices, and thus influence the practice of others. We encourage you to view the enhancement of feedback processes as the shared responsibility of yourself and your students in partnership. The strength and authenticity of the relationships between teachers and students are a crucial facilitator to learning through feedback. Finally, we encourage you to revisit your own approach to feedback in the courses that you teach. The impact of feedback on student learning rarely happens by chance; student uptake builds upon meaningful feedback design.

Box 10.5 Questions for reflection and debate

- What is the most important thing you could do to enhance feedback processes in your teaching or your institution?
- How might students react to new paradigm feedback practices? To what extent and how would teachers need to convince them of the benefits?
- To what extent are discourses of students as consumers a barrier to the development of feedback practices which demand active student involvement? How might barriers be overcome? Are staff-student partnership approaches a potential way forward?
- How could you promote new paradigm feedback practices to a senior leader in your institution?

Box 10.6 30 key ideas in designing for uptake of feedback

Designs: design assessment tasks to encourage students to seek, generate, and use feedback.

Assessment sequences: design iterative sequences of assessment tasks to encourage students to use feedback from one task to another.

Student feedback literacy: design assessment and feedback to encourage students to appreciate feedback, make judgements, manage affective factors, and take action.

Social constructivism: individual and shared feedback interpretations are co-constructed through interaction.

Rubrics and criteria: enable students to appreciate expectations by involving them actively in co-constructing or making sense of criteria and standards.

Exemplars: discuss a range of exemplars of different qualities to enable students to appreciate what good work looks like.

Exams: clarify expectations through discussion of exemplars of prior performance; design latent feedback from coursework to apply to exam tasks; provide generic feedback on previous year's exam as part of revision strategies.

Engagement: design feedback processes to promote student engagement, sense-making, and action.

Turn-around times: less important than opportunities to act; design sequences where feedback informs next task.

Technology: design technology use for students to seek, generate, and act on feedback; use e-portfolios as opportunities for student self-evaluation and for revisiting and synthesising previous feedback.

Audiovisual tools: use audio, video, and screencast modes of feedback to promote student sense-making, response and uptake.

Self-regulation: good feedback practice enhances students' capacities to self-evaluate performance and self-regulate their own learning.

Sustainable feedback: design feedback so that students take responsibility for their own learning.

Dialogue: design user-friendly opportunities for students to interact with peers and teachers.

Interactive coversheets: invite students to state on the assignment coversheet what feedback they would most like to receive; require them to state on the coversheet what previous feedback they are acting upon.

Large classes: clarify expectations; share exemplars; design rich tasks which engage and motivate students; use technology to promote interaction; provide opportunities for peer feedback.

Low achievers: provide mentoring through peer learning, exposure to exemplars, and supportive feedback.

Peer feedback: both composing and receiving peer feedback are beneficial; train and coach students to appreciate peer feedback and do it better.

Modelling: share with students your own experiences of peer review in academia including emotional reactions, perseverance, and a focus on uptake.

Relational: feedback needs to be honest and shared with empathy in ways which support students to grow.

Students as co-researchers: involve students in research and development projects on assessment and feedback.

Students as partners: negotiate assessment tasks; give students the opportunity to co-construct criteria; provide feedback that addresses students' needs and interests.

Resources: reduce comments at times when they cannot reasonably be taken up and devote more resources to feedback designs to support student action.

Programme-level: develop a more connected flow of assessments across a programme to facilitate more effective cycles of feedback.

Feedback awards: surface, recognise, reward, and disseminate principled feedback designs through Faculty and institutional awards for good feedback practice.

Scaling up: use informal networks to encourage a climate of innovation; promote the role of champions in leading change; solicit support from colleagues, middle and senior management.

Shared feedback literacy: embed the co-development of staff and student feedback literacy through a selected sample of the above, including at a programme-based level.

Feedback cultures: develop environments where innovation is promoted and celebrated; provide informal learning opportunities; facilitate opportunities for cross-disciplinary dialogue.

Marginal gains: consider making small changes to feedback practices that can add up to an overall shift towards new paradigm practices.

New paradigm: comments on student work are just information until they are used by students.

References

Adcroft, A. (2011). The mythology of feedback. *Higher Education Research and Development*, 30(4), 405–419.

Ajjawi, R., & Boud, D. (2017). Researching feedback dialogue: An interactional analysis approach. *Assessment and Evaluation in Higher Education*, 42(2), 252–265.

Ajjawi, R., & Boud, D. (2018). Examining the nature and effects of feedback dialogue. *Assessment and Evaluation in Higher Education*, 43(7), 1106–1119.

Ajjawi, R., Molloy, E., Bearman, M., & Rees, C. E. (2017). Contextual influences on feedback practices: An ecological perspective. In D. Carless, S. M. Bridges, C. K. Y. Chan & R. Glofcheski (Eds.), *Scaling up assessment for learning in higher education* (Vol. 5, pp. 129–143). (The enabling power of assessment; Vol. 5). Singapore, Asia: Springer.

Ajjawi, R., Schofield, S., McAleer, S., & Walker, D. (2013). Assessment and feedback dialogue in online distance learning. *Medical Education*, 47(5), 527–528.

Alvarez, I., Espasa, A., & Guasch, T. (2012). The value of feedback in improving collaborative writing assignments in an online learning environment. *Studies in Higher Education*, 37(4), 387–400.

Anderson, C. (2014). Only connect? Communicating meaning through feedback. In C. Kreber, C. Anderson, N. Entwistle & J. McArthur (Eds.), *Advances and innovations in university assessment and feedback* (pp. 131–151). Edinburgh, UK: Edinburgh University Press.

Andrade, H. (2010). Students as the definitive source of formative assessment: Academic self-assessment and the self-regulation of learning. In H. Andrade & G. Cizek (Eds.), *Handbook of Formative Assessment* (pp. 90–105). New York: Routledge.

Anson, C. M., Dannels, D. P., Laboy, J. I., & Carneiro, L. (2016). Students' perceptions of oral screencast responses to their writing: Exploring digitally mediated identities. *Journal of Business and Technical Communication*, 30(3), 378–411.

Askew, S., & Lodge, C. (2000). Gifts, ping-pong and loops – linking feedback and learning. In S. Askew (Ed.), *Feedback for Learning* (pp. 1–18). London: Routledge Falmer.

Ballantyne, R., Hughes, K., & Mylonas, A. (2002). Developing peer assessment procedures for implementing peer assessment in large classes using an action research process. *Assessment and Evaluation in Higher Education*, 27(5), 427–441.

Balloo, K., Evans, C., Hughes, A., Zhu, X., & Winstone, N. (2018). Transparency isn't spoon-feeding: How a transformative approach to the use of explicit assessment criteria can support student self-regulation. *Frontiers in Education*, 3(69), 1–11.

Bandura, A. (1997). *Self-efficacy: The exercise of control*. New York: Freeman.

Barton, K. L., Schofield, S. J., McAleer, S., & Ajjawi, R. (2016). Translating evidence-based guidelines to improve feedback practices: The interACT case study. *BMC Medical Education*, 16(1), 53–64.

Beaumont, C., O'Doherty, M., & Shannon, L. (2011). Reconceptualising assessment feedback: A key to improving student learning? *Studies in Higher Education*, 36(6), 671–687.

Bevitt, S. (2015). Assessment innovation and student experience: A new assessment challenge and call for a multi-perspective approach to assessment research. *Assessment and Evaluation in Higher Education*, 40(1), 103–119.

Blair, A., Goodwin, M., Shields, S., & Wyburn-Powell, A. (2014). Can dialogue help to improve feedback on examinations? *Studies in Higher Education*, 39(6), 1039–1054.

Blair, A., & McGinty, S. (2013). Feedback-dialogues: Exploring the student perspective. *Assessment and Evaluation in Higher Education*, 38(4), 466–476.

Bloxham, S., & Campbell, L. (2010). Generating dialogue in assessment feedback: Exploring the use of interactive cover sheets. *Assessment and Evaluation in Higher Education*, 35(3), 291–300.

Bloxham, S., & West, A. (2004). Understanding the rules of the game: Marking peer assessment as a medium for developing students' conceptions of assessment. *Assessment and Evaluation in Higher Education*, 29(6), 721–733.

Bloxham, S., & West, A. (2007). Learning to write in higher education: Students' perceptions of an intervention in developing understanding of assessment criteria. *Teaching in Higher Education*, 12(1), 77–89.

Boud, D. (1995a). Assessment and learning: Contradictory or complementary. In P. Knight (Ed.) *Assessment for Learning in Higher Education* (pp. 35–48). London: Kogan Page.

Boud, D. (1995b). *Enhancing learning through self-assessment*. London: Kogan Page.

Boud, D. (2000). Sustainable assessment: Rethinking assessment for the learning society. *Studies in Continuing Education*, 22(2), 151–167.

Boud, D., & Brew, A. (2013). Reconceptualising academic work as professional practice: Implications for academic development. *International Journal for Academic Development*, 18(3), 208–221.

Boud, D., Cohen, R., & Sampson, J. (1999). Peer learning and assessment. *Assessment and Evaluation in Higher Education*, 24(4), 413–426.

Boud, D., & Falchikov, N. (2006). Aligning assessment with long-term learning. *Assessment and Evaluation in Higher Education*, 31(4), 399–413.

Boud, D., & Falchikov, N. (2007). Developing assessment for informing judgment. In D. Boud & N. Falchikov (Eds.), *Rethinking Assessment in Higher Education* (pp. 181–197). London: Routledge.

Boud, D., Lawson, R., & Thompson, D. (2013). Does student engagement in self-assessment calibrate their judgement over time? *Assessment and Evaluation in Higher Education*, 38(8), 941–956.

Boud, D., Lawson, R., & Thompson, D. (2015). The calibration of student judgement through self-assessment: Disruptive effects of assessment patterns. *Higher Education Research and Development*, 34(1), 45–59.

Boud, D., & Molloy, E. (2013). Rethinking models of feedback for learning: The challenge of design. *Assessment and Evaluation in Higher Education*, 38(6), 698–712.

Bounds, R., Bush, C., Aghera, A., Rodriguez, N., Stansfield, R. B., & Santen, S. A. (2013). Emergency medicine residents' self-assessments play a critical role when receiving feedback. *Academic Emergency Medicine*, 20(10), 1055–1061.

Bourke, R. (2014). Self-assessment in professional programmes within tertiary institutions. *Teaching in Higher Education*, 19(8), 908–918.

Bovill, C., Cook-Sather, A., Felten, P., Millard, L., & Moore-Cherry, N. (2016). Addressing potential challenges in co-creating learning and teaching: Overcoming resistance, navigating institutional norms and ensuring inclusivity in student-staff partnerships. *Higher Education*, 71(2), 195–208.

Bretag, T., Harper, R., Burton, M., Ellis, C., Newton, P., van Haeringen, K., Saddiqui, S., & Rosenberg, P. (2019). Contract cheating and assessment design: Exploring the relationship. *Assessment and Evaluation in Higher Education*, (44)5, 676–691.

Broadbent, J., Panadero, E., & Boud, D. (2018). Implementing summative assessment with a formative flavour: A case study in a large class. *Assessment and Evaluation in Higher Education*, 43(2), 307–322.

Bronfenbrenner, U. (1979). *The ecology of human development*. Cambridge, MA: Harvard University Press.

Brown, G. T. L., & Harris, L. (2013). Student self-assessment. In J. McMillan (Ed.), *The SAGE handbook of research on classroom assessment* (pp. 367–393). Thousand Oaks, CA: SAGE.

Brown, G. T. L., Peterson, E., & Yao, E. (2016). Student conceptions of feedback: Impact on self-regulation, self-efficacy and academic achievement. *British Journal of Educational Psychology*, 86(4), 606–629.

Brown, J. (2007). Feedback: The student perspective. *Research in Post-Compulsory Education*, 12(1), 33–51.

Burke, D. (2009). Strategies for using feedback students bring to higher education. *Assessment and Evaluation in Higher Education*, 34(1), 41–50.

Butler, D., & Winne, P. (1995). Feedback and self-regulated learning: A theoretical synthesis. *Review of Educational Research*, 65(3), 245–274.

Cadinu, M. R., & Cerchioni, M. (2001). Compensatory biases after ingroup threat: 'Yeah, but we have a good personality'. *European Journal of Social Psychology*, 31(4), 353–367.

Calvo, R. A., & Ellis, R. A. (2010). Students' conceptions of tutor and automated feedback in professional writing. *Journal of Engineering Education*, 99(4), 427–438.

Carless, D. (2006). Differing perceptions in the feedback process. *Studies in Higher Education*, 31(2), 219–233.

Carless, D. (2013). Trust and its role in facilitating dialogic feedback. In D. Boud & E. Molloy (Eds.), *Feedback in higher and professional education* (pp. 90–103). London: Routledge.

Carless, D. (2015a). *Excellence in university assessment: Learning from award-winning practice*. London: Routledge.

Carless, D. (2015b). Exploring learning-oriented assessment processes. *Higher Education*, 69(6), 963–976.

Carless, D. (2017). Students' experiences of assessment for learning. In D. Carless, S. Bridges, C. K. W. Chan & R. Glofcheski (Eds.), *Scaling up assessment for learning in higher education* (pp. 113–126). Singapore: Springer.

Carless, D. (2019). Feedback loops and the longer-term: Towards feedback spirals. *Assessment and Evaluation in Higher Education*, 44(5), 705–714.

Carless, D., & Boud, D. (2018). The development of student feedback literacy: Enabling uptake of feedback. *Assessment and Evaluation in Higher Education*, 43(8), 1315–1325.

Carless, D., & Chan, K. K. H. (2017). Managing dialogic use of exemplars. *Assessment and Evaluation in Higher Education*, 42(6), 930–941.

Carless, D., Salter, D., Yang, M., & Lam, J. (2011). Developing sustainable feedback practices. *Studies in Higher Education*, 36(4), 395–407.

Cartney, P. (2010). Exploring the use of peer assessment as a vehicle for closing the gap between feedback given and feedback used. *Assessment and Evaluation in Higher Education*, 35(5), 551–564.

Cassidy, J., Ziv, Y., Mehta, T. G., & Feeney, B. C. (2003). Feedback seeking in children and adolescents: Associations with self-perceptions, attachment representations, and depression. *Child Development*, 74(2), 612–628.

Chalmers, C., Mowat, E., & Chapman, M. (2018). Marking and providing feedback face-to-face: Staff and student perspectives. *Active Learning in Higher Education*, 19(1), 35–45.

Chanock, K. (2000). Comments on essays: Do students understand what tutors write? *Teaching in Higher Education*, 5(1), 95–105.

Cho, K., & MacArthur, C. (2010). Student revision with peer and expert reviewing. *Learning and Instruction*, 20(4), 328–338.

Cho, K., & MacArthur, C. (2011). Learning by reviewing. *Journal of Educational Psychology*, 103(1), 73–84.

Clarke, J. L., & Boud, D. (2018). Refocusing portfolio assessment: Curating for feedback and portrayal. *Innovations in Education and Teaching International*, 55(4), 479–486.

Clear, J. (2018). *Atomic habits*. New York: Random House.

Court, K. (2014). Tutor feedback on draft essays: Developing students' academic writing and subject knowledge. *Journal of Further and Higher Education*, 38(3), 327–345.

Crommelinck, M., & Anseel, F. (2013). Understanding and encouraging feedback-seeking behaviour: A literature review. *Medical Education*, 47(3), 232–241.

Crook, A., Mauchline, A., Maw, S., Lawson, C., Drinkwater, R., Lundqvist, K., … & Park, J. (2012). The use of video technology for providing feedback to students: Can it enhance the feedback experience for staff and students? *Computers & Education*, 58(1), 386–396.

Dawson, P., Henderson, M., Mahoney, P., Phillips, M., Ryan, T., Boud, D., & Molloy, E. (2019). What makes for effective feedback: Staff and student perspectives. *Assessment and Evaluation in Higher Education*, 44(1), 25–36.

Dawson, P., & Sutherland-Smith, W. (2018). Can markers detect contract cheating? Results from a pilot study. *Assessment and Evaluation in Higher Education*, 43(2), 286–293.

Debuse, J., & Lawley, M. (2016). Benefits and drawbacks of computer-based assessment and feedback systems: Student and educator perspectives. *British Journal of Educational Technology*, 47(2), 294–301.

Deeley, S. J. (2018). Using technology to facilitate effective assessment for learning and feedback in higher education. *Assessment and Evaluation in Higher Education*, 43(3), 439–448.

Deeley, S., & Bovill, C. (2017). Staff student partnership in assessment: Enhancing assessment literacy through democratic practices. *Assessment and Evaluation in Higher Education*, 42(3), 463–477.

Dekker, H., Schonrock-Adema, J., Snoek, J., van der Molen, T., & Cohen-Schotanus, J. (2013). Which characteristics of written feedback are perceived as stimulating students' reflective competence: An exploratory study. *BMC Medical Education*, 13(1), 1–7.

Dochy, F., Segers, M., & Sluijsmans, D. (1999). The use of self-, peer and co-assessment in higher education: A review. *Studies in Higher Education*, 24(3), 331–350.

Doria, M., O'Neill, T., & Brutus, S. (2018). The longitudinal effects of peer feedback in the development and transfer of student teamwork skills. *Learning and Individual Differences*, 61, 87–98.

Douglas, T., Salter, S., Iglesias, M., Dowlman, M., & Eri, R. (2016). The feedback process: Perspectives of first and second year undergraduate students in the disciplines of education, health science and nursing. *Journal of University Teaching & Learning Practice*, 13(1), 3.

Duncan, N. (2007). 'Feed-forward': Improving students' use of tutors' comments. *Assessment and Evaluation in Higher Education*, 32(3), 271–283.

Eddy, P., & Lawrence, A. (2013). Wikis as platforms for authentic assessment. *Innovative Higher Education*, 38(4), 253–265.

Edwards, M. R., & Clinton, M. E. (2019). A study exploring the impact of lecture capture availability and lecture capture usage on student attendance and attainment. *Higher Education*, 77(3), 403–421.

Enomoto, K. (2012). A study skills action plan: Integrating self-regulated learning in a diverse higher education context. In X. Song & K. Cadman (Eds.), *Bridging transcultural divides: Asian languages and cultures in global higher education* (pp. 101–130). Adelaide, Australia: University of Adelaide Press.

Esterhazy, R. (2018). What matters for productive feedback? Disciplinary practices and their relational dynamics. *Assessment and Evaluation in Higher Education*, 43(8), 1302–1314.

Esterhazy, R., & Damşa, C. (2019). Unpacking the feedback process: An analysis of undergraduate students' interactional meaning-making of feedback comments. *Studies in Higher Education*, 44(2), 260–274.

Evans, C. (2013). Making sense of assessment feedback in higher education. *Review of Educational Research*, 83(1), 70–120.

Falchikov, N. (2003). Involving students in assessment. *Psychology Learning and Teaching*, 32(2), 102–108.

Falchikov, N., & Boud, D. (1989). Student self-assessment in higher education: A meta-analysis. *Review of Educational Research*, 59(4), 395–430.

Ferguson, P. (2011). Student perceptions of quality feedback in teacher education. *Assessment and Evaluation in Higher Education*, 36(1), 51–62.

Fernández-Toro, M., & Furnborough, C. (2014). Feedback on feedback: Eliciting learners' responses to written feedback through student-generated screencasts. *Educational Media International*, 51(1), 35–48.

Fishbach, A., & Finkelstein, S. R. (2012). How feedback influences persistence, disengagement, and change in goal pursuit. In H. Aarts & A. J. Elliot (Eds.), *Frontiers of social psychology. Goal-directed behavior* (pp. 203–230). New York, NY: Psychology Press.

Fong, C. J., Patall, E. A., Vasquez, A. C., & Stautberg, S. (2019). A meta-analysis of negative feedback on intrinsic motivation. *Educational Psychology Review*, 31(1), 121–162.

Fong, C. J., Schallert, D. L., Williams, K. M., Williamson, Z. H., Warner, J. R., Lin, S., & Kim, Y. W. (2018). When feedback signals failure but offers hope for improvement: A process model of constructive criticism. *Thinking Skills and Creativity*, 30, 42–53.

Fong, C. J., Warner, J. R., Williams, K. M., Schallert, D. L., Chen, L. H., Williamson, Z. H., & Lin, S. (2016). Deconstructing constructive criticism: The nature of academic emotions associated with constructive, positive, and negative feedback. *Learning and Individual Differences*, 49, 393–399.

Förster, M., Weiser, C., & Maur, A. (2018). How feedback provided by voluntary electronic quizzes affects learning outcomes of university students in large classes. *Computers & Education*, 121, 100–114.

Forsythe, A., & Johnson, S. (2017). Thanks, but no-thanks for the feedback. *Assessment and Evaluation in Higher Education*, 42(6), 850–859.

Fullan, M., & Langworthy, M. (2013). Towards a new end: New pedagogies for deep learning. Seattle, WA: Creative Commons. Retrieved 26/01/19from www.newpeda gogies.nl/images/towards_a_new_end.pdf.

Fung, D. (2016). *A connected curriculum for higher education*. London: UCL Press.

Gibbs, G. (1988). *Learning by doing: A guide*. Birmingham, UK: SCED.

Gibbs, G., & Dunbar-Goddet, H. (2009). Characterising programme level assessment environments that support learning. *Assessment and Evaluation in Higher Education*, 34 (4), 481–489.

Gibson, L., & Musti-Rao, S. (2016). Using technology to enhance feedback to student teachers. *Intervention in School and Clinic*, 51(5), 307–311.

Ginns, P., Kitay, J., & Prosser, M. (2010). Transfer of academic staff learning in a research-intensive university. *Teaching in Higher Education*, 15(3), 235–246.

Ginsburg, S., van der Vleuten, C., Eva, K. W., & Lingard, L. (2016). Hedging to save face: A linguistic analysis of written comments on in-training evaluation reports. *Advances in Health Sciences Education*, 21(1), 175–188.

Glofcheski, R. (2017). Making assessment for learning happen through assessment task design in the law curriculum. In D. Carless, S. Bridges, C. K. W. Chan & R. Glofcheski (Eds.), *Scaling up assessment for learning in higher education* (pp. 67–80). Singapore: Springer.

Guasch, T., Espasa, A., & Martinez-Melo, M. (2019). The art of questioning in online learning environments: The potentialities of feedback in writing. *Assessment and Evaluation in Higher Education*, 44(1), 111–123.

Hadwin, A. F., Järvelä, S., & Miller, M. (2018). Self-regulation, co-regulation and shared regulation in collaborative learning environments. In D. H. Schunk & J. A. Greene (Eds.), *Handbook of self-regulation of learning and performance* (2nd ed.; pp. 83–106). New York: Routledge.

Hadwin, A. F., & Oshige, M. (2011). Self-regulation, coregulation, and socially shared regulation: Exploring perspectives of social in self-regulated learning theory. *Teachers College Record*, 113(2), 240–264.

Handley, K., Price, M., & Millar, J. (2011). Beyond 'doing time': Investigating the concept of student engagement with feedback. *Oxford Review of Education*, 37(4), 543–560.

Handley, K., & Williams, L. (2011). From copying to learning: Using exemplars to engage students with assessment criteria and feedback. *Assessment and Evaluation in Higher Education*, 36(1), 95–108.

Harrison, C. J., Könings, K. D., Schuwirth, L., Wass, V., & van der Vleuten, C. (2015). Barriers to the uptake and use of feedback in the context of summative assessment. *Advances in Health Sciences Education*, 20(1), 229–245.

Hattie, J., & Timperley, H. (2007). The power of feedback. *Review of Educational Research*, 77(1), 81–112.

Henderson, M., Ajjawi, R., Boud, D., & Molloy, E. (forthcoming, 2019). Feedback that makes a difference. In M. Henderson, R. Ajjawi, D. Boud, & E. Molloy (Eds.), *The impact of feedback in higher education*. London: Palgrave Macmillan.

Henderson, M., & Phillips, M. (2015). Video-based feedback on student assessment: Scarily personal. *Australasian Journal of Educational Technology*, 31(1), 51–66.

Hendry, G., Armstrong, S., & Bromberger, N. (2012). Implementing standards-based assessment effectively: Incorporating discussion of exemplars into classroom teaching. *Assessment and Evaluation in Higher Education*, 37(2), 149–161.

Hepplestone, S., & Chikwa, G. (2014). Understanding how students process and use feedback to support their learning. *Practitioner Research in Higher Education*, 8(1), 41–53.

Hepplestone, S., Holden, G., Irwin, B., Parkin, H. J., & Thorpe, L. (2011). Using technology to encourage student engagement with feedback: A literature review. *Research in Learning Technology*, 19(2), 117–127.

Higgins, R., Hartley, P., & Skelton, A. (2001). Getting the message across: The problem of communicating assessment feedback. *Teaching in Higher Education*, 6(2), 269–274.

Higgins, R., Hartley, P., & Skelton, A. (2002). The conscientious consumer: Reconsidering the role of assessment feedback in student learning. *Studies in Higher Education*, 27(1), 53–64.

Honicke, T., & Broadbent, J. (2016). The influence of academic self-efficacy on academic performance: A systematic review. *Educational Research Review*, 17, 63–84.

Hounsell, D. (2003). Student feedback, learning and development. In M. Slowey & D. Watson (Eds.), *Higher education and the lifecourse* (pp. 67–78). Maidenhead, UK: Society for Research into Higher Education.

Hounsell, D. (2007). Towards more Sustainable Feedback to Students. In D. Boud & N. Falchikov (Eds.), *Rethinking assessment in higher education* (pp. 101–113). London: Routledge.

Hounsell, D., McCune, V., Hounsell, J., & Litjens, J. (2008). The quality of guidance and feedback to students. *Higher Education Research and Development*, 27(1), 55–67.

Howe, P., McKague, M., Lodge, J., Blunden, A., & Saw, G. (2018). PeerWise: Evaluating the effectiveness of a web-based learning aid in a second year psychology subject. *Psychology Learning and Teaching*, 17(2), 166–176.

Hu, G. (2005). Using peer review with Chinese ESL student writers. *Language Teaching Research*, 9(3), 321–342.

Hu, G., & Lam, S. T. E. (2010). Issues of cultural appropriateness and pedagogical efficacy: Exploring peer review in a second language writing class. *Instructional Science*, 38(4), 371–394.

Hughes, G., Smith, H., & Creese, B. (2015). Not seeing the wood for the trees: Developing a feedback analysis tool to explore feed forward in modularised programmes. *Assessment and Evaluation in Higher Education*, 40(8), 1079–1094.

Huisman, B., Saab, N., van Driel, J., & van den Broek, P. (2018). Peer feedback on academic writing: Undergraduate students' peer feedback role, peer feedback perceptions and essay performance. *Assessment and Evaluation in Higher Education*, 43(6), 955–968.

Hung, S. T. A. (2016). Enhancing feedback provision through multimodal video technology. *Computers & Education*, 98, 90–101.

Hunsu, N. J., Adesope, O., & Bayly, D. J. (2016). A meta-analysis of the effects of audience response systems (clicker-based technologies) on cognition and affect. *Computers and Education*, 94, 102–119.

Huntsinger, J. R. (2013). Does emotion directly tune the scope of attention? *Current Directions in Psychological Science*, 22(4), 265–270.

Ilgen, D., & Davis, C. (2000). Bearing bad news: Reactions to negative performance feedback. *Applied Psychology*, 49(3), 550–565.

Jessop, T., El Hakim, Y., & Gibbs, G. (2014). The whole is greater than the sum of its parts: A large-scale study of students' learning in response to different programme assessment patterns. *Assessment and Evaluation in Higher Education*, 39(1), 73–88.

Jessop, T., McNab, N., & Gubby, L. (2012). Mind the gap: An analysis of how quality assurance processes influence programme assessment patterns. *Active Learning in Higher Education*, 13(2), 143–154.

Jessop, T., & Tomas, C. (2017). The implications of programme assessment patterns for student learning. *Assessment and Evaluation in Higher Education*, 42(6), 990–999.

Jolly, B., & Boud, D. (2013). Written feedback: What is it good for and how can we do it well? In D. Boud & E. Molloy (Eds.), *Feedback in higher and professional education* (p. 104–124). London: Routledge.

Jönsson, A. (2013). Facilitating productive use of feedback in higher education. *Active Learning in Higher Education*, 14(1), 63–76.

Jönsson, A., & Panadero, E. (2017). The use and design of rubrics to support assessment for learning. In D. Carless, S. Bridges, C. K. W. Chan & R. Glofcheski (Eds.), *Scaling up assessment for learning in higher education* (pp. 99–111). Singapore: Springer.

Kabilan, M. K., & Khan, M. A. (2012). Assessing pre-service English language teachers' learning using e-portfolios: Benefits, challenges and competencies gained. *Computers and Education*, 58(4), 1007–1020.

Kahu, E., Stephens, C., Leach, L., & Zepke, N. (2015). Linking academic emotions and student engagement: Mature-aged distance students' transition to university. *Journal of Further and Higher Education*, 39(4), 481–497.

Kearney, S., Perkins, T., & Kennedy-Clark, S. (2016). Using self- and peer-assessments for summative purposes: Analyzing the relative validity of the AASL (Authentic Assessment for Sustainable Learning) model. *Assessment and Evaluation in Higher Education*, 41(6), 840–853.

Kim, M. (2009). The impact of an elaborated receiver's role in peer assessment. *Assessment and Evaluation in Higher Education*, 34(1), 105–114.

Lam, R. (2014). Promoting self-regulated learning through portfolio assessment: Testimony and recommendations. *Assessment and Evaluation in Higher Education*, 39(6), 699–714.

Lave, J., & Wenger, E. (1999). Learning and pedagogy in communities of practice. In J. Leach & B. Moon (Eds.), *Learners and pedagogy* (pp. 21–33). London: Paul Chapman.

Lea, M. R., & Street, B. V. (1998). Student writing in higher education: An academic literacies approach. *Studies in Higher Education*, 23(2), 157–172.

Levy, D., SvoronosT., & Klinger, M. (in press). Two-stage examinations: Can examinations be more formative experiences? *Active Learning in Higher Education*.

Liu, N. F., & Carless, D. (2006) Peer feedback: The learning element of peer assessment. *Teaching in Higher Education*, 11(3), 279–290.

Liu, X., & Li, L. (2014). Assessment training effects on student assessment skills and task performance in a technology-facilitated peer assessment. *Assessment and Evaluation in Higher Education*, 39(3), 275–292.

Lizzio, A., & Wilson, K. (2008). Feedback on assessment: Students' perceptions of quality and effectiveness. *Assessment and Evaluation in Higher Education*, 33(3), 263–275.

Ludvigsen, K., Krumsvik, R., & Furnes, B. (2015). Creating formative feedback spaces in large lectures. *Computers & Education*, 88, 48–63.

Luo, L., Kiewra, K. A., Flanigan, A. E., & Peteranetz, M. S. (2018). Laptop versus longhand note taking: Effects on lecture notes and achievement. *Instructional Science*, 46(6), 947–971.

MacDonald, H., Sulsky, L., Spence, J., & D. J. Brown, D. (2013). Cultural differences in the motivation to seek performance feedback: A comparative policy-capturing study. *Human Performance*, 26(3), 211–235.

Magin, D., & Helmore, P. (2001). Peer and teacher assessments of oral presentation skills: How reliable are they? *Studies in Higher Education*, 26(3), 289–298.

Mahoney, P., Macfarlane, S., & Ajjawi, R. (2019). A qualitative synthesis of video feedback in higher education. *Teaching in Higher Education*, 24(2), 157–179.

Mayhew, E. (2017). Playback feedback: The impact of screen-captured video feedback on student satisfaction, learning and attainment. *European Political Science*, 16, 179–192.

McConlogue, T. (2012). But is it fair? Developing students' understanding of grading complex written work through peer assessment. *Assessment and Evaluation in Higher Education*, 37(1), 113–123.

McConlogue, T. (2015). Making judgements: Investigating the process of composing and receiving peer feedback. *Studies in Higher Education*, 40(9), 1495–1506.

McCune, V., & Rhind, S. (2014). Understanding students' experiences of being assessed: The interplay between prior guidance, engaging with assessments and receiving feedback. In C. Kreber, C. Anderson, N. Entwistle & J. McArthur (Eds.), *Advances and innovations in university assessment and feedback* (pp. 246–263). Edinburgh, UK: Edinburgh University Press.

McLean, A. J., Bond, C. H., & Nicholson, H. D. (2015). An anatomy of feedback: A phenomenographic investigation of undergraduate students' conceptions of feedback. *Studies in Higher Education*, 40(5), 921–932.

Merisier, S.Larue, C., & Boyer, L. (2018). How does questioning influence nursing students' clinical reasoning in problem-based learning? A scoping review. *Nurse Education Today*, 65, 108–115.

Merry, S., & Orsmond, P. (2008). Students' attitudes to and usage of academic feedback provided via audio files. *Bioscience Education*, 11(1), 1–11.

Miller, T. (2009). Formative computer-based assessment in higher education: The effectiveness of feedback in supporting student learning. *Assessment and Evaluation in Higher Education*, 34(2), 181–192.

Min, H. T. (2005). Training students to become successful peer reviewers. *System*, 33(2), 298–308.

Min, H. T. (2006). The effects of trained peer review on EFL students' revision types and writing quality. *Journal of Second Language Writing*, 15(2), 118–141.

Min, H. T. (2008). Reviewer stances and writer perceptions in EFL peer review training. *English for Specific Purposes*, 27(3), 285–305.

Min, H. T. (2013). A case study of an EFL writing teacher's belief and practice about written feedback. *System*, 41(3), 625–638.

Min, H. T. (2016). Effect of teacher modeling and feedback on EFL students' peer review skills in peer review training. *Journal of Second Language Writing*, 31, 43–57.

Molloy, E., Borrell-Carrió, F., & Epstein, R. (2013). The impact of emotions in feedback. In D. Boud & E. Molloy (Eds.), *Feedback in higher and professional education* (pp. 60–81). London: Routledge.

Molloy, E., & Boud, D. (2013). Changing conceptions of feedback. In D. Boud & E. Molloy (Eds.), *Feedback in higher and professional education* (pp. 11–23). London: Routledge.

Moore, C., & Teather, S. (2013). Engaging students in peer review: Feedback as learning. *Issues in Educational Research*, 23(2), 196–211.

Mostert, M., & Snowball, J. (2013). Where angels fear to tread: Online peer assessment in a large first-year class. *Assessment and Evaluation in Higher Education*, 38(6), 674–686.

Mulliner, E., & Tucker, M. (2017). Feedback on feedback practice: Perceptions of students and academics. *Assessment and Evaluation in Higher Education*, 42(2), 266–288.

Mutch, A. (2003). Exploring the practice of feedback to students. *Active Learning in Higher Education*, 4(1), 24–38.

Nash, G., Crimmins, G., & Oprescu, F. (2016). If first-year students are afraid of public speaking assessments what can teachers do to alleviate such anxiety? *Assessment and Evaluation in Higher Education*, 41(4), 586–600.

Nash, R. A., & Winstone, N. E. (2017). Responsibility-sharing in the giving and receiving of assessment feedback. *Frontiers in Psychology*, 8, 1519.

Nash, R. A., Winstone, N. E., Gregory, S. E. A., & Papps, E. (2018). A memory advantage for past-oriented over future-oriented performance feedback. *Journal of Experimental Psychology: Learning, Memory, and Cognition*, 44(12), 1864–1879.

Nicol, D. (2007). Laying a foundation for lifelong learning: Case studies of e-assessment in large 1st-year classes. *British Journal of Educational Technology*, 38(4), 668–678.

Nicol, D. (2009). Assessment for learner self-regulation: Enhancing achievement in the first year using learning technologies. *Assessment and Evaluation in Higher Education*, 34(3), 335–352.

Nicol, D. (2010). From monologue to dialogue: Improving written feedback processes in mass higher education. *Assessment and Evaluation in Higher Education*, 35(5), 501–517.

Nicol, D. J., & Macfarlane-Dick, D. (2006). Formative assessment and self-regulated learning: A model and seven principles of good feedback practice. *Studies in Higher Education*, 31(2), 199–218.

Nicol, D., Thomson, A., & Breslin, C. (2014). Rethinking feedback practices in higher education: A peer review perspective. *Assessment and Evaluation in Higher Education*, 39(1), 102–122.

O'Donovan, B., Price, M., & Rust, C. (2008). Developing student understanding of assessment standards: A nested hierarchy of approaches. *Teaching in Higher Education*, 13(2), 205–217.

O'Donovan, B., Rust, C., & Price, M. (2016). A scholarly approach to solving the feedback dilemma in practice. *Assessment and Evaluation in Higher Education*, 41(6), 938–949.

Orr, S., & Shreeve, A. (2018). *Art and design pedagogy in higher education*. New York: Routledge.

Orr, S., Yorke, M., & Blair, B. (2014). 'The answer is brought about from within you': A student-centred perspective on pedagogy in Art and Design. *International Journal of Art and Design Education*, 33(1), 32–45.

Orsmond, P., & Merry, S. (2011). Feedback alignment: Effective and ineffective links between tutors' and students' understanding of coursework feedback. *Assessment and Evaluation in Higher Education*, 36(2), 125–136.

Orsmond, P., & Merry, S. (2013). The importance of self-assessment in students' use of tutors' feedback: A qualitative study of high and non-high achieving biology undergraduates. *Assessment and Evaluation in Higher Education*, 38(6), 737–753.

Orsmond, P., Merry, S., & Reiling, K. (2002). The use of exemplars and formative feedback when using student derived marking criteria in peer and self-assessment. *Assessment and Evaluation in Higher Education*, 27(4), 309–323.

Orsmond, P., Merry, S., & Reiling, K. (2005). Biology students' utilization of tutors' formative feedback: A qualitative interview study. *Assessment and Evaluation in Higher Education*, 30(4), 369–386.

Palincsar, A. S. (1998). Social constructivist perspectives on teaching and learning. *Annual Review of Psychology*, 49(1), 345–375.

Panadero, E. (2016). Is it safe? Social, interpersonal, and human effects of peer assessment: A review and future directions. In G. T. L. Brown & L. R. Harris (Eds.), *Handbook of human and social conditions in assessment* (pp. 247–266). New York: Routledge.

Panadero, E. (2017). A Review of self-regulated learning: Six models and four directions for research. *Frontiers in Psychology*, 8(422).

Panadero, E., Brown, G. T. L., & Strijbos, J.-W. (2016). The future of student self-assessment: A review of known unknowns and potential directions. *Educational Psychology Review*, 28(4), 803–830.

Panadero, E., & Jönsson, A. (2013). The use of scoring rubrics for formative assessment purposes revisited: A review. *Educational Research Review*, 9, 129–144.

Panadero, E., Jönsson, A., & Botella, J. (2017). Effects of self-assessment on self-regulated learning and self-efficacy: Four meta-analyses. *Educational Research Review*, 22, 74–98.

Panadero, E., Jönsson, A., & Strijbos, J.-W. (2016). Scaffolding self-regulated learning through self-assessment and peer assessment: Guidelines for classroom implementation. In D. Laveault & L. Allal (Eds.), *Assessment for learning: Meeting the challenge of implementation* (pp. 311–326). Boston: Springer.

Pardo, A., Jovanovic, J., Dawson, S., Gašević, D., & Mirriahi, N. (2019). Using learning analytics to scale the provision of personalised feedback. *British Journal of Educational Technology*, 50(1), 128–138.

Parker, M., & Winstone, N. E. (2016). Students' perceptions of interventions for supporting their engagement with feedback. *Practitioner Research in Higher Education*, 10(1), 53–64.

Parkin, H. J., Hepplestone, S., Holden, G., Irwin, B., & Thorpe, L. (2012). A role for technology in enhancing students' engagement with feedback. *Assessment and Evaluation in Higher Education*, 37(8), 963–973.

Patton, C. (2012). 'Some kind of weird, evil experiment': Student perceptions of peer assessment. *Assessment and Evaluation in Higher Education*, 37(6), 719–731.

Pekrun, R. (2006). The control-value theory of achievement emotions: Assumptions, corollaries, and implications for educational research and practice. *Educational Psychology Review*, 18(4), 315–341.

Pekrun, R., Elliot, A. J., & Maier, M. A. (2006). Achievement goals and discrete achievement emotions: A theoretical model and prospective test. *Journal of Educational Psychology*, 98(3), 583–597.

Pekrun, R., Frenzel, A. C., Goetz, T., & Perry, R. P. (2007). The control-value theory of achievement emotions: An integrative approach to emotions in education. In P. A. Schutz & R. Pekrun (Eds.), *Emotions in education* (pp. 13–36). Cambridge, MA: Academic Press.

Pekrun, R., Goetz, T., Frenzel, A. C., Barchfeld, P., & Perry, R. P. (2011). Measuring emotions in students' learning and performance: The Achievement Emotions Questionnaire (AEQ). *Contemporary Educational Psychology*, 36(1), 36–48.

Peterson, E. R., Brown, G. T., & Jun, M. C. (2015). Achievement emotions in higher education: A diary study exploring emotions across an assessment event. *Contemporary Educational Psychology*, 42, 82–96.

Pintrich, P. (2000). The role of goal orientation in self-regulated learning. In M. Boekaerts, P. Pintrich & M. Zeidner (Eds.), *Handbook of self-regulation* (pp. 451–502). San Diego, CA: Academic Press.

Pitt, E., & Norton, L. (2017). 'Now that's the feedback I want!' Students' reactions to feedback on graded work and what they do with it. *Assessment and Evaluation in Higher Education*, 42(4), 499–516.

Pitt, E., & Winstone, N. (2018). The impact of anonymous marking on students' perceptions of fairness, feedback and relationships with lecturers. *Assessment and Evaluation in Higher Education*, 43(7), 1183–1193.

Pitt, E., & Winstone, N. (forthcoming, 2019). Dialogic feedback in a digital world. In M. Bearman, P. Dawson, J. Tai, R. Ajjawi, & D. Boud (Eds.), *Re-imagining university assessment in a digital world*. New York: Springer.

Poulos, A., & Mahony, M. J. (2008). Effectiveness of feedback: The students' perspective. *Assessment and Evaluation in Higher Education, 33*(2), 143–154.

Price, M., Handley, K., & Millar, J. (2011). Feedback: Focusing attention on engagement. *Studies in Higher Education, 36*(8), 879–896.

Price, M., Handley, K., Millar, J., & O'Donovan, B. (2010). Feedback: All that effort, but what is the effect? *Assessment and Evaluation in Higher Education, 35*(3), 277–289.

Price, M., Rust, C., O'Donovan, B., Handley, K., & Bryant, R. (2012). *Assessment literacy: The foundation for improving student learning*. Oxford: Oxford Centre for Staff and Learning Development.

Prowse, S., Duncan, N., Hughes, J., & Burke, D. (2007). '… do that and I'll raise your grade'. Innovative module design and recursive feedback. *Teaching in Higher Education, 12*(4), 437–445.

Purchase, H., & Hamer, J. (2018). Peer review in practice: Eight years of Aropa. *Assessment and Evaluation in Higher Education, 43*(7), 1146–1165.

Quinton, S., & Smallbone, T. (2010). Feeding forward: Using feedback to promote student reflection and learning – A teaching model. *Innovations in Education and Teaching International, 47*(1), 125–135.

Raftery, J. N., & Bizer, G. Y. (2009). Negative feedback and performance: The moderating effect of emotion regulation. *Personality and Individual Differences, 47*(5), 481–486.

Rand, J. (2017). Misunderstandings and mismatches: The collective disillusionment of written summative assessment feedback. *Research in Education, 97*(1), 33–48.

Reddy, Y., & Andrade, H. (2010). A review of rubric use in higher education. *Assessment and Evaluation in Higher Education, 35*(4), 435–448.

Reynolds, M., & Trehan, K. (2000). Assessment: A critical perspective. *Studies in Higher Education, 25*(3), 267–278.

Rigney, D. (2010). *The Matthew effect: How advantage begets further advantage*. New York: Columbia University Press.

Rowe, A. (2011). The personal dimension in teaching: Why students value feedback. *International Journal of Educational Management, 25*(4), 343–360.

Rowe, A. D., Fitness, J., & Wood, L. N. (2014). The role and functionality of emotions in feedback at university: A qualitative study. *The Australian Educational Researcher, 41*(3), 283–309.

Rust, C., O'Donovan, B., & Price, M. (2005). A social constructivist assessment process model: How the research literature shows us this could be best practice. *Assessment and Evaluation in Higher Education, 30*(3), 231–240.

Ryan, T., & Henderson, M. (2018). Feeling feedback: Students' emotional responses to educator feedback. *Assessment and Evaluation in Higher Education, 43*(6), 880–892.

Sadler, D. R. (1989). Formative assessment and the design of instructional systems. *Instructional Science, 18*(2), 119–144.

Sadler, D. R. (2010). Beyond feedback: Developing student capability in complex appraisal. *Assessment and Evaluation in Higher Education, 35*(5), 535–550.

Sadler, D. R. (2015). Backwards assessment explanations: Implications for teaching and assessment practice. In D. Lebler, G. Carey, & S. Harrison. (Eds.), *Assessment in music education: From policy to practice* (pp. 9–19). Cham, Switzerland: Springer.

Sambell, K., McDowell, L., & Montgomery, C. (2013). *Assessment for learning in higher education*. London: Routledge.

Sanders, M., & George, A. (2017). Viewing the changing world of educational technology from a different perspective: Present realities, past lessons, and future possibilities. *Education and Information Technologies*, 22(6), 2915–2933.

Sargeant, J., Mann, K., Sinclair, D., Van der Vleuten, C., & Metsemakers, J. (2008). Understanding the influence of emotions and reflection upon multi-source feedback acceptance and use. *Advances in Health Sciences Education*, 13(3), 275–288.

Schrand, T. & Eliason, J. (2012). Feedback practices and signature pedagogies: What can liberal arts learn from the design critique? *Teaching in Higher Education*, 17(1), 51–62.

Scoles, J., Huxham, M., & McArthur, J. (2013). No longer exempt from good practice: Using exemplars to close the feedback gap in exams. *Assessment and Evaluation in Higher Education*, 38(6), 631–645.

Sedrakyan, G., Malmberg, J., Verbert, K., Järvelä, S., & Kirschner, P. A. (in press). Linking learning behavior analytics and learning science concepts: Designing a learning analytics dashboard for feedback to support learning regulation. *Computers in Human Behavior*.

Sendziuk, P. (2010). Sink or swim? Improving student learning through feedback and self-assessment. *International Journal of Teaching and Learning in Higher Education*, 22(3), 320–330.

Shields, S. (2015). 'My work is bleeding': Exploring students' emotional responses to first-year assignment feedback. *Teaching in Higher Education*, 20(6), 614–624.

Shute, V. J. (2008). Focus on formative feedback. *Review of Educational Research*, 78(1), 153–189.

Sinclair, H. K., & Cleland, J. A. (2007). Undergraduate medical students: Who seeks formative feedback? *Medical Education*, 41(6), 580–582.

Sitzmann, T., & Ely, K. (2011). A meta-analysis of self-regulated learning in work-related training and educational attainment: What we know and where we need to go. *Psychological Bulletin*, 137, 421–442.

Sluijsmans, D., Brand-Gruwel, S., & Van Merriënboer, J. (2002). Peer assessment training in teacher education: Effects on performance and perceptions. *Assessment and Evaluation in Higher Education*, 27(5), 443–454.

Small, F., & Attree, K. (2016). Undergraduate student responses to feedback: Expectations and experiences. *Studies in Higher Education*, 41(11), 2078–2094.

Smith, C. D., & King, P. E. (2004). Student feedback sensitivity and the efficacy of feedback interventions in public speaking performance improvement. *Communication Education*, 53(3), 203–216.

Smith, C. D., Worsfold, K., Davies, L., Fisher, R., & McPhail, R. (2013). Assessment literacy and student learning: The case for explicitly developing students 'assessment literacy'. *Assessment and Evaluation in Higher Education*, 38(1), 44–60.

Steen-Utheim, A., & Hopfenbeck, T. (2019). To do or not to do with feedback: A study of undergraduate students' engagement within a portfolio assessment design. *Assessment and Evaluation in Higher Education*, 44(1), 80–96.

Steen-Utheim, A., & Wittek, A. (2017). Dialogic feedback and the potentialities for student learning. *Learning, Culture and Social Interaction*, 15, 18–30.

Sutton, P. (2012). Conceptualizing feedback literacy: Knowing, being, and acting. *Innovations in Education and Teaching International*, 49(1), 31–40.

Sutton, P., & Gill, W. (2010). Engaging feedback: Meaning, identity and power. *Practitioner Research in Higher Education*, 4(1), 3–13.

Tai, J., Ajjawi, R., Boud, D., Dawson, P., & Panadero, E. (2018). Developing evaluative judgment: Enabling students to make decisions about the quality of work. *Higher Education*, 76(3), 467–481.

Telio, S., Ajjawi, R., & Regehr, G. (2015). The 'educational alliance' as a framework for reconceptualizing feedback in medical education. *Academic Medicine*, 90(5), 609–614.

Telio, S., Regehr, G., & Ajjawi, R. (2016). Feedback and the educational alliance: Examining credibility judgements and their consequences. *Medical Education*, 50(9), 933–942.

Thomas, R. A., West, R. E., & Borup, J. (2017). An analysis of instructor social presence in online text and asynchronous video feedback comments. *The Internet and Higher Education*, 33, 61–73.

Thomson, K. E., & Trigwell, K. R. (2018). The role of informal conversations in developing university teaching? *Studies in Higher Education*, 43(9), 1536–1547.

Thurlings, M., Vermeulen, M., Bastiaens, T., & Stijnen, S. (2013). Understanding feedback: A learning theory perspective. *Educational Research Review*, 9, 1–15.

Tian, M., & Lowe, J. (2013). The role of feedback in cross-cultural learning: A case study of Chinese taught postgraduate students in a UK university. *Assessment and Evaluation in Higher Education*, 38(5), 580–598.

To, J., & Carless, D. (2016). Making productive use of exemplars: Peer discussion and teacher guidance for positive transfer of strategies. *Journal of Further and Higher Education*, 40(6), 746–764.

Topping, K. (2009). Peer assessment. *Theory into Practice, 48*(1), 20–27.

Torrance, H. (2007). Assessment as learning? How the use of explicit learning objectives, assessment criteria and feedback in post-secondary education and training can come to dominate learning. *Assessment in Education*, 14(3), 281–294.

Tweed, R. G., & Lehman, D. R. (2002). Learning considered within a cultural context: Confucian and Socratic approaches. *American Psychologist*, 57(2), 89–99

Van den Berg, I., Admiraal, W., & Pilot, A. (2006a). Peer assessment in university teaching: Evaluating seven course designs. *Assessment and Evaluation in Higher Education*, 31(1), 19–36.

Van den Berg, I., Admiraal, W., & Pilot, A. (2006b). Design principles and outcomes of peer assessment in higher education. *Studies in Higher Education*, 31(3), 341–356.

van der Schaaf, M., Donkers, J., Slof, B., Moonen-van Loon, J., van Tartwijk, J., Driessen, E., ... & Ten Cate, O. (2017). Improving workplace-based assessment and feedback by an e-portfolio enhanced with learning analytics. *Educational Technology Research and Development*, 65(2), 359–380.

van Dinther, M., Dochy, F., Segers, M., & Braeken, J. (2014). Student perceptions of assessment and student self-efficacy in competence-based education. *Educational Studies*, 40(3), 330–351.

Van Gennip, N. A. E., Segers, M. S. R., & Tillema, H. H. (2010). Peer assessment as a collaborative learning activity: The role of interpersonal variables and conceptions. *Learning and Instruction*, 20(4), 280–290.

Van Zundert, M., Sluijsmans, D., & Van Merriënboer, J. (2010). Effective peer assessment processes: Research findings and future directions. *Learning and Instruction*, 20(4), 270–279.

Värlander, S. (2008). The role of students' emotions in formal feedback situations. *Teaching in Higher Education*, 13(2), 145–156.

Villamil, O., & de Guerrero, M. (2006). Sociocultural theory: A framework for understanding the social-cognitive dimensions of peer feedback. In K. Hyland & F. Hyland

(Eds.), *Feedback in second language writing: Contexts and issues* (pp. 23–41). Cambridge: Cambridge University Press.

Vincelette, E. J., & Bostic, T. (2013). Show and tell: Student and instructor perceptions of screencast assessment. *Assessing Writing*, 18(4), 257–277.

Vrieling, E., Stijnen, S., & Bastiaens, T. (2018). Successful learning: Balancing self-regulation with instructional planning. *Teaching in Higher Education*, 23(6), 685–700.

Walker, M. (2015). The quality of written feedback on undergraduates' draft answers to an assignment and the use made of feedback. *Assessment and Evaluation in Higher Education*, 40(2), 232–247.

Wanner, T., & Palmer, E. (2018). Formative self- and peer assessment for improved student learning: The crucial factors of design, teacher participation and feedback. *Assessment and Evaluation in Higher Education*, 43(7), 1032–1047.

Watling, C., Driessen, E., van der Vleuten, C. P., & Lingard, L. (2014). Learning culture and feedback: An international study of medical athletes and musicians. *Medical Education*, 48(7), 713–723.

Watling, C. J., & Ginsburg, S. (2019). Assessment, feedback and the alchemy of learning. *Medical Education*, 53(1), 76–85.

Weaver, M. R. (2006). Do students value feedback? Student perceptions of tutors' written responses. *Assessment and Evaluation in Higher Education*, 31(3), 379–394.

West, J., & Turner, W. (2016). Enhancing the assessment experience: Improving student perceptions, engagement and understanding using online video feedback. *Innovations in Education and Teaching International*, 53(4), 400–410.

Weston, M. E., & Bain, A. (2010). The end of techno-critique: The naked truth about 1:1 laptop initiatives and educational change. *The Journal of Technology, Learning and Assessment*, 9(6), 5–25.

Wiener, N. (1968). *The human use of human beings: Cybernetics and society*. London: Sphere.

Winstone, N. E. (2017). The three 'R's' of pedagogic frailty: Risk, resilience and reward. In I. M. Kinchin & N. E. Winstone (Eds.), *Pedagogic frailty and resilience in the university* (pp. 33–48). Rotterdam: Sense.

Winstone, N. E. (2019). Improving student capacity to understand the impact of feedback: The value of systems that capture and track impact. In M. Henderson, R. Ajjawi, E. Molloy & D. Boud (Eds.), *The impact of feedback in higher education*. London: Palgrave Macmillan.

Winstone, N., & Boud, D. (2019). Exploring cultures of feedback practice: The adoption of learning-focused feedback practices in the UK and Australia. *Higher Education Research and Development*, 38(2), 411–425.

Winstone, N. E., & Boud, D. (forthcoming, 2019). Developing assessment feedback: From occasional survey to everyday practice. In S. Lygo-Baker, I. Kinchin & N. Winstone (Eds.), *Engaging student voices in higher education: Diverse perspectives and expectations in partnership*. London: Palgrave.

Winstone, N. E., Mathlin, G., & Nash, R. A. (2019). Building feedback literacy: Students' perceptions of the developing engagement with feedback toolkit. Frontiers in Education.

Winstone, N. E., & Nash, R. A. (2016). The developing engagement with feedback toolkit. York, UK: Higher Education Academy. Retrieved 26/01/19from www.heacademy.ac.uk/knowledge-hub/developing-engagement-feedback-toolkit-deft.

Winstone, N. E., Nash, R. A., Parker, M., & Rowntree, J. (2017a). Supporting learners' agentic engagement with feedback: A systematic review and a taxonomy of recipience processes. *Educational Psychologist*, 52(1), 17–37.

Winstone, N. E., Nash, R. A., Rowntree, J., & Menezes, R. (2016). What do students want most from written feedback information? Distinguishing necessities from luxuries using a budgeting methodology. *Assessment and Evaluation in Higher Education*, 41(8), 1237–1253.

Winstone, N. E., Nash, R. A., Rowntree, J., & Parker, M. (2017b). 'It'd be useful, but I wouldn't use it': Barriers to university students' feedback seeking and recipience. *Studies in Higher Education*, 42(11), 2026–2041.

Winstone, N., & Pitt, E. (2017). Feedback is a two-way street. So why does the NSS only look one way? *Times Higher Education Supplement*, 2323(30). Retrieved 26/01/19from www.timeshighereducation.com/opinion/feedback-two-way-street-so-why-does-nss-only-look-one-way.

Withey, C. (2013). Feedback engagement: Forcing feed-forward amongst law students. *The Law Teacher*, 47(3), 319–344.

Xu, Y., & Carless, D. (2017). 'Only true friends could be cruelly honest': Cognitive scaffolding and social-affective support in teacher feedback literacy. *Assessment and Evaluation in Higher Education*, 42(7), 1082–1094.

Yan, Z., & Brown, G. T. L. (2017). A cyclical self-assessment process: Towards a model of how students engage in self-assessment. *Assessment and Evaluation in Higher Education*, 42(8), 1247–1262.

Yang, M., & Carless, D. (2013). The feedback triangle and the enhancement of dialogic feedback processes. *Teaching in Higher Education*, 18(3), 285–297.

Young, P. (2000). 'I might as well give up': Self-esteem and mature students' feelings about feedback on assignments. *Journal of Further and Higher education*, 24(3), 409–418.

Yu, S., & Hu, G. (2017). Understanding university students' peer feedback practices in EFL writing: Insights from a case study. *Assessing Writing*, 33, 25–35.

Yucel, R., Bird, F., Young, J., & Blanksby, T. (2014). The road to self-assessment: Exemplar marking before peer review develops first year students' capacity to judge the quality of a scientific report. *Assessment and Evaluation in Higher Education*, 39(8), 971–986.

Zhu, Q. (2018). *Chinese undergraduates' engagement with peer feedback: Perceptions and practices*. Unpublished doctoral dissertation, The University of Hong Kong.

Zhu, Q., & Carless, D. (2018). Dialogue within peer feedback processes: Clarification and negotiation of meaning. *Higher Education Research and Development*, 37(4), 883–897.

Zimbardi, K., Colthorpe, K., Dekker, A., Engstrom, C., Bugarcic, A., Worthy, P., … & Long, P. (2017). Are they using my feedback? The extent of students' feedback use has a large impact on subsequent academic performance. *Assessment and Evaluation in Higher Education*, 42(4), 625–644.

Zimmerman, B. (2000). Attaining self-regulation: A social cognitive perspective. In M. Boekaerts, P. Pintrich, & M. Zeidner (Eds.), *Handbook of self-regulation* (pp. 13–40). San Diego, CA: Academic Press.

Zimmerman, B., & Schunk, D. (Eds.) (2001). *Self-regulated learning and academic achievement: Theoretical perspectives* (2nd ed.). Mahwah, NJ: Erlbaum.

Zimmerman, B., & Schunk, D. (2011). Self-regulated learning and performance. In B. Zimmerman & D. Schunk (Eds.) *Handbook of self-regulation of learning and performance* (pp. 1–12). New York: Routledge.

Author Index

Subject Index